PURITANS IN BABYLON

PURITANS IN BABYLON

THE ANCIENT NEAR EAST
AND AMERICAN INTELLECTUAL LIFE,
1880–1930

Bruce Kuklick

PRINCETON UNIVERSITY PRESS

PRINCETON, NEW JERSEY

LIBRARY OF CONGRESS CATALOGING-IN-PUBLICATION DATA

KUKLICK, BRUCE, 1941–

PURITANS IN BABYLON : THE ANCIENT NEAR EAST AND

AMERICAN INTELLECTUAL LIFE, 1880–1930 / BRUCE KUKLICK.

P. CM.

INCLUDES BIBLIOGRAPHICAL REFERENCES AND INDEX.

ISBN 0-691-02582-7 (ALK. PAPER)

1. UNITED STATES—INTELLECTUAL LIFE—1865–1918.

2. UNITED STATES—INTELLECTUAL LIFE—20TH CENTURY.

3. MIDDLE EAST—CIVILIZATION—STUDY AND TEACHING—

UNITED STATES.   4. MIDDLE EAST—CIVILIZATION—

RESEARCH—UNITED STATES.

I. TITLE.

E169.1.K78   1996   973.8—DC20   95-43979

THIS BOOK HAS BEEN COMPOSED IN BERKELEY MEDIUM

PRINCETON UNIVERSITY PRESS BOOKS ARE PRINTED

ON ACID-FREE PAPER AND MEET THE GUIDELINES FOR

PERMANENCE AND DURABILITY OF THE COMMITTEE ON

PRODUCTION GUIDELINES FOR BOOK LONGEVITY

OF THE COUNCIL ON LIBRARY RESOURCES

PRINTED IN THE UNITED STATES OF AMERICA

BY PRINCETON ACADEMIC PRESS

1   3   5   7   9   10   8   6   4   2

For E. B.

For nothing is lost, nothing is ever lost. There is always the clue. . . .
And all times are one time, and all those dead in the past never
lived before our definition gives them life, and out of
the shadow their eyes implore us.
That is what all of us historical researchers believe.
And we love truth.
(Robert Penn Warren, *All the King's Men*)

CONTENTS

LIST OF MAPS AND ILLUSTRATIONS   xi

ACKNOWLEDGMENTS   xiii

Introduction   3

PART ONE: FROM THE UNITED STATES
TO BABYLONIA   11

Main Characters in the Story   17

ONE
The Boys of Sumer, 1876–1888   19

TWO
In Their Ruins, 1889–1892   35

THREE
A Tale of Two Cities, 1893–1896   58

FOUR
Hilprecht's Triumphs, 1897–1902   78

PART TWO: FROM BABYLONIA TO THE AMERICAN
ANCIENT NEAR EAST   93

FIVE
The Organization of Knowledge   99

SIX
The Peters-Hilprecht Controversy, 1903–1910   123

SEVEN
Archaeology and Objectivity   141

EIGHT
Intellectual Property   158

NINE
Orientalists and Their Civilizations   176

Conclusion   196

ABBREVIATIONS 204

NOTES 205

ESSAY ON METHODS AND SOURCES 235

INDEX 247

LIST OF MAPS AND ILLUSTRATIONS

Maps

Map 1	Travelers' Europe about 1900	13
Map 2	The Near East about 1900	14
Map 3	The Ancient Near East as known about 1900	15

Illustrations

Fig. 1	Nippur, photographed by John Henry Haynes (Museum of the University of Pennsylvania)	53
Fig. 2	Nippur, sketched by Joseph Meyer (Museum of the University of Pennsylvania)	70
Fig. 3	Cassandria Haynes at Nippur (Museum of the University of Pennsylvania)	86
Fig. 4	Friedrich Delitzsch (Yale Babylonian Collection)	95
Fig. 5	Hermann Hilprecht (Museum of the University of Pennsylvania)	95
Fig. 6	Albert Clay (Yale Babylonian Collection)	95
Fig. 7	Paul Haupt (Yale Babylonian Collection)	95
Fig. 8	John Peters (Yale Babylonian Collection)	96
Fig. 9	George Andrew Reisner (Boston Museum of Fine Arts)	96
Fig. 10	James Henry Breasted (Oriental Institute of the University of Chicago)	97
Fig. 11	William Foxwell Albright (Ferdinand Hamburger, Jr., Archives of The Johns Hopkins University)	97
Fig. 12	Petrie's Cross Section at Tell el Hesy, 1890 (Sir Flinders Petrie, *Tell El Hesy (Lachish)* [London, 1891], 32, plate 3)	148
Fig. 13	Styles of cuneiform transcription: Lyon (David G. Lyon, *An Assyrian Manual* [Chicago, 1886], 62)	179
Fig. 14	Styles of cuneiform transcription: Hilprecht (H. V. Hilprecht, *Old Babylonian Inscriptions, Chiefly from Nippur . . .* [Philadelphia, 1893], plate 16)	180

Fig. 15   Styles of cuneiform transcription: Radau (Hugo Radau,
          Sumerian Hymns and Prayers . . . [Philadelphia, 1911],
          plate 13)   181

Fig. 16   Styles of cuneiform transcription: Clay (Albert Clay,
          Documents from the Temple Archives of Nippur . . .
          [Philadelphia, 1906], plate 37)   182

ACKNOWLEDGMENTS

I WOULD LIKE to thank all the scholars mentioned in the Essay on Methods and Sources, as well as the librarians and archivists at the various depositories cited in the notes, but special mention needs to be made of Douglas Haller and Alessandro Pezzati of the University Museum Archives, Benjamin Foster of Yale, and Jerrold Cooper of Johns Hopkins.

I have another debt to Walter Lippincott and his staff at Princeton University Press.

In addition to the people noted in the Essay on Methods and Sources, a number of others read the manuscript in various stages of completion, some several times: Jeffrey Abt, Elizabeth Block, Steven Conn, Richard Freeland, David Hollinger, Walter McDougall, Suzanne Marchand, Henry May, Leo Ribuffo, Charles Rosenberg, Jean Strouse, and Marc Trachtenberg.

Lloyd Daley, now deceased, originally spurred my interest in this topic when he told me about his work organizing the then-closed materials on the Nippur Expedition. Michael McGuire assisted me with translations from the German. Rosemarie D'Alba, as well as two work-study students, Marc Stanislawczyk and Caitlin Portnoy, will be pleased to see their maps in print.

The National Endowment for the Humanities supported this project with a Senior Fellowship, and the University of Pennsylvania has, as usual, demonstrated enormous generosity in its support of my work.

It is important in this book that I take responsibility for all mistakes and errors of judgment.

PURITANS IN BABYLON

INTRODUCTION

IN THE UNITED STATES the fields of inquiry that produced our knowledge of what we now call the ancient Near East arose from the 1880s through the 1920s. This book narrates three interconnected stories. First, it tells how an odd collection of scholars, soldiers of fortune, educational bureaucrats, and financiers mounted the initial American exploration in the Near East. Philadelphia's Babylonian Exploration Fund paid for the explorers. They dug off and on for twelve years near the biblical Babylon, at Nippur, a religious and educational center of the oldest civilizations. The recovery of Nippur is the prism through which my other stories are refracted.

The long adventure shaped America's institutional and intellectual understanding of the ancient Near East. My second story is about the creation of the academic specialties that study this part of the world. The growth of these interwoven fields of knowledge typified the professionalization of knowledge and the maturation of the American university, particularly in contrast to its German counterpart.

The ancient Near Eastern specialities are peculiar because they have a connection to museums. They are also peculiar because they grew up in the shadow of explicit Judeo-Christian interests. Indeed, well into the twentieth century, open sectarian commitments sometimes drove scholars' work. A concern for the history and meaning of humankind was frequently just beneath the surface of scholarship. The final story in this book is about the conflict between the religious and the secular. The modern notions that came out of this conflict involved the premises of historical thinking and the way in which Western scholarship appropriated or appreciated other cultures.

The first story centers on the Babylonian Exploration Fund. The BEF conducted its work from 1888 until 1900. The effort was not only the first but also the most sustained exploration carried on by the United States in the Near East through World War I. At Nippur the BEF unearthed tens of thousands of clay tablets inscribed with wedge-shaped symbols—cuneiform writing. Since that time the tablets have given scholars the basic evidence for their knowledge of Sumer, generally regarded as the world's oldest civilization.

It took two months to make the trip from the United States to Nippur. The travelers went first to England, then to Germany and through south central Europe to Constantinople, then the capital of the Turkish-governed Ottoman Empire; next through the empire to its distant province, Iraq, then called Mesopotamia, the land of the ancient Assyrians and Babylonians; on to the chief Mesopotamian city, Baghdad; and at last to Nippur in southern Mesopotamia. Each successive leg of the trip took comparatively more time, and travel conditions were increasingly arduous. Supplies were purchased in the United States, London, Berlin, or Constantinople and shipped to Baghdad. The Americans in some cases shortened portions of the journey. Stopovers in Constantinople and Baghdad were mandatory, however— sometimes to secure necessary permits, always to placate functionaries of the government.

Once the explorers got to their destination, disease, loneliness, and hostile locals took their toll. Months would pass in Mesopotamia before a response came even to promptly answered mail. The diaries and letters of the participants show that they were soon engaged in a war of each against all. Self-promotion and the desire for preferment overcame joint aspirations. Harsh living conditions and ambition exacerbated petty animosities. Personal idiosyncrasies flowered in an exotic environment that undermined Victorian propriety. As one of the explorers put it, "This is a queer world and when you put 7 persons together out in the desert on a little mound, they are sure to scratch each others' eyes out."[1]

The Americans had a taste for this kind of drama, but many soon had their bellies full. The BEF waged four campaigns, as they were called, in the desolate surroundings of the buried city. Yet only one man was associated with the work in the field for the entire time. Other explorers and hangers-on came and went, unable or unwilling to stick it out in the Near East. Some sickened; one died in the desert; a few were fired; others quit; one was only willing to return with his wife; two desired glory but insisted on staying in East Coast parlors.

The drama in these parlors equaled that in the Near East. The expedition spawned unseemly fights among the University of Pennsylvania (Penn), Johns Hopkins, Yale, and Chicago for institutional leadership in the study of the ancient Near East. Various academic factions warred with one another, as did competing social elites. Many of the participants at home also left records of what happened. Although their manners were sometimes more refined than those of the explorers, they too were a remarkable assemblage of human types. The administrators were spiteful, power craving, and imperious, yet also resourceful, intelligent, and energetic.

On nineteenth-century maps, lands to the east of Europe were known as "the Orient," all of it strange and exotic. Nonetheless, the Near Orient was distinguished from the Far East of China and Japan.[2] In the American view the Near Orient was inferior and backward but also old, and vaguely but unmistakably connected to the progressive, superior "West."[3] Inspired by Europeans and driven by Judeo-Christian zeal, American "Orientalists" started seriously to think about this area of the world in the last third of the nineteenth century. My second story is about how their thinking was institutionalized.

By the time of the Civil War, the scholarly American Oriental Society promoted the interests of Orientalists inside and outside American colleges, and made India central to the idea of Orientalism. By the twentieth century a new generation of men in universities had created the ancient Near East. Mesopotamia became the core of the American conception of the ancient Near East, though both Palestine and Egypt made bids for primacy. India remained a separate field of endeavor because it had no role in the Bible, which came to dominate the scholarly geography. But not only the Bible was at issue. The pivots of inquiry in the American ancient Near East derived from scriptural study, but researchers wanted to be known as scientists and not Biblicists. Mesopotamia and not Palestine became the focus of scholarship. Indeed, tourists may have rendered the Holy Land too familiar and even too popular for the more sober students, who preferred the least-traveled place in the East and the heartland of this book, Babylonia. Over time, Egypt and later Palestine challenged the concentration on Mesopotamia. The pyramids and the Sphinx, and then the splendor of the tombs of ancient kings, attracted attention that was wider and more secular than what Mesopotamia could muster. Nonetheless, Assyria and Babylonia had an academic advantage that was never relinquished. The languages of these civilizations were more easily acquired if another Semitic language had been mastered. The Americans trained in divinity and biblical Hebrew in the nineteenth century turned their communal attention to the Semitic language of Assyrian (now called Akkadian). The interest in hieroglyphics was no match for this attention. Bible study in America had formidable consequences for academic organization well into the twentieth century, and in the 1920s resulted in a resurgence in the importance of Palestine.

I have most often used the term *ancient Near Eastern studies* to refer to this web of inquiries intellectually centered in Mesopotamia.[4] At most universities these research areas did not easily identify themselves as "departments." This standard administrative rubric housed "disciplines" that were more codified and easily specified, such as physics, English, or political science. Instead, a unique constellation of academic specialties emerged. *Semitic studies* focused on the languages—Hebrew, Arabic, Aramaic, and Akkadian—with Akkadian becoming the lingua franca. *Assyriology*, which became limited to the study of the languages of old Mesopotamia, began by joining philology with the excavation of the ancient civilizations of Assyria and Babylonia. *Egyptology* remained a term covering the study of both hieroglyphic writing and Egyptian exploration, although philology and exploration diverged as specialties. *Archaeology*, sometimes specified as biblical or Near Eastern, grew out of the more general adventuring of explorers and came into being as a distinct scholarly endeavor. All these fields developed their own bureaucratic niches in which scholars could find employment. These niches enabled academics to train in the living and dead languages of the Near East and in its exploration and history, concentrating on the orientation of the old cultures to Judeo-Christian values.[5]

In the late nineteenth century some young Americans interested in the life of the mind left the moorings of the Protestant church for study in the new social sciences or in a philosophy increasingly divorced from theology. Other would-be scholars, however, turned to the Orientalist fields that linked the prestige of science to a concern for the Western religious tradition. Another learned constituency was drawn to Semitic studies in particular. American Jewry had developed among the rabbinate its own tradition of Hebrew scholarship. At the end of the nineteenth century American Jews for the first time stopped looking to Germany for advanced academic training and opened their own central institutions for the training of rabbis.[6] More important, some Jewish men of intellect who would earlier have become rabbis and students of the Talmud sought university positions. The field of Semitic studies gave them an opportunity to use the linguistic skills they had acquired as children. It also permitted them to feel that they were still in the Jewish tradition, although they were more secular and modern in the growing university system. Semitic studies became one of the premier wedges with which Jews penetrated the hitherto Protestant world of higher learning. In the late nineteenth century, sixteen positions in the field, a notable number at the time, were held by men of Jewish background.[7]

To understand the growth of ancient Near Eastern studies is to understand the maturation of the American university and its connection to Germany. German scholars in the nineteenth century were the bright stars of the learned world. Their ideals attracted many American schools that aspired to greatness and competed to secure *Doktors* educated in German seminars. The Germans who came to the United States were a fascinating lot. They were, overall, intelligent and well trained. But they had to be powerfully motivated to uproot their lives and come to a provincial academic culture of second-rate status. Their motivation was often a desire for recognition coupled with a sense of the impediments that the German system would throw up to them (especially because some of them were Jewish). The German Americans were successful in scholarly terms in the United States. They were also, by and large, ultimately German in their loyalty and contemptuous of the culture that had given them the opportunity they sought. Their foreign accents were noticeable, as were their Kaiser Wilhelm mustaches.

The most important exemplar of this German American type in Oriental studies was Hermann Hilprecht. Like almost everyone who became prominent in the field of ancient Near Eastern studies, Hilprecht was trained by Friedrich Delitzsch at Leipzig. Authoritarian and hierarchical, Delitzsch's seminar typified the German system of doctoral training. It embodied an apprenticeship in which young men were dependent on the wisdom and goodwill of a single older mentor. Hilprecht had absorbed these ideas by the time he came to the University of Pennsylvania as its first expert in the ancient Near East and secured a place on the BEF's expedition. Hilprecht detested the gritty work in the field but did pontificate about the need for *wissenschaftliche* excavation and the (obvious) inadequacies of those Americans charged to do it. The Nippur dig gave the United States credit in the international scholarly community. But soon after the expedition ended in the early 1900s, Hilprecht publicly complained about the abilities of his colleagues. His complaints provoked a bitter dispute over who was the worse exemplar of digging methods, Hilprecht or his American foes. The "Hilprecht Controversy" became a local scandal; an institutional battle touching the erudite at Harvard, Yale, Johns Hopkins, Columbia, and Chicago; and an international incident, finally pitting the British and the Americans against the Germans. Hilprecht's shadow over this book, sometimes dark, is always long. The controversy about him displayed national academic and social divisions and cultural differences between the United States and Europe. It dramatized the issues that allowed the university to dominate intellectual life in the United States.

The complexities of the specific endeavor that uncovered Nippur and illustrated the professionalization of knowledge had, in the end, a deeper significance. Inquiries into the ancient world played a part in creating the modern idea of the West and the West's notion of history. This is my third story.

Secularization was a critical aspect of intellectual life at the turn of the twentieth century, and it effected radical changes in studies of the past. The deep Christian commitment of many Near Eastern explorers was striking. They wished to secure the truth of the Old Testament, and from their purpose comes the title of this book. Yet their attempt to comprehend the ancient world sometimes led these pious men of knowledge away from religion. The paradox in the evolution of Near Eastern studies was the manner in which the pursuit of Bible truth might undermine the truth of the Bible.

The negative impact of nineteenth-century historical studies on the sacred is well known, but no one has written on the contribution of ancient studies to this tale. Excavations and decipherment aided in a new understanding of the past and a new way of grasping the human role in the universe.

The Americans went to these far-off sites just when intellectuals who had discovered the end of their own domestic frontier began to look abroad at the possibility of an American empire. Although some thinkers were anti-imperialists, they also believed that the torch of Western civilization had made its way from Greece and Rome to Britain and now, about 1900, to the United States. The Americans in the Near East believed in the greatness of their own culture, distinguished by economic strength, martial capacity, and an enduring religion and form of government. These beliefs perhaps helped convince them that the ancient states were great. The explorers unearthed physical remains, literature, and art. This material showed that Egypt and Assyria had characteristics similar to what Americans thought defined civilization in the United States. But the decay and waste around them also made these explorers at times reflect morbidly about the impermanence of human things. They quoted the biblical prophecies about the destruction that fell on Assyria. As one historian has said, the adventurers knew their Shelley, and one explorer in Egypt recited "Ozymandias" to his son:

> I met a traveller from an antique land
> Who said: Two vast and trunkless legs of stone
> Stand in the desert. . . .
> And on the pedestal these words appear:
> "My name is Ozymandias, king of kings:
> Look on my works, ye Mighty, and despair!"
> Round the decay
> Of that colossal wreck, boundless and bare
> The lone and level sands stretch far away.[8]

The Americans often contrasted the transience of non-Christian spirituality in the Near East to the eternal verities of Jesus. Some students of the ancient Near East thus held on to their religious commitment. They are a stunning counterexample to easy generalizations about the secularization of higher education in America in the twentieth century. To analyze the careers of these religiously oriented specialists is complicated. The analysis involves the bureaucratic structure of their fields of inquiry as well as their own intellectual fearfulness. We need also to comprehend the authority of their leader, the Johns Hopkins scholar William Foxwell Albright, and the work of speculative historians such as Arnold Toynbee.

On the other hand, the vivid experience of impermanence in the Near East could lead to uncertainty about received creeds. Many savants forsook the faith of their fathers. The tale of the doubters is more conventional because they went down a more well-trod path. Scholars such as the Egyptologist James Henry Breasted of Chicago followed easily in the tradition of John Dewey's liberal pragmatism. But more than convention was at work. The historical and linguistic reasoning that came to the fore in uncovering ancient cities and deciphering their documents had a cruel impact on religion. Those who took the well-trod path were not merely technocrats or superficial humanists. Their craft depended on principles that made religious worldviews unpromising and unsatisfying; it also depended on certain compelling claims about historical knowledge and the connection of the West to other cultures. Overall, the professional lives of the faithful and those of little faith illuminate the crablike movement that took the intellectual world away from religious belief.

This book divides without difficulty into two parts. The first part is mainly but not exclusively about the early expeditions. It gives an account of American Orientalism in the nineteenth century and of the campaigns, from the initial planning in the mid-1880s to their formal end in 1900. Much in this narrative has, for me, the quality of a novel by Anthony Trollope: it is filled with incident, an unpredictable plot, and (most characteristically) lively but flawed protagonists. The documents of the period show, from various angles, ambition, betrayal, courage, greed, and—perhaps most consistently—imperfection. At the same time the story illustrates the growth of ancient Near Eastern studies in the United States and the way in which secular reasoning challenged the affirmations of faith.

The second part of the book examines the bureaucratic and intellectual impact that the exploration had on learning in the United States and in the rest of the world. The larger academic context in which the campaigns took place is at center stage. Although the repercussions of the first American expeditions are still significant, the story shifts to the more inclusive scholarly and institutional changes. The narrative emphasizes the administration of ancient Near Eastern studies and the religious and methodological problems that this novel professorial area generated.

I have occasionally examined threads of the story that were significant before the 1880s or that extended beyond the 1920s, yet essentially these fifty years were the formative time in the history of the fields associated with the ancient Near East. Although my concentration is on American scholarship, I am aware that national boundaries do not adequately define the limits of learning. But these boundaries molded traditions of knowledge. This book ties the earliest campaigns to the broader history of ancient Near Eastern studies in the United States in a critical era. In learning how a connected set of inquiries arose, one can finally learn something about the presuppositions of historical understanding, and so about our place in the scheme of things.

PART ONE

FROM THE UNITED STATES TO BABYLONIA

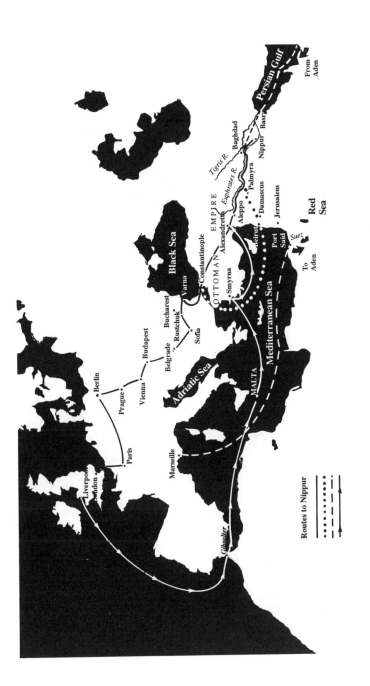

Map 1 Travelers' Europe about 1900

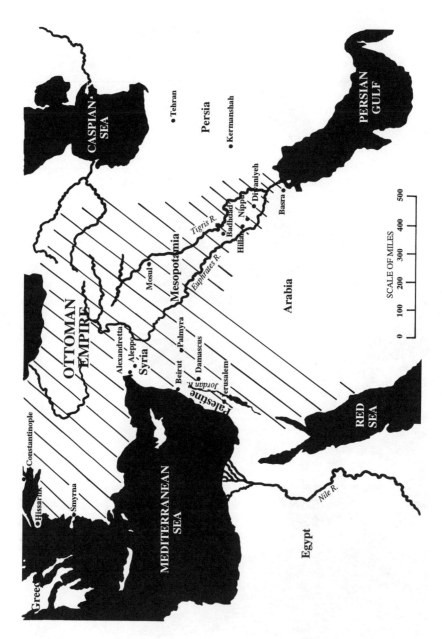

Map 2 The Near East about 1900

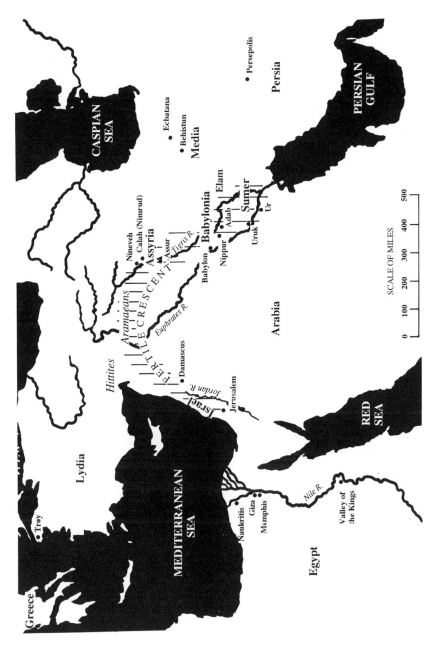

Map 3 The Ancient Near East as known about 1900

MAIN CHARACTERS IN THE STORY

Scholars and Explorers

William Dwight WHITNEY, student of Sanskrit and ancient India in Yale University; the leading American Orientalist in the second half of the nineteenth century.

Dr. William Hayes WARD, clergyman and religious journalist; leader of the initial American expeditionary force to Mesopotamia.

Dr. John Punnett PETERS, clergyman and Old Testament scholar; sometime professor of Semitics in the University of Pennsylvania and first director of American exploration in Mesopotamia in 1889 and 1890.

John Henry HAYNES, business manager and photographer in Mesopotamia in 1889 and 1890; director of exploration, 1893–1900.

Cassandria Artella HAYNES, wife of John HAYNES; in Mesopotamia from 1899 to 1900.

Dr. William Rainey HARPER, student of WHITNEY, professor of Semitics in Yale University; first president of the University of Chicago, established in 1892.

Dr. Robert Francis HARPER, brother of Rainey HARPER and one of two Assyriologists of equal rank in Mesopotamia in 1889; later called to be professor of Assyriology in the University of Chicago.

Dr. Hermann (or Herman) V. HILPRECHT (German national), clergyman; one of two Assyriologists of equal rank in Mesopotamia in 1889, and scientific director in 1899 and 1900; professor of Assyriology in the University of Pennsylvania.

Dr. Paul HAUPT (German national), professor of Assyriology in the Johns Hopkins University.

Sara Yorke STEVENSON, amateur Egyptologist; sometime president of the Museum of the University of Pennsylvania.

Sir Flinders PETRIE (English), leading Egyptologist at the end of the nineteenth century; sometime employee of the University of London.

Clarence FISHER, student of HILPRECHT; architect in Mesopotamia from 1899 to 1900, and later a prominent archaeologist in Palestine.

Dr. Albert CLAY, clergyman and student of HILPRECHT; called to be professor of Assyriology in Yale University.

Dr. Edgar James BANKS, explorer in Mesopotamia for the University of Chicago, 1904–5.

Dr. Morris JASTROW, Jr. (Jewish), professor of Semitics in the University of Pennsylvania.

Dr. Friedrich DELITZSCH (German), leading trainer of Assyriologists—including Frank HARPER, HILPRECHT, HAUPT, BANKS, and JASTROW—first in Leipzig, then in Berlin.

Dr. George Andrew REISNER, leading archaeologist in Egypt and professor in Harvard University; excavator for Harvard and the Boston Museum of Fine Arts.

Dr. James Henry BREASTED, student of Rainey HARPER and foremost authority on Egyptian hieroglyphics; professor of Egyptology in the University of Chicago and founder of its Oriental Institute.

Dr. William Foxwell ALBRIGHT, student of HAUPT and called to be successor to his chair in the Johns Hopkins University; premier scholar of biblical archaeology.

Various other diggers and scholars, including many pupils of DELITZSCH, HILPRECHT, and HAUPT.

University Heads

William PEPPER and Charles Custis HARRISON of the University of Pennsylvania; Rainey HARPER, formerly a professor in Yale, of the University of Chicago; Daniel Coit GILMAN of the Johns Hopkins University; Charles William ELIOT and A. Lawrence LOWELL of Harvard University; Seth LOW and Nicholas Murray BUTLER of Columbia University; and Arthur Twining HADLEY of Yale University.

Gentlepeople of Wealth

Catherine Lorillard WOLFE, of New York, patron of that city's cultural endeavors; Edward White CLARK of Philadelphia and his brother Clarence CLARK, patrons of the University of Pennsylvania and the University Museum; Jacob SCHIFF (Jewish) of New York and Gardiner Martin LANE of Boston, patrons of Harvard; J. P. MORGAN of New York, patron of the Metropolitan Museum, Yale University, and the Morgan Library; John D. ROCKEFELLER and his son, John D. ROCKEFELLER, Jr., of New York, patrons of the University of Chicago; and Phoebe Apperson HEARST of San Francisco, patron of the University of Pennsylvania Museum and the University of California.

1

THE BOYS OF SUMER, 1876–1888

A FULL-BLOODED Protestant Christianity dominated educated life in nineteenth-century America.[1] For the professional classes the Holy Land was an important reality. American missionary activity in the Near East, and in Palestine in particular, was intense, and by the 1820s hardy American Protestants had begun to uplift the Arab world. Later, they went to Egypt. By the second half of the nineteenth century, genteel but serious American tourists were trekking to Palestine.[2] This desire of the college-trained middle class to appropriate the ancient East had a manifestation in the academic culture that lies at the heart of this book.

This culture of learning and intellect was located in the schools of New England and the Northeast, many of which had been founded as ministerial training centers, and all of which had curricula devoted to the education of Christian gentlemen. Divinity schools were America's first institutions offering instruction for graduates of these colleges. The institutions taught the history of the church, theology and the Bible, and Latin and the biblical languages, Hebrew and Greek. Aside from schools of law and medicine, seminaries were the only places for American young men to receive advanced, "graduate" training until late in the nineteenth century. These seminaries were not replaced as repositories of the highest learning until the beginning of the twentieth century. By that time scholars-to-be conventionally went to graduate schools in what would later be called the disciplines of the social sciences or humanities.

Outside the colleges, the interest of literary figures was more likely to gravitate to ancient Egypt than to the Bible lands. Indeed, Egypt attracted wide attention, as attested to by a nineteenth-century vogue for an Egyptian style in architecture and by the large audiences that lectures and collections of antiquities attracted. From early in the nineteenth century mummies and the representations of Egypt—the Sphinx, the pyramids, and hieroglyphics—engaged a less clerical public. From the available evidence, this public was also more popular than the one that pressed for Americans to master the knowledge of the peoples of the Bible. Over the course of the century, however, the inability of Egypt to engage a more scholarly clientele worked to its disadvantage when the American university, at the end of century, became synonymous with the life of the mind.[3]

In most ways the United States in the nineteenth century was an intellectual province shared by Britain and Germany. Yet in their colleges and divinity schools the Americans had produced an independent and respected tradition of Bible scholarship. Moses Stuart, the Old Testament student at Andover Theological Seminary in Massachusetts, had earned the respect of the European professoriate in the first half of the nineteenth century. In 1841, Stuart's student, Edward Robinson, published *Biblical Researches in Palestine, Mount Sinai, and Arabia Petraea in 1838.*[4] Robinson had studied in Germany and later taught at Union Theological Seminary in New York City. For two and a half months he had surveyed the Holy Land, the region in and around Jerusalem and the Red Sea. His book founded the modern study of biblical topography, the historical geography of the area. Robinson identified many sites and pointed out the errors of generations of seekers after Bible wisdom who had toured these places. In the United States Robinson's pathbreaking work lent honor to the "scientific" study of religion that did not compromise Scripture.

In 1841 Yale had appointed Edward Elbridge Salisbury, America's first European-trained Orientalist in Arabic and Sanskrit, an ancient language of India. William Dwight Whitney studied with Salisbury; when Whitney later assumed a professorship at Yale, New Haven was recognized for an Orientalism that extended beyond the Bible lands to India. Whitney and his student, William Rainey Harper, put American training in ancient languages on a level with that of Europe, although German universities persistently drew Americans until the end of the century.[5] With his idiosyncratic and barely Christian religious ideas, Whitney gave many young Americans an enthusiasm for ancient India and the Vedas, the sacred writings of Hinduism.[6] Harper, whose forte was biblical Hebrew, explicitly defended the Christian tradition, although he read the Bible "liberally."[7] Harper studied Hebrew as it had been studied in the past, to explicate the Old Testament. He also wished to show how the language was connected to other old Semitic tongues and to shed light on the cultures of the Orient.

Both Harper and Whitney were interested in comparative philology, which essentially tried to connect the long-extinct languages. Scholars knew that French and Italian were more closely joined than French and German. What were the relations of the world's oldest languages? How had they evolved? How had older forms developed into more recent ones? Questions of this kind absorbed comparative philologists in much technical detail and argument. But high stakes were involved. Philologists who examined the oldest dead languages, such as Sanskrit, were looking for the ur-language, the presumed first tongue that human beings had spoken, and thus for the whereabouts of the first group of people who had a language. The comparative philologists were investigating the geographical origins of humankind in what the Bible said was Eden and the confusion of dialects that the book said spread from Babylon.[8] Much modern research derived from biblical preconceptions. But just as surely, it seemed to American savants, scholarship might confirm what the Bible told us in picturesque language.

The more or less conservative Calvinist theology of the divinity schools was slowly transformed during the nineteenth century. The new ideas in the life sciences, and surely the publications of Charles Darwin, negatively affected traditional Christian certainties. Science questioned a literal understanding of Genesis's tale of creation and of the origin of humanity. Educated Americans were reconfiguring their Christian views. The growth of graduate study outside the schools of theology signaled the secularization of scholarship in the humanities and social sciences. Yet the decline of creedal conviction must not be overstated. Scholars had worried about Genesis long before Darwin and had "figurative" interpretations of the Bible available. Beliefs were given up gradually. Various strategies combated the corrosive impact of nineteenth-century thought. A massive commitment to Christianity remained intact.

Academic students of the Bible, the ancient world, and its languages had claims to legitimacy antedating those of scholars who went into the newer disciplines. The American Oriental Society (AOS) was founded in 1842–43 and began to publish the proceedings of its meetings and then a periodical, the *Journal of the American Oriental Society*.[9] This was before the founding of the German Oriental Society in 1844, and more than a generation before the founding in 1869 of the organization with which the AOS had most commerce in the nineteenth century, the American Philological Association. The AOS initially supported the investigation of the Bible lands and much else that was exotic—non-European, and therefore Oriental. It was "a place where the grammatical, geographical, and historical studies of missionaries could be received and published."[10] Egypt was conspicuously missing as an area of interest. But for a time the AOS had a "classical section," hoping to use the prestige of Greek and Latin, well institutionalized in colleges, to bolster the claims of Oriental languages.

Other local and national groups followed the AOS and its *Journal*.[11] The American Palestine Exploration Societies of the early 1870s were not wealthy or outstanding or durable institutions, but they did evince the strength of concern for Bible scholarship.[12] At the end of the century, a young American of scholarly religious bent no longer needed to look for a career in the rabbinate or ministry or in the teaching of one of the various areas of divinity, but could look to the growing academic world of the Orient, which already had a fifty-year history and a record of accomplishment.[13]

By the latter part of the century the array of Orientalist concerns had the backing of a new generation of university presidents. Along the East Coast, in the Midwest, and in California, public and private institutions of higher learning were founded. Many imbibed an ideal of research from Germany, and at older (Protestant) colleges this ideal often altered traditional conceptions of higher education. The University of Chicago, newly financed by John D. Rockefeller, was supposed to be a Baptist school, whereas Johns Hopkins had less sectarian aims. But science enthralled the administrators of these schools and others like them. Moreover, although from a later perspective the ascension to leadership of this group of bureaucrats was an important moment in the secularization of the academy, the administrators also believed in divine truth. They did not want religion to intrude into the expert work of the university in any controversial, untoward way; they did want religiously safe researchers who upheld Judeo-Christian convictions.[14] Even at the anamalous if preeminent Harvard (always on the American Protestant "left"), professors self-consciously imparted Protestant cultural values if not a devotion to the religion of Christ.

The students of Robinson, Salisbury, Whitney, and Harper were not at odds with the American university of the late nineteenth century. The younger men closely analyzed texts to ascertain historical truth. Yet at the same time, they frequently worked to credit Holy Writ. American scholars carefully exposed the Bible and its traditions to critique, yet their research tended to verify the book's status as a more or less reliable guide to the civilizations it described. The Bible's historicity could be challenged, yet scholars found intellectually stimulating but comforting ways to explain away what was not corroborated by the evidence extant in the nineteenth century.

A major test came in the 1870s and 1880s when Americans encountered the work of the German Julius Wellhausen. His magnum opus, *Prolegomena to the History of Israel*, was available in English in 1878.[15] Wellhausen challenged Moses' authorship of the Pentateuch, the first five books of the Bible. He argued that they were composed from four other sources. Moses himself might never have existed.[16] Overall, the books of the Old Testament almost all came from compilers rather than a single author, said Wellhausen. The reason was that the Old Testament had begun as a body of oral traditions and brief documents handed down from generation to generation. At certain periods scribes collected these and put them into a single account. Evidence for different traditions behind the Old Testament stories could be detected through variations and duplications in the biblical books themselves. For example, in Genesis two tales of the Creation appeared. Genesis 2:4–3:24 told the well-known story of Adam and Eve. But before this story, there was another version—probably of later vintage—in Genesis 1–2:4.[17]

As was true throughout much of the nineteenth century, intellectual advances depended on the willingness of the learned to accept the legitimacy of hypotheses in their investigations. Wellhausen said the Pentateuch derived from documents that no one had seen, just as Darwin had inferred the existence of certain antique life forms. Both naturalists and scholars in libraries had similarly postulated texts, languages, cultures, or species that existed before the rise of present civilized humanity.

Wellhausen brought to fruition what was known as the "higher criticism" of the Bible.[18] Scholars such as Moses Stuart had once been content to examine biblical texts and sources to discover what they really said, practicing the "lower criticism." Wellhausen additionally subjected the texts to "literary" analysis. He wanted to know how they got to us in the state that they were in, and so presumed that repetitions and different styles mingled in a single existing document indicated the compound nature of biblical writing.

Wellhausen had not gone so far as had his fellow German, D. F. Strauss, who was famous for giving higher criticism notoriety. His *Leben Jesu* of 1835–36 was translated into English and available in the United States in the 1840s. Strauss had called into question the miracles of Christ and so the divinity of Jesus and the crux of Christianity. He examined the New Testament stories suggesting Jesus' divinity in light of his own best knowledge of the way the world was. Multitudes could not be fed with a few bits of food, nor did people rise from the dead. Scholars must reinterpret a history that asserted such occurrences in order to uncover what ancient authors were about. Perhaps they really had meant something else, or perhaps their beliefs had to be translated in the way a twentieth-century anthropologist would, with sympathy, explain a rain dance.

Wellhausen was not so radical as Strauss, but the reasoning involved was similar for both students of the Old and New Testaments. These scholars would treat the Bible as they did any other book. Wellhausen concentrated on grasping the true history of the composition of the Old Testament, rather than the religious truth of what the documents said. But his work was still unsettling, given the earlier example of Strauss. Influential in the United States, Wellhausen's scholarship was, if not irrefutable, at least compelling in its general outline: it seemed most unlikely that a single hand had authored the Pentateuch.

Together, Strauss and Wellhausen defined the higher criticism, gave it a reputation for ruthlessness, and made it a potent force in America. Scholars were permitted to subject the Bible's arrangement and factual claims to scrutiny identical to that which any history written in the nineteenth century would undergo.

Although not so challenging as the higher criticism, classical studies in Great Britain also put American scholars of the Near East on their mettle. The growing knowledge of ancient cultures had prompted British thinkers to place the oldest religious impulses neither in reason nor in revelation, but in primitive magic or tribal ritual.[19] James Frazer's *Golden Bough* (the first edition of which was published in 1890) accumulated a great deal of information for theoreticians, along with a secular and negative appraisal of religious faith.[20] In . . . *The Religion of the Semites* (1889) the erudite and more orthodox Robertson Smith wrote about the start of the Hebraic tradition. His theories, however, still led to trials for heresy in his Scottish presbytery, while arousing admiration in America. Not exactly a higher critic in the style of Wellhausen, Smith argued that the Old Testament could best be understood by extrapolating backward from the practices of nineteenth-century Arabian nomads. He concluded that Judaism had sprung from ancient rites and sacrifices that bore little relation to the elevated conceptions of monotheism.[21] Additionally, in the United States, some Jewish and Christian scholars found the study of "comparative religion" appealing. This field joined the list of Bible-oriented areas of inquiry even though it in some measure presupposed that the Judeo-Christian system was on a more or less equal plane with other religions.[22]

European scholars raised issues that could rarely be examined with full candor in America. The British and the German academics did not usually intend to destroy the Judeo-Christian order. Yet their substantive findings damaged the historical trustworthiness of the Bible. The principles behind the higher criticism were more disquieting, for the reasoning prohibited any recourse to the divine. On the one hand, the Germans claimed that investigation of the human past could not include the supernatural. On the other hand, human beings had to experience religious truth in temporal terms. For many scholars Old Testament history still revealed a deity. Thoughtful Americans could barely suppress this tension when they reflected on the higher criticism.[23]

By the 1880s, scholars of the Near Orient in the United States saw their studies in the front lines of a defense of the Old Testament. They also believed that a scientifically defended history of the Israelites would fit in with the histories of other ancient peoples and merge with the story of the West. They wanted a defensible spiritual basis for human history and sought to link it to a story that would explain present society. For a variety of reasons, they were persuaded that they would make the most progress if they could actually explore the Orient. Yet the erudite made a number of false starts.

Johns Hopkins University was founded in 1876, largely to promote graduate study. Its president, Daniel Coit Gilman, wanted to establish the Near East as an area of scholarship. He appointed Thomas Chalmers Murray in Semitics to one of his initial faculty posts and planned a full set of courses. But Murray died soon thereafter. Gilman did not get Johns Hopkins back into the area until several years later, when he hired a young German scholar, Paul Haupt. Haupt was a major acquisition and eager to excavate overseas, but by the time he had gotten his sea legs in America, Johns Hopkins had lost crucial time.

In the meanwhile, early in 1880, President Charles William Eliot of Harvard offered a professorship in Oriental languages to the uniquely talented Robertson Smith, who was then being tried for heresy in Presbyterian Scotland. Eliot was already the dominant academic administrator in the United States, and Smith a scholar of international fame. He was not an armchair theorist like many British Victorians working in the history of religion. Fluent in Arabic, Smith traveled in the Arabian peninsula. He questioned the "contemporary primitives" about their customs and kinship. He then made conjectures about the evolution of religion in these cultures, using the Old Testament records as a documentary base point. Smith had a keen interpretative bent; he juxtaposed social and literary analysis to produce a new perspective on the Israelite faith, first embodied in an 1875 article, "Bible," in the *Encyclopaedia Britannica*. Smith was not a proto-anthropologist; rather, he blended speculative history, Old Testament criticism, and participant observation in an altogether innovative species of scholarship. In offering him employment at Harvard, Eliot took a dramatic initiative that would have given Oriental studies in the United States a unique direction: Smith wanted to depict a historically evolving hierarchy of different cultures but was unusual in the way he linked the more developed to the less. Eliot rightly told Smith that a job in Cambridge was "the best position in America in your department of scholarship" and hoped Smith would create "a fresh start" for Harvard.

Unfortunately for Eliot, the 1880 trial was resolved in Smith's favor, and his Scottish supporters convinced Smith that he would be unhappy in Cambridge, teaching only "amateurs and Unitarians." Eliot was successful in appointing his next choice, Crawford Toy, but Toy made little impact.[24] Harvard's failure to persuade Smith, like Murray's untimely death at Johns Hopkins, retarded progress at these two institutions.

Another aborted effort was centered in New York City. Meeting in New Haven in 1884, members of the American Oriental Society proposed a reconnoitering expedition to the Near East. This proposal received the formal sponsorship of the Archaeological Institute of America, an organization interested primarily in the heritage of Greek and Rome. Later that year, in September, a little band of Americans set out for the Near East to survey various sites for the full-fledged exploration that, it was hoped, would come later. Catherine Lorillard Wolfe, a wealthy New York patron of elite religious causes, put up five thousand dollars for the trip. Leading it was William Hayes Ward, an older clergyman-scholar. He was nearing fifty—overage for a pilgrim to the Near East. Ward edited a religious newspaper, the *Independent*, in New York, and advised the financier J. P. Morgan, who was acquiring Mesopotamian antiquities for the Metropolitan Museum. Esteemed for his understanding of the lands and peoples of the Old Testament, Ward—like Robertson Smith—had apparently refused a call to Harvard in Oriental languages. He desired that a consortium of cultured New Yorkers, both in and out of the academic world, might sponsor further investigation in the Near East. The so-called Wolfe Expedition first extended the scholarly reach of the United States to the ancient Near East.[25]

When the travelers came back in 1885, a learned group based in New York immediately sought funds for a more sustained tour that would involve excavation. Ward reported positively on the benefits to American culture of such excavation and suggested possible places.[26] The reconnaissance showed that determination could overcome the practical problems of planning and making a trip.

Foremost in pressing for a successor to the Wolfe Expedition was a New York Episcopal clergyman, John Punnett Peters,[27] the son of the rector of St. Michael's Church, the affiliation of the wealthiest and most prominent families on the West Side of Manhattan. The scion of an old New England family with ties to Yale, Peters was graduated in 1873; he played on Yale's first football team and befriended his fellow student William Rainey Harper. Both Peters and Harper worked with William Dwight Whitney, and Peters received a Ph.D. in 1876 in Semitic languages, specializing in Hebrew. At the same time Peters was ordained in the Episcopal church. Rather than choosing the ministry, he tutored at Yale for three years and then studied Semitic languages for four more years in Germany. In 1883 he returned to the United States to help his father at St. Michael's.

From this New York base, Peters pushed for American exploration in Mesopotamia. In his early thirties, he argued vigorously that the United States should lead in this sort of Old Testament scholarship. In a variety of popular New York publications, he urged on a literate upper-middle-class public the importance of the ancient Near East. "Liberal-minded men," wrote Peters, must be found to pay for excavations for the benefit of the New World.[28] Americans could raise the level of their civic life and gain trophies for the United States.

In 1884 Peters moved for a time to Philadelphia to be a professor of Old Testament languages at the Episcopal Divinity School. He promoted in Philadelphia, as he had in New York, an American role in Babylonia. He had no luck until the summer of 1887 when he enlisted the aid of Edward White Clark, whose father had been a Philadelphia banker before the Civil War. After the war, Clark and his brother Clarence emerged as important figures on the national financial scene. In the 1870s and 1880s their interests came to include coal, iron, steel, and railroads as well as the stock market and finance. Both men, however, desired more than the respect given to the rich and powerful.

Edward Clark had visited the Orient as a young man, spending time in Palestine and Damascus. He became fascinated with the Near East and the ancient world that Europeans were exploring. In the Clarks John Punnett

Peters struck pay dirt in his search for "liberal-minded men" to finance excavation. Philadelphia would reap the benefit from a plan that New Yorkers conceived. The Clarks had found a vehicle for the recognition they wanted.

With the Clarks' influence and money behind him, Peters mobilized more donors and created the Babylonian Exploration Fund to pay for an expedition. In addition to money from the wealthy, Clark and Peters wanted to engage scholars from many institutions and walks of life, and by the fall of 1887 had drawn the University of Pennsylvania into their enterprise. The subscribers to the BEF signed a contract with the university. Any finds from the expedition were to be sent to Philadelphia as property of the university, if it provided a "fireproof building" to house them.[29]

The decision of Clark and Peters to ally themselves to Penn was both astute and predictable. For more than a year Peters had been jointly appointed to the Episcopal Seminary and the university. Yet more important was the character of the university's chief officer, Provost William Pepper.[30]

Pepper came from a well-to-do medical family and made money himself from a practice that throve on a charming bedside manner especially irresistible to wealthy women. He also taught medicine at Penn. In 1881, still under the age of forty, Pepper was inauguarated as provost, head of the institution, despite the hesitations that many had about the soundness of his character and rumors about his personal morality. At that time Pennsylvania was a small and sleepy place dominated by its well-known medical school. Pepper's energy and genius transformed Penn into a bustling institution of national and international renown. Much of the story of the growth of the school is similar to that of other emerging American universities: local entrepreneurs smitten by European scholarship and mindful of the prestige of high culture invested their profits in an unusual way. The money generated in the Northeast and the Midwest after the Civil War turned provincial academies into great centers of learning. Penn's story differed to the extent that Pepper's vision was different.

Pepper had nothing of the more enduring repute of Harvard's Charles William Eliot. In his time, however, people often thought of Pepper as the Benjamin Franklin of the nineteenth century. He modeled himself on the young Franklin, someone active in national urban affairs but eager to give others credit. Ambitious, he believed glory would accrue to him if he mastered the appearance of selflessness. Like Franklin before him, Pepper thought that higher education should be practical, a notion that fit in well with the primacy of the growing professional schools in medicine, law, and business at his university. But the weakness of "the College," Penn's department that bestowed the arts degree, did not escape him.

Pepper pursued a consistent modus operandi in his thirteen years as provost. An early biographer noted that he was "a money earning machine" for

Penn. Nonetheless, he was convinced that many prospective donors, as well as the city and the state, might wish to support high-toned endeavors without desiring specifically to aid the school. Penn did not have the soaring local influence that Yale and Harvard, for example, could command in their communities. In raising money, Pepper left ambiguous the exact connection of various benefactions to the university, or promoted organizations whose links to Penn were weak.[31]

His attachment to the BEF exemplified this strategy. The fund encouraged the generosity of moneyed citizens who felt a nagging uncertainty about a mere financial career and wanted a connection to something ethically superior.[32] For such men the hope of scientifically establishing the truth of the Old Testament was comfortingly high-minded in an age troubled by Darwin yet unwilling to give up religious verities. The lure of the distant past, the search for antiquities that fascinated nineteenth-century Europeans, and queries about the beginnings of their own societies might move people of wealth to contribute to entities like the Babylonian Exploration Fund. Pepper knew that the subscribers did not desire simply to assist an institution of higher education; he did not press the BEF to clarify its relation to Penn, and encouraged the independence of the donors.

The European quest for the origins of civilized life did not merely indicate Victorian imperialism. Many thinking members of a culture share a concern for the past and the meaning of the human story. The rise of interest in ancient life struck deep chords in the minds of many people. One of the explorers eloquently caught this complex of motives. Such people went to Babylonia, he said, "in the spirit of Christian enlightenment and scientific inquiry to bring forth from its ancestral home, now desolate and forsaken, the heritage of forgotten ages to be entailed forever, with all that is valuable in the deeds, thoughts and aspirations of the human race, to succeeding generations . . . as long as history shall endure."[33] Speaking of one of the rich Philadelphians he hoped to tap for funds, Pepper was more direct: "He is of ripe age and needs some dignified opportunity of reaching a broader fame."[34]

At the same time, Pepper created the Semitic languages program to strengthen the College at the university and to make the study of the ancient world attractive. In 1886 Peters was one of just three people appointed in this field. In that year the entire graduate program awarding degrees beyond the bachelor of arts had five students. The following year, with instruction in Hebrew, Aramaic, and Akkadian, the university enrolled thirty-two graduate students in Semitic languages, as well as thirty-one others in thirteen other disciplines. In 1887, as the work of the BEF got off the ground, Pepper established, on paper at least, a museum in which he could put treasures found in Mesopotamia and elsewhere. Soon thereafter, in 1888 and 1889, the university constructed a new library and moved antiquities into it. This fulfilled the pledge to the BEF to give a home to the Near Eastern collection. Pepper anticipated displaying in the library any finds that the explorers might acquire or dig up in Mesopotamia; soon additional objects made the institution a repository for material from all over the globe.[35] On paper, in borrowed rooms or in the library, and finally in a building of its own, the entity was known as "the University Museum."

In the nineteenth century experts first formulated ideas pertinent to the BEF about how knowledge was linked to museums. The learned classified museums into two groups. The natural history, or scientific, collections were gatherings of objects interesting to geologists, botanists, and zoologists. The fine arts collections housed paintings and portraits. But the BEF positioned itself between these two sorts of institutions. This was the realm of *Kulturgeschichte*, the natural history of civilization. The University Museum would "reconstruct and illustrate the life history of the human race."[36] Objects of various kinds would illustrate the development of human culture and of civilization in the ancient world and elsewhere. In some ways this purpose was sophisticated and easy to grasp. The University Museum was initially concerned with paleontology, the study of fossils, as well as with the work of explorers in the BEF. But by the mid-1890s paleontology had a minor role and, by the turn of the century, it had vanished as a concern. It was not part of "the human story," which would tie together objects and the societies that produced them. The University Museum would house what was necessary to a general historical social science, a cultural archaeology.[37]

Experts sometimes thought of such museums as home to the science of ethnology, which synthesized the material and cultural evidence for studying civilizations. The material evidence came from explorers—archaeologists in the making—who dug up the remains of lost societies. The cultural evidence was gathered by adherents to the fledgling field of anthropology who examined still-existing "primitive" cultures or lost cultures similar to still-existing primitive ones.

Such thinking, however, was theoretical. In practice, scholars found it perplexing to put human cultures on display. Early on, experts easily accepted crude evolutionist, if not Darwinian, ideas: some races or cultures were superior to others, and progress could be limned by looking at, say, the western European nations in contrast to those of the Orient. An even lower stage of development could be charted by showing off peoples who lived in the present but at a visibly more backward phase of civilization; they represented an inferior state of culture from which even Orientals had evolved. Such tribal groups were often found in the Americas, but (as Robertson Smith had shown) in the Near East the scholar could locate Arab nomads. Existing cultures could thus illustrate the advance that had occurred over time, the sequence from hunter to nomad, to villager, to various levels of urban dweller. Such a process was famously—and notoriously for historians—displayed at the World's Columbian Exposition, the White City of 1893.[38]

In scholarly settings, however, it was more difficult to carry out such a plan. To begin with, students of the Old World, whose discoveries at places like Troy and Nineveh had captured the public imagination, fought with those who attended to the "uncivilized" groups in the Americas. The former looked to the past and to ancient art and literature. They had great status. The latter were drawn to the connection of past and present and the existing backward peoples in the New World. These "Americanists" were less honored than students of Greece, Egypt, or Mesopotamia and labored under the burden of studying "savages."[39] That is, issues of prestige mixed with disagreements about which groups to study and how to study them. Scholars of the New World were affiliated with anthropology, which was unique among the new social sciences in its links to museums. Yet by examining primitives in the present instead of digging up relics of the past, anthropologists (in contrast to Old World explorers) came to have less need for museums. The anthropologists also were less interested in exhibiting and comparing cultures to the detriment of their own field of study. Some explorers, on the other side, were zealous for discovery in the Old World and had only a vague sense of what scholarship was about, as opposed to the craving for adventure. They never lost their sense, however, of the critical need for museums for monetary support and for showing off what exploration had unearthed.[40]

Although this dispute between archaeology and anthropology was fundamental, it played itself out in various ways in the context of other, equally divisive, conflicts. Within the ranks of explorers were those most interested in the recovery of ancient civilizations, field archaeologists. They sometimes opposed those interested in the interpretation of the artistic and literary remains recovered, chiefly the epigraphers or decipherers. The epigraphers were most comfortable in their offices translating texts. Like anthropologists, epigraphers came to have fewer links with museums and with public display.

Conflicts also occurred between the increasingly professional academics who inhabited museums and the individuals like Pepper who administered the institutions. The provost and the wealthy people around him hoped to make a genteel culture available to a wider if still select public. The archaeologists, anthropologists, classicists, and other students of the ancient world who had access to some essential ingredients of this culture were building careers. Their world was one of expertise and long training programs. The amateurs and professionals were heading in different directions: one group was in the business of acquainting people with the world, the other of controlling access to knowledge. As the administration of museums grew more complicated, their management too became a profession. At times archivists and curators found their own welfare at odds with that of the scholarly professionals; at other times, the scholars complained that curatorial or archival duties compromised their responsibilities as teachers and researchers.[41] This was most apparent in the many museums that grew up without any university affiliation at all—for example, the Metropolitan in New York and the Museum of Fine Arts in Boston.

By early 1888 the structure that would pay for the first American exploration of the ancient Near East was in place. Pepper chaired the BEF, and Clark was its treasurer, while Peters followed up suggestions for contributors with interviews and a talk about the proposed undertaking. An executive committee of the BEF, composed of some of the most generous donors, met regularly to plan the expedition and, later, to disperse funds and dispose of the finds.

Finances required the exchange of currency in England, Germany, Turkey, and Mesopotamia. The BEF had to allocate money for warranted expenses and to discriminate between them and improvident and even self-interested requests. Administrators and explorers might legitimately disagree on what was needed. Both those in the field and those at home also underestimated the frustration and misunderstanding that would occur because of the mails, which were slow in conveying instructions from the one side and information from the other. Once the exploring had begun, the turnaround time for letters was three months.

The staffing and organization of the campaign were most onerous. The BEF named Peters scientific director and engaged John Dyneley Prince as Peters's secretary. Having just been graduated from Columbia College in New York, Prince paid his own way. The trip was his first step in a university career in Assyriology at Columbia. Peters's knowledge of Akkadian—as opposed to Old Testament Hebrew—was limited,[42] and with little sense of national loyalty he first proposed that an English Assyriologist accompany him. When this plan fell through, Peters attached Robert Francis Harper of New Haven to the expedition as Assyriologist and second in command. Al though he had a doctorate in Assyriology from Leipzig, Frank Harper was not much of a scholar. His most important recommendation was his famous older brother, William Rainey Harper, a friend of Peters and professor of Semitic studies at Yale, who was soon to become the first president of the new University of Chicago. One shrewd observer of the little brother said "he is not an Assyriologist at all. Give him plenty to eat and all the beer and pale ale that he wants and pretty girls and no work to do and he is a very pretty good big boy."[43] Frank Harper had a mercurial and immature disposition. One was never sure from one moment to the next whether he would seek a belligerent confrontation or smoke an expensive cigar with his would-be enemy. His elder brother saw to it that Frank was always gainfully employed, while Frank regularly wrote asking Rainey to "send some money" so that he could buy cigars.[44]

In addition to Harper, the BEF hired Perez Hastings Field as an architect, and John Henry Haynes as business manager and photographer. Field was in his early twenties and lasted only one season. He turned out to be unreliable and frivolous, more suited to Paris, where he liked to spend his time, than to the desert. Haynes, however, remained in the field for more than a decade.[45] Almost forty and by far the oldest member of the expedition, he was the only American to go to Mesopotamia in the late nineteenth or early twentieth century who approached William Hayes Ward in years. It was not a country for the middle-aged. Haynes was a solitary man not given to speed in thought or action. He covered his dull-wittedness with portentous sermonizing, but he was not without the virtue of dogged fidelity. After a desultory career as a secondary-school educator in Massachusetts, he went to the Mediterranean in 1880 and made it his home. In Athens he apprenticed himself to an early photographer of note, William James Stillman, and learned the tasks necessary to taking and developing pictures. This skill and his stolid reliability made him a useful member of the 1881 expedition of the Archaeological Institute of America to Assos in Turkey, and he was also a member of the Wolfe Expedition. When not employed as a photographer, he taught at Protestant mission schools, Robert College in Constantinople, and Central Turkey College in Aintab. Haynes was selected to be photographer. His sober and plodding reputation for probity made him a good choice as business manager, bookkeeper, and disperser of funds. "O' how slow . . . in action" Haynes was, someone said. Another said he was "a common uneducated man," "of very small knowledge" and "very slow in his action." But Peters argued that although Haynes was "slow almost to exasperation," he was "faithful, honest, loyal, self-sacrificing & he knows how to manage the Turks & a caravan & to *photograph*."[46]

The BEF thus selected a group on rational principles in accord with the most up-to-date notions of "scientific" excavation. The director was supposed to concentrate on the actual excavation, assisted by a photographer, an architect, and an Assyriologist. The role of the last was clear. He could read the documents taken from the earth and thus had a unique area of expertise. The photographer and architect also had skills that were not duplicated, but their duties were less clear. After the turn of the century, as archaeology grew into a distinct specialty, its central task became the reconstruction of the living arrangements at an ancient site. An excavator knew the specialized techniques that enabled him to do this job. Trained architects were also crucial because they could help in determining the layout of an ancient town and the way it might have been built and rebuilt. Photographers were useful later, too, because pictures could permanently document what matters looked like at any given time as ongoing excavation progressively altered the landscape. But the Americans had only the vaguest notions of this division of labor when they went to Mesopotamia. The main goal was to get valuable material out of the ground, and the method was the use of many shovels. The notion that the explorers should in addition learn about the contours of old cities was rudimentary at best. If the architect and the photographer had a defined duty, it was to identify and take pictures of works of art or interesting objects that were dug up. Indeed, although he was the boss, the director was the only man without a specialty. He was no better at digging than any of the others, and a case could be made that the Assyriologist or the architect might do better than the director.

At the last minute Provost Pepper added significantly to his cadre of explorers. Hermann Vollrath Hilprecht was a young and talented German Assyriologist.[47] He had come to America in 1886 to edit the *Sunday School Times*, a religious newspaper published in Philadelphia that combined popular and scholarly journalism. In the fall of 1886, shortly after Peters took jobs at both the university and the Episcopal Seminary, Hilprecht joined Semitic languages at Penn with a year-long job as lecturer in Egyptology, the first such position in the United States. A few months later, however, the university approved him as professor of Assyriology, although the *Sunday School Times* still employed him. While his professorship, like that of Peters, was irregular, Hilprecht committed himself to Pepper's institution building. Because of his "delicate health" he declined at first to go to the Near East. Then Pepper appointed him "co-assyriologist" for the exploration and, without initially informing the others, made him second in command:[48] he and Harper would equally share the Assyriological responsibilities, and Hilprecht would take over if something happened to Peters.

Here was room for squabbling. Peters was most capable of heading a practical project, but he had only a lay knowledge of the archaeological discoveries in Mesopotamia. Both Hilprecht and Harper denigrated his learning and felt that he disregarded their expert opinions. Peters's disability in their field exacerbated all the tensions that any leader engaged in a new and exacting activity would have encountered. Hilprecht and Harper, however, were often themselves at odds. Both were in their twenties and eager for rank. Each had reason to think of himself as above the other in the explorers' little hierarchy. Hilprecht perhaps overvalued his skills as a philological scholar. Nevertheless, he was not ungifted, and everyone agreed that his competence exceeded that of Harper. On the other side, Harper was a well-connected Ph.D., less troublesome than Hilprecht, who combined a rude condescension toward his American peers with a whining, hypochondriacal personality. The younger Harper, who claimed on the expedition to think well of Hilprecht, said the German was "the most baby-ish and jealous boor I have ever seen." As Pepper put it, "Hilprecht will die if he does go, and he will die if he does not."[49]

Structural cleavages were as important as personal clashes. Peters's first loyalty was not to the university but rather to Clark and the BEF. On the other hand, Hilprecht saw his future with Provost Pepper and Pennsylvania. Although Pepper and Clark worked closely, the vague allocation of respon-sibilites between Penn and the BEF developed into a conflict between the chief lieutenants.

These differences were suppressed at the start. Peters scored an initial victory for Penn and the BEF against Johns Hopkins University and the Smithsonian Institution, the "national museum" in Washington, D.C. In 1883 Hopkins replaced its first Semiticist with Paul Haupt. The twenty-four-year-old was a German almost as exasperating as Hilprecht. Although they were as one in exulting over the excellence of German scholarship, they dismissed each other's abilities as soon as they reached the United States.[50] In 1888 and 1889, however, Haupt and Peters squared off.

Haupt's hopes for Mesopotamian exploration went back to his time in Göttingen. He came to America in part "to excite an interest in the subject among the men with dollars, & to get them to start an excavation fund."[51] Haupt's model for this sort of endeavor was Germany, where the state pro-vided funds for exploring and for a building to house antiquities. Since Johns Hopkins from its inception had decided not to have a museum of its own but to cooperate with the Smithsonian, Haupt believed that the Smith-sonian and federal dollars would get Johns Hopkins to the Near East. The choice was the old city of Ur. However, Haupt lagged behind Peters and his group and apparently was only prompted to act when he learned that prep-arations in Philadelphia for an expedition were far along. Haupt quickly worked up a formal tie with the Smithsonian as curator and denigrated Peters's efforts as "local" in scope whereas what was wanted should have a "*decidedly national character.*"[52]

It is unclear whether Haupt and willing Smithsonian officials could have pulled off an expedition. There is no evidence that money would have been forthcoming or, for example, that Haupt could have procured the assistance of the American army and navy, as he assumed. But he was overly aggressive in drumming up support and had gotten underway only after Peters had successfully organized his group; Haupt alienated a number of sympathizers and made Baltimore look like an interloper covetous of the recognition others deserved. With some work, Peters won a bruising encounter with officials at Johns Hopkins and the Smithsonian over who had prior claims. In a final triumph for Peters and Hilprecht, the BEF even denied Haupt a place on the expedition,[53] which, at long last, was now ready to leave.

2

IN THEIR RUINS, 1889–1892

IN THE SUMMER of 1888 Peters traveled by ship from the United States, going first to London and Berlin, where he purchased supplies and consulted with various academic authorities. Then, in September, he made his way south by train on the Orient Express—Prague, Vienna, Budapest, Belgrade, Sofia—to Constantinople and the lands of the Ottoman Empire. Like other Americans Peters ruminated on passing "from civilization to semi-barbarism, . . . from Occident to Orient."[1]

Of the many jobs Peters undertook, none was more critical than obtaining permission to excavate and to export the results. The Turks, who governed Mesopotamia, had to grant this permission (or *firman*), as well as the right to travel and set up shop somewhere in Mesopotamia. The Turkish capital, Constantinople, now became an important stopping place for the Americans. The Ottoman Empire was famous as "the sick man of Europe," a pawn in the power struggles of the English, French, Germans, and Russians. The political and military defects of Constantinople meant that the Great Powers treated its concerns cavalierly when they came in conflict with the growing scholarly demands of the Europeans. The Ottomans were bearers of an inferior Muslim culture. The West must heed Turkish prerogatives but could not accept them as equal to those of the Europeans.

This disparity in the respect due to the Turks and to the Europeans increased as one journeyed to the southern portions of the empire, including Mesopotamia. Here were the degenerate Arabs, whose civilization had declined from an earlier golden era.[2] They were dangerous, hostile to Westerners, ill governed, and only nominally in the hands of Ottoman authorities.

The Ottoman Empire was, to an extent, wretchedly and inefficiently managed. But, to an extent, the Turks used their cumbersome bureaucracy to bend to their purposes various Western designs, including scholarly ones. The disorder of the Turks' distant Mesopotamian province abetted this strategy, for the Ottomans could count on the unfriendly and anarchic Arabs to create sympathy for the tribulations of the empire.[3]

Peters first had to secure Turkish acquiescence in the American plan, which the Ottomans must have looked on with apprehension. The Americans were from yet another strong country demanding favors from the beleaguered Constantinople officialdom. Yet Turkey could benefit. The Americans would pay not only their own expenses but also those of the Turkish officials assigned to them. In addition, another player in what the English called the "great Eastern game" might allow the Ottomans to divide the Western opposition further. If they could not conquer the West, the Turks might still be left with a modicum of autonomy proportional to the number of countries competing for favors. Finally, in exchange for permission to dig, the Ottomans could require the Americans to give up at least some of the finds. From Mesopotamia, the Westerners would send back whatever they found to Constantinople, where a division of the spoils would take place. The United States would enhance the cultural influence of the Turks, who had opened their own museum.

Ottoman rulers might issue various types of permits—simply to explore, to excavate, or to excavate and take what one found. From the American perspective the final sort—the Americans always referred to it as "the firman"—was crucial. For three months Peters negotiated in Constantinople and corresponded regularly with Clark.

Correct in his dealings with Clark, Peters was straightforward yet upbeat. He described his doings clearly and concisely. Full of goodwill, benign yet not uncritical, he depicted his fellow explorers authoritatively. He concentrated on his hardest task. The firman might be forthcoming, he said, if the president sent a letter. The Americans at home were informed of the sultan's interest in a phonograph, and Thomas Alva Edison was drafted to aid American exploration. For a time Peters wrote to the banker Clark about a possible American loan to the Turkish government; such business dealings might ease the way to excavation.[4] Hilprecht complained that Peters did not understand "the fundamental principle" of Ottoman politics: "Refuse never a thing but say smilingly 'yes' to every request. Simply delay the grant till eternity."[5] As time went by Peters acknowledged that things were "dark & mysterious." One lived "in the midst of trickery & intrigue." Soon Peters and his associates were complicit in the system of petty bribery, or baksheesh. Officials of all sorts enabled the Americans to evade administrative rulings, customs regulations, and even significant laws.[6] "The absolute *status quo* is the thing desired here," Peters said. "Houses fall to pieces, ships decay, roads are worn to chasms; so Turkey is wearing out & cannot be repaired." Meanwhile, as Pepper put it, all effort had to be "concentrated upon securing the one prime essential—the firman."[7]

It was not to be. In December Peters and his secretary, John Prince, left for Mesopotamia with documents allowing them to dig and to purchase any excavated antiquities the Turkish authorities did not want, a weak kind of permit. Peters was still optimistic. No more favorable contract was possible. If the campaign prospered, the Americans could arrange matters more agreeably when Constantinople inspected the finds. The Ottomans would violate their own cautious written word. Peters also notified Philadelphia that the Turks had approved digging some one hundred miles from

Baghdad, at Niffar. This was the old Nippur, a religious center of the ancient civilization and now an enormous mound near the comparable ruins of Babylon.

The other members of the expedition had traveled from London to Marseilles, then by ship to the city of Smyrna on the west coast of Turkey, and then to Alexandretta (now Iskenderun), the Mediterranean port entrée to the southeastern parts of the Ottoman Empire. There they waited for Peters and Prince. Then the whole group went inland to Aleppo in Syria. The caravan of sixty-one horses and mules and a crew of local guides made its slow way, eight hours a day, at a little less than three miles per hour, along the Euphrates to Baghdad. Each step of the journey seemed to carry them more deeply into the past, the contemporary signs of which they were looking for. The desolation oppressed them. Everywhere around them was devastation, particularly the mounds, or *tells*, that were the sites of buried cities.

Peters and his associates were rightly nervous about their undertaking but invigorated by the historic nature of their enterprise. They often reflected that they were taking the first American place in a modern Western tradition of exploration that extended back almost a hundred years. In their thoughts was a living vision of European discoveries and triumphs to which, the Americans hoped, they would soon contribute.

In 1798 Napoleon's troops invaded Egypt. At war with England, the French hoped to disrupt British trade with India, but Napoleon also took with him a small army of scholars—the Commission of Arts and Sciences—who studied the land and people of Egypt. Preserved both in the Bible and in the writings of the Greek and Roman authors, the glory of Egypt's past had never been completely forgotten. The pyramids and the Sphinx of Giza in particular had intimated the magnificence of this civilization. The publications and engravings of Napoleon's experts added substantively to the European and American grasp of Egypt. In the 1810s, Giovanni Belzoni, a circus strong man who worked in England, explored and pillaged in Egypt. He shipped pieces of art back to the British Museum, including the colossal granite head and upper torso of a pharaoh. This art stirred Western imaginations about lost peoples in a way that engravings could not.

More important for interpreting the East was the French recovery in 1799 of a slab of polished black basalt. This volcanic rock, found near Rosetta about forty miles east of Alexandria, contained a bilingual inscription in Greek and two varieties of ancient Egyptian—hieroglyphics. By the 1820s scholars had used the Rosetta stone to decipher the hieroglyphics. Orientalists began to reconstruct the history of the Egyptian political dynasties. They learned that Egypt had once been a great power and had dominated other states. Its civilization, however, had decayed until, like the other Near

Eastern countries of the nineteenth century, Egypt was characterized by inefficiency and decadence and disregarded as a sovereign entity. The decline raised troubling but stimulating questions: How had the transformation occurred? What had made the Near Orient great before Europe itself had become civilized? How had culture come to Europe? Could France or England or Germany fall into the desuetude of the East?

The case of Greece underlined the salience of these questions. Both Greece and Egypt were so weak as to be subject to the nominal rule of the Ottomans, themselves sliding toward a slothful anarchy. After the British defeated the French in Egypt at the turn of the nineteenth century, the Turks gave the English ambassador, Thomas Bruce, the earl of Elgin, permission to take Greek "antiquities"—material remains of these lost worlds. Between 1803 and 1812 the earl removed much material from the Parthenon in Athens. Even in the early nineteenth century, the morality of this activity was debated. Greece was a vassal state but everyone knew its historical significance for the West.

In the long run, the "Elgin marbles" influenced European and American taste and increased interest in the sculpture of long-ago societies—certainly in whatever could be exported to England or France. Aesthetes and historians of Greece and Rome investigated the art and literature of the ancient world as a sort of teacher to the contemporary age. They also transported to European centers as many Greco-Roman objects as they could.

Much later in the century Heinrich Schliemann enlarged this concern. Schliemann was a self-taught classicist, particularly fond of Homer's epic poems, the *Iliad* and the *Odyssey*. The *Iliad* was the story of the Trojans' war against the Greeks. Schliemann was determined to find Troy, the capital of the Greek enemy, located somewhere in northwest Turkey on the east coast of the Aegean. With *Iliad* in hand he excavated at Hissarlik in the early 1870s. Although Schliemann mistook an earlier "level" of the remains of the city for the Troy of the *Iliad*, he did discover the city and a treasure that he claimed belonged to Homer's Trojan king, Priam.

Later Schliemann dug at Mycenae in Greece. This time he vindicated Homer's view that the city was home to Agamemnon, leader of the Greek expedition against Troy. And this time Schliemann argued that he had found the grave of Agamemnon, with valuable burial offerings. This argument, too, proved false, but Schliemann had corroborated the general accuracy of the Homeric tales and proved again that works of art could be found in the earth.[8]

Mesopotamia and Persia also attracted European exploration.[9] Adventurers in the desert used newly discovered literary sources to grasp a fragment of the history of old civilizations that did not seem unlike present states. From Mesopotamia, too, scholars and swashbucklers brought home the remains of its peoples, visual monuments to past imperial times.

In the eighteenth and early nineteenth centuries, Orientalists had begun to puzzle out the meaning of the texts on monuments at Persepolis. The city was located in Persia, what is now southwestern Iran, east of Mesopotamia, and was a center of the Persian Empire. This ruling political unit had arisen in the sixth century B.C., and it lasted some two hundred years. Western travelers in Persia had found inscriptions that were apparently written in three different languages. All were in the wedge-shaped writing inscribed on ancient bricks and tablets found throughout Mesopotamia itself. The signs had usually been impressed on soft clay tablets with a sharp, pointed wooden stick or stylus. Baked or hardened in the sun, the clay was the equivalent of books or paper covered with writing and might survive indefinitely. The tablets turned up as European travelers poked around in the wastes of Mesopotamia. The markings were given the scholarly name "cuneiform," from the Latin for wedge, *cuneus*.

As it turned out, many cultures had borrowed the cuneiform script in the ancient Near East. In the early nineteenth century, because the Persepolis inscriptions were located in Persia, savants assumed that one of the languages of the "trilinguals" might be Persian in wedge-shaped characters and corectly guessed that the Persian would be in the simplest of the cuneiform scripts. With the help of those who had mastered Old Persian, students began to decipher that third of the inscriptions that was Old Persian written in cuneiform.[10]

This triumph culminated in the astounding work of Henry Creswicke Rawlinson, an English civil servant in India. Rawlinson had a gift for languages and in India had learned Persian. In 1835 he was transferred to Persia itself. There he was lured to another set of trilingual inscriptions on a rock face at Behistun, twenty miles east of Kermanshah in northwestern Iran, south of Teheran and north of Baghdad. These inscriptions were enormous and long, illustrated by an eighteen-foot-wide bas-relief, a huge sculpture that projected only slightly from the smooth rock. Three hundred feet above the ground, the Behistun inscriptions were also dangerously inaccessible.

From 1835 to 1837 and again on repeated trips in the 1840s Rawlinson transcribed much of the material on the face of the cliff. His achievement was so extraordinary and had such status among American Orientalists that his description of his work bears quoting at length:

> On reaching the recess which contains the Persian text of the record, ladders are indispensable in order to examine the upper portion of the tablet; and even with ladders there is considerable risk for the foot-ledge is so narrow, about eighteen inches or at most two feet in breadth, that with a ladder long enough to reach the sculptures sufficient slope cannot be given to enable a person to ascend, and, if the ladder be shortened in order to increase the slope, the upper

inscription can only be copied by standing on the topmost step of the ladder, with no other support than steadying the body against the rock with the left arm, while the left hand holds the note-book, and the right hand is employed with the pencil. In this position I copied all the upper inscriptions, and the interest of the occupation entirely did away with any sense of danger.[11]

Decipherment of some of the Old Persian cuneiform printed in the *Journal of the Royal Asiatic Society* in 1837 made Rawlinson's reputation in a growing international community. Then, in 1847, he published a transliteration and translation of all the Persian and a copy of the cuneiform original.

The Old Persian script was syllabic, with thirty-two characters; their values were relatively easy to work out. The erudite were more concerned about the third inscription, recognized to be in the same language as the writing on the inscribed tablets found throughout Mesopotamia. In the late nineteenth and early twentieth centuries this language was known as Assyrian, because the major early finds of documents in Mesopotamia were made in the north at the capital cities of the old Assyrian Empire. But as I have noted, later scholars universally adopted the name *Akkadian* for the Semitic script of ancient Mesopotamia that, over the millenia, had many variant dialects, several of which had been used by the Assyrians. The symbols of Akkadian had two nonalphabetic values. Some of its cuneiform signs stood for syllables—indeed, different syllables. The same signs, however, could stand for multiple words. This was what scholars at first got at by talking about "ideograms" or signs for ideas; they later referred to "logographic" signs for words. Finally, combinations of two or three signs might have new values different from those suggested by the single signs in succession. There were hundreds of these characters, and penetrating their meaning was difficult. Interpretation of the Akkadian was facilitated because it was a member of the Semitic linguistic family, akin to Hebrew, Arabic, and Syriac. Yet in the 1840s the complexities of the tongue puzzled many students, despite the translation from the Old Persian. Other scholars made critical advances in deciphering the language. Rawlinson, however, got the credit with an 1851 publication of the Akkadian on the cliff—the text, a transliteration, and a translation. The basic translation of the second, or Elamite, version—named after the people who had lived in Elam, in what is now southern Iran—followed the Akkadian; the Elamite derived from a list of syllables, or syllabary, connected to the Akkadian.

In 1857 the Royal Asiatic Society tested the progress that had been made on Akkadian. It asked four experts, including Rawlinson, independently to translate a hitherto unpublished text. When the society opened the sealed envelopes containing the separate translations, it found that the experts more or less agreed. The secrets of the main extant cuneiform language were claimed to have been discovered, although the decipherment of texts and the training of scholars in techniques remained a demanding job for the next 150 years.

The Bible supplied the intellectual framework for most Near Eastern scholarship. As the sacred book of the Judeo-Christian tradition, it had propelled many Western visitors to the East and, indeed, had given the learned most of the information they had about the ancient history of that part of the world. For the Americans, the Bible was a more fundamental text than it was for the Europeans.

The Christian Bible has two major parts. The New Testament contained the teaching of God's son, the Savior. It tended to overshadow in importance the Old Testament, which was the whole of the Jewish Bible. But the Old Testament was crucial for Westerners interested in the beginnings of human society. Its thirty-nine books chronicled the relationship between God and his people, the people of Israel, before the time of Christ. The Old Testament was not only the cornerstone of Judaism but also a history of the human race from its origins in the Garden of Eden and a record of Israel's religious aspirations and development. The text meditated on human character and destiny and included prayers of sorrow and thanksgiving. For those committed to Judeo-Christianity, the Old Testament showed something of God's plan for humankind. The history of the Jews demonstrated how God worked in time, revealing the nature of existence, the trials of believers, and the progressive direction of history.[12]

The first five books of the Old Testament (the Pentateuch) told of the Creation, the spread of mankind, and the early history of Israel. Genesis, the first book, related how God constructed the world and placed Adam and Eve in Eden, somewhere in the ancient East. But Adam and Eve disobeyed God, who sent them from Eden. Their progeny proved so wicked that they provoked God's wrath in the form of a great flood, survived only by Noah and his family. After the flood, according to Genesis, Noah's descendants lived together and spoke the same language. They settled in a southern Mesopotamian plain and planned "a city and a tower with its top reaching to heaven." Their presumption again displeased God. He confused their speech so that they could no longer understand one another. Humankind was scattered over the earth and stopped building the city. The unfinished tower was called Babel—meaning confusion—since there the Lord had multiplied the languages of the whole world (Genesis 11:1–9). The then unfinished city was the biblical Babylon, even in its infancy a symbol of human arrogance.

The story of the Hebrew people followed the story of Babel. The biography of Abram (later Abraham) was that of the patriarch of a new religion and society seeking its identity. Abraham migrated from his birthplace in the most southern part of Mesopotamia, Ur, home of the Chaldees (the name for the most-ancient southern Mesopotamians). By the late nineteenth century, Abraham's hometown was associated with origins that were of the most ancient vintage—*ur*. Abraham's people began a long nomadic existence. Centuries later, their great legislator and prophet Moses led the Israelites out of Egypt in the Exodus and authored the story that appeared in the Petateuch. Moses died before his people reached the Promised Land—in Palestine, between Egypt and Mesopotamia. But he defined the idea of monotheism and gave them God's law in the Ten Commandments. In the nineteenth century many Americans knew in detail the history of the Jewish quest for a permanent home, and their learned compatriots worried about Julius Wellhausen's arguments that Moses had not written it.

Later books of the Bible railed against the wickedness of the cultures that grew up in Mesopotamia. Each biblical author reviled them for their treatment of Israel, which even scholars in the nineteenth century could see as a minor power in the imperial conflicts of the oldest societies in the world. The Bible hated and condemned the power of Assyria and decried its capital (in the seventh century B.C.) Nineveh.

Assyria's empire collapsed and Nineveh fell (in 612 B.C.) twenty years after the death of its great king, Assurbanipal. The Old Testament had prophetically celebrated: "All who hear the news of you clap their hands at your downfall. For who has not felt your unrelenting cruelty?" (Nahum 3:18–19).

A coalition of Medes and Babylonians defeated the Assyrians, and the Babylonians, further south in Mesopotamia, gained the major victories. Historians knew this empire as *Neo*-Babylonian because Babylonia had been a great power much earlier; people had first tried to build the tower there. The Bible, which hated the Assyrians, also told of the troubles of the Israelites with the Babylonians, and called their capital city of Babylon the "great whore."

While the Bible set the context for the investigation of Near Eastern cultures, intellectual curiosity moved Rawlinson and the other experts. The uncovering of much new cuneiform material assisted their labors. In the 1840s and 1850s French and English explorers in northern Mesopotamia near Mosul were digging tablets and much else from the earth. European visitors had long inquired about the tells rising out of the plains, composed of debris and dirt over the remains of old dwelling sites. Local lore linked many of them with places mentioned in the Bible, and in times past they had drawn the faithful. Now explorers dug into these mounds, trenching and tunneling to see what they held. Europeans wanted to learn more about their history in conjunction with what the Bible said and hoped to discover antiquities to send back to Paris and London.

In the early 1840s Paul Emile Botta, the French consul in Mosul, in the north of Mesopotamia, excavated at the nearby mound of Kuyunjik. In addition to inscribed tablets he unearthed rooms filled with sculptures, lime-stone slabs with bearded men in long gowns, winged animals, and other wild beasts—the home of an ancient monarch. Indeed, Botta had found the palace of the Assyrian king, Sargon II. Although it was some time before Europeans knew exactly what Botta had uncovered, the Mesopotamians of old were clearly worthy of respect, like the Egyptians with their pyramids. The little-known Assyrian Empire, dreaded and scorned in the Old Testa-ment, actually had the character the Israelites attributed to it. In spite of its greatness, the empire had, in fact, vanished from the face of the earth just as the biblical prophets had said it would, until Botta's exploration.

Although a French museum, the Louvre, first benefited from what Botta shipped back, the British Museum in London soon had even more spectacu-lar finds. It sustained the English preeminence among the European nations in displaying the dead societies.

Austen Henry Layard was a young English adventurer without employ-ment or experience as an explorer when he met Botta in 1842. Soon there-after, Layard's energy and enthusiasm brought him even more fame than Botta.[13] At the end of 1845, after Botta had left Mosul, Layard dug there. For the next several years, off and on, he unearthed treasure after treasure from Assyrian palaces, limestone friezes and sculptures of huge animals, many of which later adorned the British Museum. Layard was hailed for the redis-covery of Nineveh itself. Although European exporters of antiquities had preceded Layard in the East, the insouciance with which he took objects typified the attitude of Westerners toward ancient Near Eastern artifacts. Layard's shipments to London, along with Rawlinson's heroic scholarship, impressed on the English-speaking world the power of the West in the East.

In his written work, *Nineveh and Its Remains . . .* (1849) and *Discoveries among the Ruins of Nineveh and Babylon . . .* (1853), Layard made the great Assyrian cities of Nimrud (the biblical Calah) and Nineveh familiar to readers of English. Not incidentally, he emphasized the connection of his finds to the Old Testament, recognizing that this relation would publicize his efforts. If he "could attach a religous importance" to his discoveries, said a friend, he would "come the complete dodge over this world of fools and dreamers."[14] This cynical appraisal underestimated the independent fasci-nation that Europeans and Americans felt for the artifacts then in the Louvre and British Museum.

The French and English digging had given new impetus to archaeology, the exploration of the distant past through excavation. But most of the dis-coveries had occurred before anyone made much of the cuneiform writing. The tablets were less significant to the public than were the gigantic sculp-tures. But as scholars deciphered the cuneiform in the mid-1850s, interest turned from the sculpture to the old languages.

In 1850 Layard had increased the available documents through his own spadework. During that year his laborers came across rooms in Assurbanipal's palace that contained thousands of inscribed documents. The tablets, many in fragments because a roof had collapsed on them, filled each room more than a foot deep. Layard packed crate after crate for shipment back to London. Those who came after him in the trenches near Mosul added to this collection. In Nineveh he had dug up the library of King Assurbanipal, a collection that contained copies of literary works old even in the time of the Assyrians. Assurbanipal was a scholar and had had his scribes collect and copy the literature of Mesopotamia.

At the British Museum in the 1860s and 1870s Rawlinson presided over the cataloguing, transliteration, and translation of this material. A series of books famous to Orientalists, Cuneiform Inscriptions of Western Asia, began to appear. The Germans, who led Europe in the training of the learned, eagerly used the collections of the British Museum. Because they had few cuneiform documents themselves, German savants—such as Hilprect and Haupt—willingly traveled to London to examine and copy the tablets.

The original decipherers had proceeded on the basis of hunches and many astute preconceived ideas. Although ingenious and intelligent, the first translators, with few exceptions, did not systematically exploit philological principles. The Germans pioneered a methodical contextual analysis that derived from a long tradition of study in Greek and Latin and an exhaustive interest in taxonomy. To ascertain the meaning of Akkadian words and the structure of the grammar, they compared different uses of the same words and contrasted similar uses of different words.[15] They also taught Akkadian on the basis of a presumed knowledge of Hebrew because possession of one Semitic language made learning another far easier. Soon Germany was training American students, such as Frank Harper, in the decipherment of tablets that the English had taken from the ground.[16]

Yet a young Englishman, George Smith, made the most important discovery in 1872, still apparently relying on the intuition of English decoders. Working on the writings in the late 1860s and early 1870s, Smith found a document that gave an Akkadian version of the story of the Flood described in Genesis. Public interest in this biblical link was so great that an English newspaper paid Smith to go to Mesopotamia in search of more material related to the Flood. When he obtained additional documents about the Mesopotamian Noah, the popular appeal of archaeology jumped again. The repute of those who understood the tablets grew, particularly insofar as they could connect their work to the Bible.

Layard had writtten that his work would be "attractive, particularly in America where there are so many scripture readers."[17] Many "duplicate" sculptures that he had unearthed in Assyria wound up in the United

States.[18] Through archaeology the scholarly Christian or Jew in America could envisage the refutation of skeptics about the Bible. Scientific excavation in the Orient might corroborate the history that the Bible unfolded, and so lend authority to religion. Exploration might confute the British and German critics who were confined to scholarly libraries. If archaeology could show the Bible to be historically accurate, the reasoning went, its theological message was more likely to be true.

On the other hand, even exploration might undermine faith. George Smith's discovery of an Akkadian flood story implicitly posed hard but galvanizing questions for Americans: What did a prebiblical story of a deluge portend? Did it confirm the veracity of the Bible, or did it show that the Bible story was only one of many quasi-historical legends, integrated into the "myth-life" of a culture? The document about an Akkadian Noah also directed attention to the possibility that the ancient Near East was the *source* of a higher Israelite civilization. American scholars had to know about the Near Orient because the land would reveal the origins of the Judeo-Christian tradition. Wellhausen, Frazer, and Robertson Smith had conjectured about the nature of primitive religion in a way that cast doubt on the sacredness of Judeo-Christianity. Archaeology might corroborate them and *not* the Bible.

George Smith's finds represented great intellectual labor, but attention was focused on them because Rawlinson's and Layard's adventures had put monumental art on display in London. The learned used two sorts of objects, works of art and documents, for evaluating the nature of the ancient civilizations. One was available only after dangerous, compelling adventure but was then accessible to anyone. The other was useful only after sustained work in the scholar's library with a magnifying glass. The results of this work were open to anyone who read academic prose, but most people had also to trust expert authority. Rawlinson's exploits at Behistun had blurred the distinction between the soldier of fortune and the epigrapher, but thereafter the indelicacy of digging and trenching contrasted with the labors of the decipherer. Even as excavating became more careful and was transmuted into archaeology, the contrast remained. Simultaneously, the philologists of the ancient world depended on the explorers to obtain the documents on which they worked. Scholars and benefactors in the United States worried about the relative merits of digging and deciphering. Indeed, the attempt to satisfy both interests had already created friction between Peters and his Assyriologists.

In 1850 and 1851 Layard had gone into southern Mesopotamia hoping for further triumphs in buried cities that were even older than the Assyrian capitals to the north. Babylon held a special place, but his finds there were meager. He was not able to excavate at the other southern sites of ancient Borsippa and Uruk (then Erech and, in the twentieth century, Warka) where he had planned to dig. After unsuccessfully investigating at Niffar, formerly Nippur, where the Americans were now heading, he was "much inclined to question whether extensive excavations . . . [there] would produce any very important or interesting results."[19]

Others dug in southern Mesopotamia during this period also, but without much luck. Nonetheless, by the time Smith discovered his story of the flood in the early 1870s, the erudite better understood the cuneiform. They also realized that the "books" in Assurbanipal's library copied older texts and had sketched a nonsacred history of early Mesopotamia consistent with the Bible. The Assyrians of the seventh century B.C., in northern Mesopotamia, occupied a prominent place in this history. But they were preceded by the older Babylonians who had ruled from cities further to the south. Their empire reached back to 1500 B.C. and beyond. There was also growing evidence from the cuneiform tablets that the Assyrians and Babylonians, who were kinsmen and who occupied the country for more than a thousand years, had not invented their writing system.[20] Indeed, Rawlinson claimed that the cuneiform tablets dug up at places like Nippur were written in an entirely different, non-Semitic language.

In the latter part of the century, despite Layard's reservations, the Wolfe expedition had looked southward in Mesopotamia to the southern part of Babylonia where perhaps the most ancient civilization had left its remains. These shadowy people, whose existence was first postulated on the basis of little evidence, were the Sumerians. Tablets unearthed in southern Babylonia made their existence a reality by the 1880s.[21] The discoveries in the library of Assurbanipal at Nineveh in northern Mesopotamia, Peters had said, pointed to southern Mesopotamia as a new field for exploration. There, in Babylonia, thought Peters, scholars would find rich traces of the culture that the Assyrians had imitated and might uncover the oldest libraries and evidence of the ur-civilization of Sumer. Moreover, although the inscribed tablets would tell the learned about the history of this lost world, Babylonia might additionally yield "finer treasures of art," an "elegant and refined art" that, again, the Assyrians had merely borrowed.[22] On the scene at the end of 1888, Peters and his crew were now poised to corroborate these hypotheses.

As the Americans marched south, they met, so they thought, natives who lived much as their predecessors had. In a sense the explorers rode into ancient times. They wrote from "Babylonia," as if they were there and not in late-nineteenth-century Mesopotamia. The little group was already sacrificing for science. Far from the amenities of Europe or the United States, the Near Orient repelled the Americans. The mix of peoples was "vilely dirty . . . and forbidding." The adventurers sometimes thought the Arabs unevolved; at other times they saw "evolution in reverse" at work. They described the natives as "untutored children of the desert," a "half savage people," "unprogressive and unlovely." The locals were "degraded," with a facial type "heavy and low." "These dirty Arabs," said Peters, "whom to touch is to soil one's self, regard us as unclean."[23] Worse than the locals was the locale.

The heat was often oppressive, and the winds overwhelmed the Americans with dust. Thick clouds of sand could fill the eyes and ears, choke the throat, and make breathing close to impossible. With less sand the sun might be so bright that it was painful to see. When it rained there was rarely protection from the weather, the accompanying mud, or the chills and damp that followed. Parts of the trek were "unspeakably barren," the landscape one of "immense tracks of sand and sand hills."[24]

The Americans always had to deal with "the vermin"—insects, snakes, scorpions, lizards. The fleas, said Peters, became a matter of indifference. "But the flies were the most terrible pests. . . . The countless myriads of tickling, buzzing, biting things from which there was no escape from dawn to dusk, in house or field, in motion or at rest." Later, a summer locust plague disgusted the visitors. Millions of locusts had perished in the Euphrates, and the great river "stank like a cess-pool." The insects covered the tables where food was served. Each bite had to be preceded by brushing a free place before "another mouthful . . . was once more buried under the bodies of the locusts."[25]

The Americans also feared disease. The "Baghdad date mark" or "Aleppo button" was a disfiguring boil that appeared on the face and extremities. It lasted for a year, and Europeans often got several. More frightening were various fevers—ague, typhus, malaria. No one was immune to them, and although they generally passed, they could be dangerous. The bubonic plague had last struck the area in 1875 and had apparently been eradicated. But cholera was endemic and deadly. In 1889, shortly after the Americans had left, an epidemic had broken out near the marshes of Nippur, and spread through the whole land. Seventy-five people a day died in Baghdad, which had a population of about ninety thousand; the foreign residents left the city.[26]

Before the party arrived at Baghdad, personal tensions erupted, exacerbated by the surroundings. Smarting from his association with Harper and unused to taking orders, Hilprecht penned a torrent of letters "*Privately (& confidentially)*" to "my Provost." Hilprecht gave Pepper "a few hints" of "how matters actually stand."[27]

Hilprecht had a litany of complaints, exaggerated versions of the minor torments affecting all the explorers. The closeness of "turkish workmen & beggars" was repulsive. He was side by side "with the lowest class of Oriental paupers surrounded . . . by sheep & swine." More horrid was "a legion of mosquitos, sandflies, bedbugs and worst of all *lice*," said Hilprecht. All in all he found it "beneath my dignity & that of my University." "This country is worse than I thought. Every person speaks of our going to Babylonia as a matter of life & death."

His peers added insult to Hilprecht's troubles. They had not issued him a revolver and, he implied, had deliberately put his life at risk from lions or robbers. His complaints about his steed became legendary among later explorers. "I . . . got the worst horse in the lot for the first 8 days, and it was so weak that it fell twice with me, while walking slowly." According to Peters, Hilprecht's horse was "the fastest walker and runner . . . , but he does not like it, and I do not think he would like any horse but a strong cow."[28] Hilprecht converted his own desires into the language of universal ethical and scientific imperatives. Again and again he pleaded with Pepper to send him extra money independently of the expedition's regular channels. Only a secret and additional source of income would prevent his being shortchanged and allow him to act in the university's best interests.

More was at stake than Hilprecht's comfort. Over and over he warned Pepper "as Provost and my true friend" that Peters was sabotaging the exploration. Peters was "misus[ing] the trust of the University." His ignorance of Assyriology resulted in blunder after blunder, and he was alienating his staff. In fact, Peters's overbearing energy could evoke everyone's dislike and irritation. Someone said he had come into Baghdad "sitting on the horse like a big melon," and Peters himself later described his procession as "pompous."[29]

When the other explorers were not castigating each other, they turned on their leader. Hilprecht's animosity for Peters, with "his satanic smile," is striking well over a century later. Hilprecht lamented "the ruins of an undertaking." The expedition was "a failure," "already half wrecked" or "an entire wreck." We had "to expect nothing or very little from the work in Babylonia." He told Pepper, "as his professor who promised fidelity . . . : *stop this expedition.*"

Part of the problem was that "the Dictatoric power in the hands of one man has ruined us." Peters and Haynes "act[ed] secretly together." Hilprecht wailed that he was "entirely in their hands & power, far from civilization." He had to go "with blind eyes to Babylon." Hilprecht also thought the choice of Nippur bad, though the Wolfe expedition had recommended the site, and chance and circumstance had made it reasonable for Peters to select when he was negotiating in Constantinople. Nippur was too large, and there was no reason to think much would be found there. Extrapolating from his knowledge of Assyriology, Hilprecht repeatedly proposed instead a "most promising" and "very small" mound. Like Haupt, Hilprecht wanted the United States to take Ur, home of the biblical Abraham: "What an attraction for American Christians."

Most important, Hilprecht told Pepper, Peters could never export whatever finds there were at Nippur. "Abandon all hope for a firman." Hilprecht iterated this view to "the representative of my University which I love" from the time he arrived in the Middle East in 1888 until he left the next year. He thought the Turks would confiscate all antiquities dug up. That was why the United States effort would come to naught. Hilprecht's heart would "almost break" for "our University." *My hope is buried*," and "my mind is full of grief." "So much youthful labor, so much enthusiasm of a large city of a whole land, wasted for nothing." Overall it was a "most unscientific and deplorable expedition."

The exploration, Hilprecht wrote Pepper, should be "call[ed] back . . . at once, as being entirely wrecked." Alternatively, Pepper ought "to give full power to me to act" and to dismiss the Americans.

Hilprecht's jeremiad had a reasoned basis. Because it would be impossible to get exportable treasures from the digging, he wanted to buy them. There were "antiquities dealers" who had underlings dig up material at random in the mounds, or who bought material that Arabs had secured for them. The dealers sold these antiquities and guaranteed their illegal transport from the Ottoman Empire to London and, later, New York. The explorers had already bought tablets and other items from dealers in London and Baghdad. Peters had shipped some of these to the United States for exhibition. Hilprecht argued that this ought be the exclusive way of procuring objects. He developed various schemes to purchase tablets and ship them illegally back to America; Hilprecht knew how to avoid Oriental regulations.

The "sincere and faithful professor" wrote that the crucial aspect of the project was not the fieldwork at all. Hilprecht cared little for what excavation might teach. Instead he wanted to stock a museum with objects and could obtain them in the Baghdad black market. The only point of excavating anyway was to show everyone "that we have actually used a spade."

Hilprecht connected his ideas on stockpiling tablets with Peters's view that the explorers make casts or samples of documents immediately available to other interested parties. This view was anathema to Hilprecht. "If you allow casts & publishing before your curator has seen the material the attractive point of our University will be taken away," "for these very tablets," he wrote Pepper, "shall be a means to get students to Philadelphia." It would be unjust "to those men who sacrifice their lives in the East, to give the results of their work into other hands." "No friend of the University," Peters did not grasp the significance of these matters. If Peters was naive about making copies of the tablets Pennsylvania had procured, Paul Haupt of Johns Hopkins "might easily get over here in his jealousy, and publish . . . the copies." Hilprecht also worried that Harper's allegiance was not to Penn but to Yale. Hilprecht, of course, wanted more than to maintain Penn as a distinctive center for the study of Assyriology. Only his students should publish the tablets "under my auspices as theses."

All this and more Hilprecht communicated to Pepper *before* anyone reached Nippur. The provost kept his head. The BEF would be making decisions about the expedition every season, each one extending from the fall until the following spring, when the heat would terminate work. Peters's lengthy stay in Constantinople had forfeited half of the initial period. Yet the fund estimated expenses through the beginning of May 1889 at about twenty thousand dollars, more than the subscribers had anticipated. Moreover, the fund had to judge even before the actual dig got underway (in February) whether to raise money for a second year. There was enough evidence of trouble—mainly but not exclusively from a hyperbolic Hilprecht—to discourage Pepper and Clark. They did not yet face a critical turning point. They nonetheless had to weigh the possible benefits of courageous commitment against the wisdom of abandoning an impossible campaign, and the dangers of foolhardy arrogance against the disgrace of giving up.

In December Pepper wrote judiciously to Hilprecht and Peters. The BEF, he told Peters, believed that he should fully use Hilprecht's "eminent scholarly abilities." More important, by the spring of 1889, Peters must make every effort to ship to America the antiquities that he had already purchased. The BEF wanted "to rouse public interest" in further funding. Moreover, "all finds and all objects" were "to be sent directly here, so that they can be edited." No one desired "to exclude . . . American scholars and . . . institutions from participation in the benefits of our permission and our work." But, said Pepper, "you can see clearly as a practical man, that at this initial stage of a difficult and costly matter, and after such unexpected and costly delays," the subscribers must be given "absolute justice." In other words, they must get what they had paid for; the university must take sole possession of the finds.

To Hilprecht, Pepper wrote that the Assyriologist correctly felt "we must be just before we are liberal." Nonetheless, as valuable as Hilprecht's sense of the scholarly jugular was, Pepper wanted no more letters indicating "divided councils" or "a carping spirit of criticism." "Don't imagine that your companions have not criticised you," he wrote Hilprecht.[30]

The explorers had reached Baghdad in early January. After another two-week postponement the group left on the last leg of the journey, the hundred-mile trip to Nippur itself. In Baghdad they left Peters's attaché John Prince, who had become so sick that he resigned from the expedition and returned to New York as soon as he was able. Prince was the first of many whose commitment to exploration was brief. Meanwhile, the rest of the party made the overland trip without incident to the mounds of Nippur, situated in the middle of desert and marshes, home to Arab nomads, a distance from even small and dreary Mesopotamian towns. At the beginning of February they had completed the building of their permanent camp of tents and reed huts. Peters named it "Castle America." Sited on the highest point of the great canal that divided Nippur in two, the camp initially included housing for the first lot of Arab workmen, some of whom had wives and children, as well as some Turkish officials.

Nippur presented more dangers than did the other tells Westerners had examined in the nineteenth century. It was far from a caravan route or a large town protected by a Turkish garrison. Nippur was located near the southern Iraqi marshes, created by the overflow of the Euphrates in the *jezireh*, or "island," between the Tigris and the Euphrates. No direct land route went through these swamps. During rainy weather, a stream of the Euphrates would take the explorers close to the ruins. In the dry season the whole area became "a pestilential mud-bed," but the explorers could march "a straight course" of five to nine hours more quickly from the town of Diwanieh, some fifteen miles away. This "miserable little collection of mud hovels more than half of them deserted" was the principal connection of the explorers to the outside world. It had a post office and a telegraph station. Perhaps two days' march away was the larger town of Hillah, with a population of some twelve thousand.[31]

The marshland, intersected by numerous canals, was inhabited by the Afej Arabs. The Afej were settled farmers surrounded by Bedouin nomads. Acccording to the Americans, fierce rivalries and outright warfare were pervasive between the Afej and their neighbors, and between the subtribes of the Afej themselves. Outlaws and robbers frequented the area, a favorite place of refuge for desperadoes; Hilprecht called them the "doubtful characters of modern Babylonia." The natives, said Peters, were not unlike "our Indians," "savage, treacherous, picturesque & the worst thieves & beggars."[32] The Americans hired native workmen and guards, and made gifts and pledges of friendship to the leaders of various subtribes. But Peters and his companions were rightfully nervous.[33]

Both the Turks who were supposed to govern the region and those who were supposed to protect the Americans added to the insecurity. The Turks "were afraid of the Arabs and the Arabs hated them." In the 1860s the Turks had had their noses bloodied in an unsuccessful attempt to levy taxes and enforce military conscription in the area. In the 1890s, Ottoman authority was nominal, and the Arabs were openly contemptuous of their overlords. The Arabs did regard the Ottoman soldiers (*zapiteh*) as a formidable force when they were assembled in large numbers. But, incompetent and ill trained, the small group squiring the Americans and the Turkish commissioner appointed by Constantinople to supervise the dig—all paid for by the Americans—were subjects of ridicule, as well as being an irritant in Arab-American relations.[34]

Here, in "cheerless swamps" in a neighborhood "inflamed by war," the Americans had pitched camp in the midst of "simple minded" yet traitorous tribespeople.[35]

The desolation and hazards muted the American quarreling. As they began to dig, the Americans forgot their differences. The risks and Pepper's gentle remonstrances brought a benign reorganization of responsibilities that made even Hilprecht speak briefly of Peters's "energy and zeal." "We are now really one large family, no longer headed by a dictator but by the most amiable leader and friend."[36] Back home the BEF made up its mind to continue for a second and even possibly a third year. A formal solicitation for contributions stated that "trained scholars" in Nippur were avoiding the problems of European expeditions.[37] When objects purchased abroad reached the United States, the Fund put on a show that stimulated continued donations.

The truce at Nippur was fragile. Harper and Hilprecht overcame their mutual dislike and agreed to publish a joint letter condemning an early interpretation of the finds that Peters had prepared for the *Nation*.[38] Hilprecht's letters to Philadelphia lapsed to their usual tone, so much so that even the sanguine Pepper scrawled on their margins "Burn!"[39]

The Americans had not settled in Nippur to dig until early February. But, as they told the BEF, up to three hundred natives were soon excavating with a modicum of care.[40] The actual work resulted from joining Hilprecht's Assyriological knowledge to Peters's practical sense.

Hilprecht liked to theorize, but he was an expert in the exploration of Mesopotamia, in its history, and in deciphering tablets. Distressed at the size of the Nippur mounds, whose circumference was estimated at some two miles, Hilprecht advocated a selective strategy. The explorers should dig trenches through promising mounds. Exposing various layers of debris, as the Germans had advocated, would reveal the different uses that successive occupiers of the city had made of a specific piece of ground. Hilprecht also wanted to exhume the most important structure at Nippur, the great temple, or *ziggurat*, that was the center of the city's life. Finally, he proposed to zero in on any site that appeared rich in tablets.[41]

Hilprecht's plan was sensible, if suitably vague. He vacillated, too: he lamented that nothing of importance would be discovered because the job was not being done as he thought the Germans would do it, and he wanted credit for whatever successes the Americans had. Yet despite his early complaints about the complete uselessness of any excavation, the quality of his scholarly instinct cannot be gainsaid. The ziggurat at Nippur became a focus of scholarly interest. Early in the dig Hilprecht was also enthusiastic about having found "an actual library" of tablets.[42] The Assyriological literature soon repeated his claim,[43] and later explorers argued that the Americans had found the remains of a scribal quarter.

Fig. 1 Nippur, photographed by John Henry Haynes

Peters was a man of greater practicality and decisiveness, but he worked under the burden of making decisions with little knowledge of his own, relying on men he did not like. He pretended to an authority he did not possess. He grudgingly followed Hilprecht's reasoning while asserting its differences from his own. He maintained that no "temple library" had been found, but Hilprecht's urging and Layard's discoveries at Nineveh made the search for such an entity Peters's top priority. At the same time Hilprecht distanced himself from the excavating decisions that Peters had derived from Hilprecht's own theories.[44]

These disputes between someone primarily in charge of digging and someone primarily an epigrapher were beside the point. The BEF underscored what was plain to all: that portable antiquities were the sine qua non. The plan for further financing centered on exhibiting the material obtained from dealers that had already been shipped to Philadelphia. Peters's and Hilprecht's ideas were subordinate to a more fundamental demand: excavation of items that the BEF could display in the United States.[45] At the same time the Americans were relinquishing the notion that their finds would include great sculptures. As they gave up hope of having large pieces of art shipped to America, their preoccupation with inscribed tablets increased.

As the last week in April, the end of the season, approached, the expedition was in unsteady equilibrium. Then, on the night of 14–15 April, one of the Turkish soldiers shot and killed an Arab fleeing after some minor theft. The shooting provoked consternation among the explorers. They feared retaliation from the tribespeople surrounding the ancient city and decided to leave as soon as they could. For the next two nights the Americans watched the war dances and native powwows apprehensively, eager to be away on 17 April. That morning, in the hustle and bustle of departure, the Arabs set fire to the camp. In the confusion natives took off with what they could, including the saddlebags of money entrusted to Haynes.[46]

The scene would have been laughable were it not for the despair of the explorers. Although they had correctly perceived the locals as possible enemies, the Americans had also denigrated the natives, whom, they assumed, a bit of Western grit could master. The Westerners always acknowledged Haynes as the authority on Arab ways. His advice to the traveler was: "Fearlessness, self-control, perfect command of one's forces and show of boldness and nerve . . . without bluster or swagger will generally win the day for the courageous."[47] Now, as one observer put it, Peters and his associates were "helpless." "Nobody had his senses on to know what to do"; "everybody cared for his own life."[48] But the incident was fatal only to American dignity. As the fire burned itself out, the excavators gathered up the remnants of their belongings and slunk from Nippur. "Our first year," said Peters, "had ended in failure and disaster."[49]

A dispirited and humiliated band made its way to Baghdad. Harper and the architect Field resigned from the expedition. They decamped for the more pleasant cities of London and Paris. Both gossiped about the short-comings of their peers and of the dig. "I had failed to win the confidence of my comrades," wrote Peters.[50] So distressed was Pepper that he had "a long and earnest talk" with Harper's older brother. William Rainey Harper allowed that Frank was probably much to blame for the expedition's troubles and telegraphed him "to keep his tongue quiet." Pepper then wrote an avuncular letter to Frank in London and admitted that the BEF was "greatly disappointed." But Pepper entreated that "the bad blood and ill feeling" must be "absolutely concealed from public notice" if American scholars were to continue in the Near East. He begged Harper to censor himself. Harper might say that the BEF was disappointed, that errors of judgment had occurred, but that no one thought of giving up American interests.[51]

Troubles harrassed Pepper and Clark, but at the risk of pouring more money into a losing undertaking they did not shrink from Nippur. Psychologically invested, they summoned Peters home. In July he gave them a hopeful report. Although Peters was shy about leading the explorers, he was committed to the digging. The fund considered having Haynes, who had remained in Baghdad, assume direction, and he spelled out his ideas in six-thousand-word dispatches.[52] At times he could rise to a heavy eloquence, but usually he had the peculiar ability to produce long letters that said almost nothing. Ultimately the BEF was not desperate enough to select Haynes as scientific director.

Except for Haynes, none of the Americans wanted to go back. At the same time all were caught between their fervor to leave the field and their protestations that they would make sacrifices for science. Hilprecht proclaimed his willingness to serve the BEF most loudly but threw up the most roadblocks to staying in Babylonia. He sent in his resignation after the attack and said he would not take it back. This decision was to help the BEF. Nothing of real value would be found at Nippur, and Hilprecht wished to save the BEF his expenses.[53] In the end, he did not resign but also did not go back to the field. His proficiency in interpreting the tablets worked with his own desires. The BEF sent him to Constantinople to inspect the documents shipped there. This job would continue for a decade. Hilprecht would divide his time among Philadelphia, his native Germany, and Constantinople, where he would examine the finds before they would be split between the Turks and the Americans.

Despite his contempt for Harper, Hilprecht recommended that he become the expedition's head.[54] Peters agreed. Even though Harper was not much of a "book scholar" and was unhelpful on Assyriological matters, Peters thought Harper should take his place. "I should rather return," Peters

wrote as early as December. "I . . . am a luxury." Harper would do "in practical matters" over Hilprecht, who was "too theoretical."[55] When Harper's
resignation thwarted the plans of Peters and Hilprecht, Peters reluctantly
agreed, as a matter of pride, to command the expedition in its second year.
But now the director would command only Haynes. The BEF had lost
Prince, Field, Harper, and Hilprecht to Babylonia.

This was not a setback to the second campaign. Expenses were reduced.
Personal conflict vanished. Haynes's intellectual somnolence and his fatalis-
tic acceptance of his role left no target for friction. Conflicts with the Arab
tribespeople diminished because, at least according to the Americans, the
natives recognized the economic benefits of the expedition and the harm-
lessness of its presence.

After his visit to the United States, Peters traveled back to the Near East,
again making the slow trip through Constantinople to Nippur. Delayed
again, he and Haynes led the digging from January to May 1890 with up to
350 workmen.[56] At the end of the season, they uncovered a multitude of
tablets. Nippur, Peters wrote excitedly, had proved itself to be a "prolific
hill," and he was distressed at having to stop on the verge of gaining an
extraordinary number of tablets.[57] One could "be proud of . . . Old Nippur.
It is doing splendidly well."[58] On a scale of zero to one hundred, Peters
exhilaratedly cabled Pepper "*90*" to indicate the importance of the finds and
his sense that support should continue for a third campaign.[59]

Now, however, the digging had to end for the second year, and in the
early summer of 1890 Peters faced his most difficult challenge. Late in 1889
he had stopped in the Turkish capital to work out the division of the tablets
before the second year's exploration had begun. This job would later fall to
Hilprecht, who was often in Constantinople examining the finds, but for the
first and second campaigns, Peters had charge of this mission.

Although he had obtained permission only to buy excess antiquities in
his firman of 1888, Peters hoped that the firman meant something other
than what it said. The Turks could gain from the presence of the explorers
through the expenditures in the empire of Western funds and the recovery
of antiquities. The Ottomans thus had to balance what percentage of the
finds they could confiscate against what percentage was necessary to give up
to the Americans to keep them coming back, as long as they were wanted
back. The Ottoman authorities could make personal gifts to the expedition's
director regardless of the nature of the permission. But the size of the gift
would be subject to complicated calculations and intense negotiation.
Peters's knowledge of what he had unearthed and shipped to Constantinople for inspection by the Turkish Museum would help him.

In the summer of 1890 Peters reported on the inevitable delays in dealing
with the Ottomans. "We say Time is Money. They say Haste is of the devil."
"Allah only knows, for the working of the Turkish mind is outside natural

law."[60] As if to force Constantinople, Pepper wrote Peters that "the turk should exhibit unusual generosity." "Press for the best possible division." Pepper was "extremely anxious." "We are committed so deeply to this business we must pull it through if at all possible."[61]

There was, nonetheless, said Peters, "no hope" of an early division.[62] So long were the delays that Peters returned to the United States and in April 1891 went back to Constantinople for final parleys. All the while the BEF held back on money for a third season. It unsuccessfully tried to involve a consortium of American universities, and not just Penn, in the digging. The BEF itself might carry on but only if the division was magnanimous: half of the finds. Even then money might be hard to come by.[63] In June, back in the Turkish capital, Peters's news on the division was unsettling. "With sinking of heart" and "deep mortification" Peters related that only about a third of the objects would be sent back. Clark cabled him at once: "Dissatisfied . . . return for Conference."[64] Then, a little later, there was a better report. As Peters put it, "roads here are very crooked."[65] By August he had obtained more than half of the tablets, and "much the best lot."[66]

Although his vindication buoyed up a distracted group of donors, adversity had chastened Peters. Before the Americans committed themselves further in Nippur, he said, they should examine what they already had. The BEF should plan new digging on the basis of its knowledge and, finally, negotiate a division before taking to the field another time. Having lost the 1890–91 season to palaver about the division, the expedition should forget about 1891–92 while it took stock of what it had accomplished. Then the explorers might set out a third time. To the question of whether he would lead these forces, Peters had a brief response: "Impossible! Let Haynes go it alone."[67]

3

A TALE OF TWO CITIES, 1893–1896

A S THE SECOND campaign ended satisfactorily, Assyriology in American scholarly circles was gaining the recognition that the achievements of exploration warranted. Since the 1860s, the Sankritist William Dwight Whitney of Yale had been one of the major forces in the American Oriental Society. He made the academic study of ancient India the chief glory of the organization and led the AOS away from its missionary foundations and from the Old Testament. Because of Dwight's idiosyncratic non-Christian sensibility and the distance of India from Bible lands, the society had thus begun the secularization of university life. The center of American orientalism became ancient India. The interest in the Near East was modest, just as concern for the Far East was small.[1] Whitney was the longtime secretary of the AOS, and in the early 1880s, his biographer has written, Whitney's drive "to suppress overtly religious topics" increased. Whitney's thrust, however, was blunted after he gave up the secretaryship in 1884.

The growing scholarly importance of Mesopotamia over India was signaled in 1890 when Whitney stepped down from his ceremonial presidential office. The Old Testament scholar and leader of the first Mesopotamian reconnoitering expedition, William Hayes Ward of New York City, took over. Ward's accession to power was part of a general geographical struggle. It pitted New England collegiate circles, where Indology was preeminent, against those of the middle states. In the cities of New York, Philadelphia, and Baltimore Assyriology was stronger. In the latter cities Jews and foreigners were a more significant force than they were in Boston and New Haven. We have already met the Germans Hilprecht and Haupt; we will later meet the important Jewish intellectuals, Haupt's student Cyrus Adler, Penn's Morris Jastrow, and Columbia University's Richard Gottheil. Whitney wrote about this group as "the Semites," not merely referring to their scholarly field but also intending to express a genteel anti-Semitism.

In this struggle among the erudite, the balance of power in the AOS swung further south. Its meetings would no longer be restricted to New Haven and the North. Moreover, the *Journal* gave more space to Assyriological topics. As the AOS became a professional academic association in the system of universities in the United States, Mesopotamia became intellectually central to a new geographic area—the American ancient Near East. This shift made the AOS converge more on biblical studies than it had previously. As the society and ancient Near Eastern studies matured, the secular (and anti-Semitic) course that Whitney had charted was ironically diverted. The study of India continued to be a field unto itself, outside the Near East. Both the location of Mesopotamia and the interests of many Assyriologists took Oriental studies in the Near East closer to the Bible than Whitney had wanted.

Overall, the more heterogeneous East Coast academic world outside New England protected genuine Christian sensibilities better than the conventionally Protestant culture of Harvard and Yale.[2] Yale would ultimately join the camp of Assyriology, while Harvard would eventually unsuccessfully try to move the axis of the ancient Near East even further west, from Mesopotamia to Egypt.

As part of the first moves away from India, the AOS lauded William Pepper and his initiatives in its first meeting in Philadelphia in the fall of 1888. Pepper used the occasion to display antiquities that Peters had purchased and shipped back to raise the standing of local donors. The meeting "marked the formal recognition of the efforts . . . by Pennsylvania to further Oriental and more particularly Semitic studies."[3]

The Philadelphia group felt its power in the AOS, and after fretting about money and administration, the BEF sent Haynes back to Mesopotamia alone in the summer of 1892. Mishaps delayed him, and the third expedition was not in the field until early 1893. In some ways the dig was uneventful. Haynes excavated in the desert almost continuously for thirty-six months. During this period most of the would-be explorers lived on the East Coast with their financial backers. The United States, not Babylonia, often occupied center stage in exploring and building ancient Near Eastern studies.

Thus, as "dirt archaeology" in America got its start, scholars subordinated fieldwork to the skills acquired in the library and the committee room. Two series of events shaped the environment from which funds and instructions flowed to Haynes. First, John Peters left Penn; as his authority waned, that of Hilprecht, for good reason, waxed. Second, Pepper resigned as provost in 1894. Although he assumed the headship of the University Museum, he struggled with Penn's new provost over the direction of the institution.

Pepper's successor, Charles Custis Harrison, was born in Philadelphia in 1844 and excelled as a scholar at Penn. He made his career as head of the Franklin Sugar Refining Company from 1862 until he sold the enterprise in 1892, when it was the largest business in Pennsylvania.

In many ways Pepper and Harrison were alike. As chair of Penn's Ways and Means Committee, Harrison had supported Pepper in expanding the university and raising the money to do it. During Harrison's regime, Penn continued to grow rapidly, adding buildings, academic departments, faculty, and students. His fund-raising skills equaled Pepper's, and Harrison's greater wealth enabled him to contribute far more to Penn than Pepper could.[4]

At the same time Pepper and Harrison differed. During Harrison's tenure, academic standards tightened as students acquired technical competence. The faculty purveyed increasingly specialized knowledge. Harrison oversaw what historians have called the professionalization of the university and distanced himself from the more gentlemanly approach of Pepper. Harrison was an efficient, hard-driving businessman whose early intellectual ability took him back to the academy; Pepper was a graceful and gracious man of culture, not a dilettante but not a scholar or an administrator either. Harrison was one of the "captains of erudition" whom social critic Thorstein Veblen criticized in his books of that period, *Theory of the Leisure Class* (1899) and *The Higher Learning in America* (1918). The contrasts were displayed in the tone of their governance and, finally, in the animosity that developed between the two men.

When Pepper left office in 1894, his graduation address asserted that his administration had converted a group of "disconnected schools" into "a great academic body." Pepper's system was "strong enough for effective central control, yet so flexible as to admit affiliation with many separate organizations." The university should "exclude rigid control and rest upon mutual confidence and a common devotion to a great cause." Pepper also said, however, that he was resigning because of "the immense extent of the University interests." They demanded "the undivided activity of the most energetic man," who would not have to choose between administration and other endeavors.[5] Harrison's great achievement, according to later university publications, was transforming "the internal organization of nearly every department, and of the University as a whole." "Symmetry of plan and unity of purpose" at last characterized the institution.[6]

When Harrison took over as provost, his centralizing vision clashed with the ideas of Pepper, now representing only the museum. From the mid-1890s on, all the run-of-the-mill troubles within that institution were secondary to a bitter struggle between Harrison and Pepper and their bureaucratic successors. Conflict between the university and the museum would be confused, complicated, and unending.

In 1892, as provost, Pepper had formed a museum building committee. The new building would replace the top floors and halls of the library, which were crowded with objects obtained by Penn's explorers. At first, Pepper was not committed to this lavish project. He worried about the effect on his other aims. He was, however, won over. The new museum would be a monument to Pepper himself. As head of a new physical plant, he would also have a base after leaving the office of the provost. But most important to Pepper's change of mind was a deepening friendship with Sara Yorke Stevenson, a Philadelphia socialite of unusual interest.

Born in Paris and raised in France and Mexico, Sara Yorke came to Philadelphia after the Civil War, at the age of twenty-one. There she resided with members of her father's family after his death. In 1870 she married Cornelius Stevenson, a prominent clubman and a colorless if well-to-do lawyer, content not to compete with his exotic and talented wife. By the early 1880s she was working with the Philadelphia gentlemen dabbling in antiquities and had taken up Egyptology. An early proponent of the university's role in the exploration of the ancient world, she had curatorial responsibilities for the Egyptian section of the museum. Through her social contacts she raised money for its Near Eastern section and maintained friendly relations with the famous British Egyptologist Sir Flinders Petrie. He regularly consulted for the museum and sent antiquities to Penn from his excavations (mainly in Egypt) because of Stevenson's support for the English Egypt Exploration Fund.[7]

Pepper's connection to Stevenson thickened in the late 1880s when she worked with the BEF. There was some indecision on her part about making this association. Friends had warned her off Pepper as a "charlatan" and a man of "corruption, lies, [and] personal ambition," presumably because of the rumors that he was "an adulterer." Perhaps with reason, Stevenson could never shake off doubts about Pepper, but she became a political and personal intimate of the provost.[8] When he left office, she received an honorary doctorate, the first one Penn had conferred on a female.

The extant record of their relationship is ambiguous. Few original letters between the two survive. Yet when Pepper died in 1898, Stevenson underwent a psychological crisis and struggled to reconfigure her life after his death had removed her principal emotional sustenance. She transcribed his correspondence to her, including the French billets-doux they had exchanged, and annotated it with recollections of what she had written to him and what the dynamics of their lives had been at the time.[9] This document displays a passionate intensity. In writing to Stevenson, Pepper committed himself to the emancipation of women. But, he said, the goal was "fearfully complicated by . . . marriage & . . . the present sociological programme." The two of them had to respect "the open, close cooperation of man & woman . . . not necessarily married to each other . . . leaving to each creature the determination of relations personal. . . . And it is here . . . that woman must lead."[10]

Inevitably the later interpreter of the material wants to know where Pepper had Stevenson lead. In one sense it does not matter if sex consummated the affair: their bond was clandestine and crucial to their lives. Nonetheless, there was a sharp boundary between physical penetration and its absence. Not knowing if the boundary was transgressed, we lack an important piece of information useful not only in grasping their relationship but also in assessing their characters and, so, other significant aspects of their lives—their willingness, or lack thereof, to disregard Victorian notions of propriety. They would have risked much with a physical liaison, and knowledge of it would facilitate our assessment of Pepper's reputation as a "charlatan."

Pepper may have been using Stevenson, as his enemies told her. But he had fits of depression about his projects and their value, and he needed the reassurance that this strong woman gave. On her side, Stevenson could not resist the attention of a powerful and famous man whose vulnerable inner life especially appealed to her.

She was also an ally in the encounters between the university and the museum. With Pepper's help, his friends, led by Stevenson, planned a grand and costly building and made complicated arrangements to fund it. As was occurring in the financing of the Nippur expedition, private donors raised money. But a museum building would be more expensive. Pepper and his associates augmented personal contributions with financing from the university, a gift of land from the city of Philadelphia, and appropriations from the state of Pennsylvania.

As the building committee carried out its plan, it ran up against the policies of Provost Harrison. He wanted the museum to be subservient to the university but did not intend to add to its resources from the university's general fund. Nor did he want the museum's solicitation of public largesse to conflict with the university's prerogatives. At this time Harrison was battling with Pennsylvania State University, in State College, Pennsylvania, for money from the state legislature. He did not want his fight compromised by distracting requests to the state by the museum, which must subordinate its desires to an overall scheme. Harrison feared a victory for Penn State: that institution had "no just claim . . . to obtain recognition as the University of the State of Pennsylvania," a distinction "to which the University [of Pennsylvania] has a prescriptive and hitherto unquestioned right."[11]

Pepper felt that the various institutions connected to the university should be modestly independent. This was true of the museum. Its instruction and antiquities belonged to Penn. Yet it "receive[d] no financial aid from the University," and had its own administrators, a president and board of managers. Under attack from Harrison, Pepper implemented a more extreme policy. With Stevenson's assistance he formed the American Exploration Society, which would raise money for the museum but would have no connection to the university; perhaps the museum would become a more freestanding entity.[12]

In January 1895 Harrison presented a policy statement to the museum. In any dispute, wrote Harrison, "the ruling body is and must be the [University] Board of Trustees." "This body must be the source and fount of all power and must represent the University to the World."[13] Harrison, indeed, demanded "written acceptance" of his communication and "the *cordial* concurrence" of the museum.[14] Pepper's friends were "furious."[15] Yet when Stevenson replied for the museum's managers a month later, Pepper maintained only a shred of dignity. The museum acknowledged Harrison's letter and expressed "its concurrence in the same."[16]

In the period of the third Nippur campaign, from 1892 to 1896, the level of flattery that Hilprecht expressed to Harrison rose as the latter's power increased. Moreover, with less authority to realize his plans, Pepper at times became pessimistic about the Near East. In addition to cultivating the new provost, Hilprecht buoyed up the old one. When Pepper's interest briefly waned, Clark led the BEF. These developments aside, the impact of the battle between Pepper and Harrison was indirect in the 1890s: people believed that tension existed between museum and university and so contributed to the reality of tension.

The differences between Peters and Hilprecht had also begun in the late 1880s as a struggle between Hilprecht's dedication to the university and Peters's to the BEF. That is, loyalty to the BEF, which formed the nucleus of the museum's board, had not in Hilprecht's eyes guaranteed loyalty to Penn. In the 1890s that fight between the two men played itself out in a more extreme way, between Penn and an outsider.

Hilprecht's stock with the BEF and the university had risen after he had gotten to know Turkish officials in Constantinople in 1889. His knowledge of cuneiform made him more valuable there than Peters, who had conducted the first negotiations for a division of the finds. Hilprecht ingratiated himself with the Ottomans overseeing Western exploration. The new Turkish museum would preserve the heritage of the empire with antiquities Europeans had dug up. If Hilprecht assisted the Turks, he reasoned correctly, his own significance in the scholarly world would jump, and the Turks would look more benignly on Pennsylvania's undertakings. An added benefit was that extended stays in Constantinople, paid for by the university, would put Hilprecht closer to Germany, a country that he often visited and that he finally made a second home.

In 1892 the Hartford Theological Seminary offered Hilprecht a position. Even Peters was moved to write that the loss of the German would be "a real calamity" and urged Harrison, then Ways and Means chairman, that it was "a matter of first importance" to retain Hilprecht. The university acted quickly. His complicated work arrangements, still split among museum, university, and the *Sunday School Times*, were regularized, and his salary increased. He stayed, as he put it, "with my dear child of sorrow and joy, our Assyrian department."[17]

Subsequently the university subsidized Hilprecht's work in Constantinople. He spent the summers of 1893 and 1894 there, went again in 1896, and yet again for the second half of 1897. He catalogued cuneiform material for the Ottoman museum and became the leading Western authority on

Turkish holdings in Assyriology. Hilprecht secured a favorable disposition of the finds from the third expedition when Haynes's boxes of antiquities arrived in Constantinople. When the first firman expired, he negotiated a new one to continue the dig.

Hilprecht astutely saw the decreasing utility of collecting all the documents pouring in from Haynes. He recognized that many were identically imprinted with conventional inscriptions or simple and similar business records, and his interest in merely having a large number of tablets waned. The university needed samples of the more common inscriptions but could generously donate many of these sorts of documents to other institutions and allow anyone to examine them. Yet literary documents that evidenced high culture—scholarship, histories, or myths—furnished the key to the earliest civilizations and must be sought after in the field and secreted at home. Hilprecht advised Haynes to be more discriminating about what he looked for, although it is difficult to know how Haynes was to do this. He was so ignorant of the cuneiform tablets when he left in 1892 that Hilprecht prepared a little guide or "King List" so that Haynes could roughly appraise the value of the tablets.[18] Additionally, Hilprecht now mentioned that Haynes should dig up "the lowest strata" at Nippur. The German never really articulated what this sort of spadework should accomplish. He nonetheless implied that the expedition should contribute to knowledge of the first advanced society in a way that went beyond the discovery of documents. Hilprecht was not involved with earth moving, and was no champion of Haynes's own ruminations on the contours of the old city. But he began to value excavation as a means of uncovering different sorts of evidence for interpreting Mesopotamian civilization.[19]

While Hilprecht's star justifiably rose in Philadelphia, that of Peters sank. After he returned from Constantinople in 1891, he maintained his affiliation with Penn but moved to New York City, a decision that itself brought negative comment. Two years later Peters cut his ties to the university, taking up his father's job. Previously assistant, he was now rector of St. Michael's.[20]

Peters stayed on as scientific director of the expedition, although the mechanics were cumbersome. In the first instance Haynes reported to Peters and received orders from him. While Peters himself consulted with Pepper and Clark in Philadelphia, the two of them worried not just about Haynes in Nippur but about Peters in New York.

Although Peters's departure complicated the work of the BEF, his resignation from Penn was not entirely unwanted. University officials regarded him as part of "the Anti Supernatural Trust" among Semitic scholars in the United States, especially those centered at Yale. His theology was "crooked" and carried the higher criticism of the Bible "to the extremest extent of destructiveness." Peters accepted the Bible's moral lessons, but only "mere

fragments are left of the Scriptures which are entitled to any belief or respect." These fragments were only those "that accord with human knowledge and experience, so that there is no need of them."

This appraisal exaggerated the radicalism of Peters's liberal ecumenical-
ism, but studying ancient civilization and religion had affected his beliefs.
Hilprecht, who was a more erudite scholar, was a much safer man. Indeed,
although no one really replaced Peters at Penn, Hilprecht, who was also a
Protestant minister, argued that the American's successor must be a Christian who could get along with the clergymen, the main suppliers of students
to the graduate program.[21]

Peters's now independent role in the BEF at first created no changes for
Haynes. Only someone of Haynes's laconic disposition could have thrived at
Nippur. Although his descriptions of his life and work linked the melodra-
matic and the prosaic, physical dangers still existed. "One day last week," he
wrote in late 1893, "an unusually hot battlefield drank the blood of 71 slain
warriors and thirsts for more today. This makes something like the fifteenth
or sixteenth war between the tribes and subtribes around Nippur . . . since
we arrived." At the end of the year he explained the irregular dispatch of his
weekly reports: "Wars, cholera, and covetous Arabs infest the desert route."
The "lawless region of ungoverned country" and the "confusion and unrest"
meant a "commingling of professed friend and unsuspected foe" in "our
little camp."[22]

Haynes's trials did not matter much to the authorities back home. They
pressed him incessantly to locate tablets, despite his growing interest in
other aspects of the digging and in unearthing the building at the center of
Nippur's religious life, the ziggurat. The Americans were reconciled to the
failure to obtain the monumental art that had made Layard famous. In
southern Mesopotamia they were uncovering a civilization older than Assyria, one that did not have imperial sculpture. Thus, whatever Hilprecht or
Haynes thought, Pepper and Clark now demanded the next best thing—the
documentary records that Layard too had found.

"Your friends here," wrote Clark to Haynes, "are very anxious for tablets
and any small objects carrying dates, and we hope that you will select a
mound that will yield such objects in abundance during the remainder of
your exploration work. What you have done [with the ziggurat] is very
important in an archaeological point of view, but the other is more interesting to us at home."[23]

In addition to facing automatic dissatisfaction in the United States with
his operation, Haynes did not know from one month to the next whether he
could go on. Badgered by complaints about expenses, he would receive orders to stop by a certain date, then to carry on, then to pack up at once, then
to continue on a reduced scale. In America the BEF struggled to find dollars

for a cause that, even after its successes, was not easy to float. Indeed, some evidence hints that Pepper got money to dig after the summer of 1894 because of a football scandal at the university. The Intercollegiate Football Association had chastised Penn, which had a powerful team with a dubious record for fair play. The moment was "ripe" for the university to assert its "scholastic side" by continuing the Nippur expedition.[24]

Although the BEF always kept Haynes in the black, the erratic nature of the fund-raising made his work difficult. The time required for mail delivery and the vagaries of the post between Constantinople and Nippur (and especially between Baghdad and Nippur) irritated each side. Often Haynes would receive instructions that developments at home had long since made obsolete. Sometimes the Americans issued and retracted commands with bewildering frequency, their meaning made even more problematic by brief cables to Baghdad (rushed to Nippur) that cryptically stated the most recent thoughts from the United States. Throughout the correspondence ran an undercurrent of vexation at Haynes's slow progress or his unwillingness to carry out orders. The BEF complained that Haynes did not give sufficiently detailed information about his daily work, and Haynes *did* report inadequately. His letters, notes, and photographs did not usually help in figuring out what he had dug up at Nippur and where. The BEF hoped in vain that on his return Haynes's "record book" and "his habit of keeping a record of everything" would allow them to reconstuct what had gone on.[25]

Another dimension of the problem was the inevitable gaps in communication and the onerous nature of the task. Haynes was intellectually deficient, but the people back home never grasped the challenges he faced. Pepper, Clark, and Hilprecht all wrote to Haynes and disparaged his weaknesses, but the burden of letter writing fell on Peters. Although he knew at first hand what Haynes confronted, his relations with Haynes frayed most quickly. Peters deplored Haynes's faults and his slowness to Haynes himself and to other members of the BEF. He berated Haynes about the poverty of his reports. He warned him not about mismanagement of money but about possible extravagance and the need for frugality. And all this came from people who had voted with their feet to stay away from Nippur. Haynes often bore nagging and veiled insults without comment. Yet over his three years in the field a growing sureness about his skills as a digger, a sense of justice, and the peculiarities of his own temperament gave his letters an edge.

Since he had made "no actual discoveries" in one period, he wrote the following week that he "did not write the customary summary of the week's doings." After excavating for well over a year, Haynes asked Peters in the summer of 1894 to have the BEF "excuse me from more minute description of the temple until its further exploration shall have given us the necessary data for deciding many points that now seem to us obscure." It was hard for him, he said later, to offer "fragmentary [weekly] descriptions" of his digging. The subjects were "difficult to comprehend, though to a theorist it may seem a simple matter." Moreover, the heat was very great. "Those blinding and burning duststorms, that make the summer months trying alike to physical endurance and to a becoming composure of mind, have begun to afflict us."[26]

In mid-1894 Peters reported to Clark that he had reprimanded Haynes. Peters had written the explorer that the dig's results "are not such as to make us assured of the great value of the work done." The committee wished "that the excavations should be conducted in other portions of the mound where there was a strong probability of the discovery of inscribed records." When Clark and his wife went to the resort at Hot Springs, Arkansas, for their health, Peters wrote him there (and not in Philadelphia) that flooding in Mesopotamia explained the recent failure in the post from Haynes. In the letter Peters had most recently received, Haynes had described conditions that had delayed every sort of mail. These most interesting details from Haynes, said Peters, "fill me with an envious desire to be in his place." At the same time Peters hoped that Clark would find his own vacation "delightful and pleasureable as well as beneficial."[27]

The summer of 1894 brought a great change for Haynes. Uncertain about continuing the dig, he had insisted on returning to the United States for consultation. Instead, in April, he went to Baghdad for a short rest. He was the only English-speaker at Nippur. In Baghdad, at least, he could relax after a "lonely and desolate life" in "Robberdom and Murderland." "Few people know what it is to live alone, and no one who has ever attempted to live without companionship among brutal, scheming, thieving, and murderous tribes of feud-brewing robbers can ever know the mental tension."[28] In Baghdad Haynes learned that more money (forthcoming perhaps because of the improprieties over football) would extend the exploration.

At the same time, he was acquainting himself with an American architect. Guaranteed financing, Haynes "induced a young man of some architectural training who is traveling through India, Turkey, and other countries to join the expedition until February 1895 without salary."

> The young man is Joseph A. Meyer, a graduate student in the Department of Architecture, Massachusetts Institute of Technology Boston. He has had a travelling fellowship for two years, and is a candidate for an advanced degree. He is a good worker and I am sure will prove to be a companionable fellow, and of great service to the expedition. With his help and companionship I am the more reconciled to return this summer to Niffer.[29]

Meyer did have architectural ability. He had been graduated from MIT in 1891. The designing competitions that he had won had gained him fellowships to pursue a doctorate and to examine building styles around the world. But Meyer was also a gentle man, a wanderer and a seeker. Hardly young at thirty-eight, he had come to architecture only after mastering engraving and studying music on the Continent. Before meeting Haynes, he had been traveling for two years in Europe, Russia, and India, and was en route to Syria and Palestine. All the while he kept a diary and illustrated it with delicate pen-and-ink sketches.[30]

The two men left Baghdad on an alternative route to their destination, overland to Hillah, some sixty miles away. Their caravan transferred its goods at Hillah to a boat headed down the Euphrates to Nippur. From the time he left a rivulet of the Euphrates to make his way to the camp, Meyer brought a new perspective to Western understanding of the site. For the next several months, his drawings illustrated life at Nippur, and his words painted a picture of hard but congenial work and of the growing intimacy between him and Haynes.

> The way led over an alluvial plain cracked by the heat and sparsely covered with a low bush. . . . All afternoon there was a straggling procession from the two masts in the distance. . . . By nightfall we were quite ready for sleep. But we had little of it—the mosquitos were fearful, even a sheet was no protection. . . .
>
> About 4:30, temperature 78, we were out and about, and about 5:45 started for the mounds with our crowd of zapitehs. Mr. Haynes put the men to work. . . . Excavating is done in gangs. The chief of the gang wields a pick, and is an expert excavator brought from Hillah. His immediate assistant fills the baskets with a small hoe. Each such gang had a number of basket carriers, who bears his basket on his hip with his hands under the basket and behind him, carries it up and out of the excavation, and empties the earth on the heap of debris. . . . We had lunch under a small tent on top of the Ziggurat, where we spent a good many hours of the afternoon. . . . As it grew cooler, Mr. Haynes and I walked over the temple. . . . We found an inscription on one of the bricks, but it was unfamiliar to Mr. Haynes. . . .
>
> 7 am, 95, The temperature rose rapidly. The feeling during the hot south wind was one of suffocation, and a slight headache soon followed. The wind lasted perhaps one hour. . . . I finished up some drawings for Mr. Haynes's report. . . . The man to Deviniah returned this afternoon. He reports a sort of religious riot in Hillah. An officer struck a Said—was called worse than a Jew, Said arrested and sentenced by the Mufti to ride facing a mule's tail through the bazaars. The people closed their shops in protest, and sent a deputation of 40 men to the governor in Baghdad. . . . The sketch on the next page is only to show the general construction of the mound that has been called "Tablet Hill." This "Hill," the two lines of shops and other unexcavated mounds towards the S.W., seem to enclose a great square 300′ × 600′, perhaps the "Festival Plain" of the temple. . . . The sketch . . . is not exactly after nature, for I have left out all dump heaps—which on this side are enormous—in order to show

the great wall, buttresses and the excavated top of the temple. Otherwise it is pretty correct.[31]

At home the Fund praised the quality of Meyer's drawings, while in the field Meyer's companionship transformed Haynes. His efforts became more "scientifically" pleasing to the BEF. Meyer reinforced Haynes's growing concern for the urban shape of Nippur, the layout of the city that would appeal to the mind of an architect. There was a shift in Haynes's interest; one aspect of the digging became to fathom what Nippur had looked like. It became desirable not merely to tunnel in the ruins for objects, but methodically to plan excavation to reveal the shape of the urban setting.

Still, Peters continued to tell Haynes that "the Committee want tablets." He repeatedly dunned Haynes to send more photographs. Haynes had promised the BEF pictures and had not come through, said Peters again and again. "Why have you not done as agreed?" Still, even Peters noted that Haynes's letters had become "most admirable and scientific reports." To Clark Peters wrote: "I cannot commend too highly the scientific manner in which this work [of excavating] has been conducted by him since he has been joined by Mr. Meyer, nor the excellence of Meyer's sketch maps and plans." Meyer was "a very great acquisition." "Very much pleased with Mr. Meyer's drawings," Clark agreed that Meyer was "valuable . . . as a companion and co-worker."[32]

In truth, Haynes's letters did become fuller and less dour in their estimates of his surroundings, the Arabs, and the expedition's prospects. When he had arrived at Nippur in early 1893, he had decided not to live in tents, as the explorers had done on the first two campaigns. Haynes built a permanent camp, called "the Castle." When Meyer joined him, they improved it. To secure the headquarters Haynes dug a well that protected the water supply from marauding Arabs and that for a time produced clean, palatable water. He and Meyer also made the roof of the Castle more desirable so that it might serve as a cool, insect-free place to sleep, and now spent their nights out under the Mesopotamian stars.[33] They enjoyed a rough but companionable existence.

In September 1894 Meyer became ill, although he was well enough to oversee the excavations and to measure and draw architectural features of interest. By mid-October, however, he often could not make his daily rounds. "I stayed at the house until 9:30," he wrote in his diary. "Then walked up to the excavations. The exertion was almost too much for me, and it was some time before I could look at what had been done." "I went back to the house without waiting for the horn for quitting." Frequently now he was not able to go out at all.

What interest can the diary of a sick person be to one who is well. He is full of his pains and discomfort and thinks of nothing else. Today I was all stomach and bowels—no train of thought but began, concentrated and ended in those

NIFFER.
NORTH-WEST FAÇADE
of the ZIGGURAT.
EXCAVATED DURING the
SUMMER of 1894.

SHEET № 26

Fig. 2 Nippur, sketched by Joseph Meyer

soul-harrowing organs. Nothing seems to bring them into a proper sense of respect for their owner and lord, who in consequence only takes interest in reading the patent medicine almanac, or in drinking inordinate quantities of warm water in vain hope of washing away the disorder.

Haynes was troubled. He wrote Peters that Meyer was "seriously ill. He has [on October 27] not left the house for nine days." Around the same time Meyer regretted that "tomorrow it must be laudanum, I suppose—as a last resort."[34]

During Meyers's illness the quality of Haynes's reporting suffered again. Peters grumbled and urged Haynes to meet the BEF's standards. Haynes's failures as a photographer particularly vexed Peters. "He ought to be brought to book on this subject," Peters told Clark. "The committee desires to have from you a report on the amount of photographing you have done. . . . The money spent for this purpose has not been properly used." Pictures were just one of many irritants:

Please give us by return mail precise and clear statements as to the position and relation of these objects. . . .

It may seem a little hard to criticize from this distance, but it has seemed to me that the removal of . . . crude bricks . . . was work of superogation. . . .

I sympathize . . . in the anxiety and distress that has come upon you in connection with Mr. Meyer's illness. . . . I do not agree with you that glass is the best material for photography in such an expedition. . . . I do not exactly understand where the terra cotta figurines . . . were found. . . . Looking for speedy news of large finds of tablets. . . .

I presume there is no need of further expressing at the present moment the deep regret of the committee at your failure to make use of photography as you should have done. . . . It is a matter of great regret to me that my affairs have not allowed me to again visit the land of the Affeck [tribe]. I would like nothing better than to be back again at Nippur, digging holes in the ground and hobnobbing with my Arab friends.[35]

If Haynes were to break the dig for the summer of 1895 and return home for a vacation, Peters thought that the BEF could see his notes and press him to elaborate on what he had done. Haynes's letters, said Peters, were "eminently unsatisfactory." "I do not wish to scold at Haynes in every letter," Peters told Clark, but he could not keep Haynes "up to the point." "He needs constant poking."[36]

On the other side, Haynes's worry over Meyer brought closer to the surface his anger at the demands made upon him. At the "wearisome end of a busy week of broken rest and hard work" he reported that Meyer, who had substantially improved, had again suffered a "serious attack."

Please excuse me to your committee, who I know are impatient of delays, and anxious for great results. We, in the field are no less impatient of the one, and no less desirous of the other . . . but are limited by the physical barriers of endurance and possibility. It is by no means easy or comfortable for any foreigner to dwell near the pestiferous insect-breeding, secreting, malarious, marshes of lower Babylonia, when the temperature in perfect shade rises above 115, and the stifling dust-storms rob the sun of shadow, and parch the skin with a furnace heat, while the ever present insects bite, and sting, and buzz, through all hours of the day and night. Please do not think me to have rejected my former opinion regarding continuous work at Niffer. . . . After a larger experience than has fallen to the lot of any other Occidental I must confess that the tension of daily life among these greedy, treacherous Arabs, through the heat and pests of a Babylonian summer often approaches uncomfortably near the breaking point; nor is the strain wholly physical. The mental organism has its peculiar burdens and tension to bear, and these are sometimes greater than it is possible to describe. . . . The relief, however, of assistance and trusted companionship has justified the decision to return on my part, while to my companion the result has been mischievous. . . .

How impossible it is for your committee at such a distance of space and time to direct my movements on the basis of my reports, which are always received several weeks after the reported work is done, and before your replies can reach me several weeks more must elapse. . . .

It is of course unfortunate, but yet I do not possess the rare genius requisite to put to practical use your weekly suggestions, which owing to the distance that separates us, only reach me three and a half to four months after the completion of the task to which they should apply. They make excellent reading and are gladly received, and my inability to apply them to some useful end, worthy of the care and forethought that called them into existence, is greatly deplored by me, and must be regarded as a loss to the expedition.[37]

Haynes's sarcasm was more or less contemporaneous with his reports of Meyer's worsening condition. In the middle of November Meyer fell "violently ill," "critical." After he improved a bit, Haynes decided, on the twenty-third, to send him to Baghdad. "He was carried in a chair from our house to the water's edge at Niffer, and comfortably placed in a boat for Hillah. . . . From Hillah he was to be carried in a covered litter." In Baghdad, Haynes arranged for Meyer to be cared for by a competent physician, John Sundberg, who corresponded with the Americans about his patient. By the middle of December Haynes wrote that Sundberg was "discouraging" about Meyer's full recovery. Sundberg, however, proposed to take Meyer in a few days to Switzerland, whence the physician was removing his own ailing wife.[38]

When Sundberg's first report about Meyer, and in passing about the trials of the third dig, reached Pepper in mid-January 1895, it provoked a significant response. "I feel that none of us have appreciated sufficiently the difficulties under which our expedition had been working in Babylonia," said Pepper. Peters's letters to Haynes, the ex-provost went on, "always produce an irritating effect upon my mind. The poor fellow is away off there, entirely alone; and every one of Dr. Peters' letters is a tirade of criticism . . . it is a source of annoyance to me. . . . However, all will come right, if only the poor man's life is spared." A clutch of sympathetic mail commiserating with Haynes went off. Although Peters mentioned again several of Haynes's defects, even he empathized with the explorer's "burden of a sick comrade" and congratulated Haynes for his "courage and persistence" and assured him of his "warm friendship."[39]

Peters's warmth came too late for the BEF. In mid-December Pepper and Clark decided that the archives of the expedition should be transferred from New York to Philadelphia. Peters would forward his letters of instruction to Philadelphia, where Clark would approve them before they went to Haynes. Six weeks later the Fund took more serious steps. Haynes received a new set of orders in which Hilprecht had a hand. Although the demands differed little from the old ones, the BEF implied that Haynes need not ever have listened to Peters. Clark told Haynes that any instructions made "through Dr. Hilprecht . . . must be followed and . . . request[s] from Dr. Peters to the contrary must be ignored." Moreover, the BEF asked Haynes to send his reports directly to Pepper or Clark. Soon Haynes stopped corresponding with Peters. With Hilprecht's aid Pepper and Clark wrote directly to Haynes. Finally, Peters lost his title as scientific director of the dig, and Haynes got it. The changes were quick and dramatic. Pepper worried that the BEF would "alienate" Peters or that he would "covertly oppos[e] us." At the same time (although I cannot see it) Pepper was delighted about the "good effect [in Haynes] the change in the manner of conducting correspondence had produced."[40]

The deterioration of Peters's connection with the BEF is an unfortunate story. Although his fellow feeling was exasperatingly nonexistent, he was an able man, as his two-volume book on the campaigns of 1889–90 demonstrated. Moreover, to some extent, he was a convenient scapegoat for a guilty BEF.

In any event the flurry of activity meant less to Haynes than it otherwise might. Shortly before Christmas Meyer had died: "A letter, dated at Baghdad on the second [of January], and received at Niffer on the eighth . . . announces the very sad death on the twentieth of December, and burial in the little English cemetery on the following day, of my late companion and friend, Joseph A. Meyer of Canton, Ohio, in the thirty-eighth year of his age."

There had been, said Sundberg, "a copious *rusty* purulent expectoration. The emaciation was extreme." "He did not want to let go of my hand even when asleep." Until a few hours before his death he had been "very melancholy and wept much." "The loss to the expedition," wrote Haynes,

> is far exceeded by the personal loss to myself of an efficient helper, and a genial companion, whose life was exceptionally free from every form of evil. The whole influence of his noble life, in every act and word, was cast on the side of right, purity, and virtue. The tenor of his speech was uplifting, nor can I recall a word or act of his, that need make him blush in presence of his holy Maker and righteous Judge. . . .

> He made a manly struggle for his ebbing life; but the odds were great against him, and he has fallen in the contest. He has paid the debt of disease. He has gone to his rest. Our desert home is afflicted with grief. A great sorrow has overtaken us in our loneliness; but the Lord God reigneth over all, and in his own time and way, He will carry on this work, though the laborers fall by the wayside. . . . Unto Him we turn for guidance, in this dark hour of need, and cheerfully take up the increased burdens thus laid upon us, to bear them according to our daily strength, trusting in Him to supply all needs, that lie beyond our own weak power to do for the essential success of the work required of us.[41]

"I fear much for Mr. Haynes," Sundberg wrote. "The climate and the *solitude* with a constant strain of anxiety are telling on him." When this mournful news reached the United States in mid-March, Pepper agreed: "No human being could stand the strain to which he has been subjected much longer." Intensely involved with Sara Stevenson at this point, Pepper recalled that Haynes had broken off an engagement in order "to go to the desert." Now Pepper worried that Haynes's relations with that young woman "may play a part in his mental condition." Clark added that he was glad to authorize a leave for Haynes. "I am not willing to assume . . . responsibility . . . [for] keeping him . . . at Niffer without rest . . . and companion." Hilprecht, who had little insight into other people's psyches, worried about Haynes. Despite his reservations about Haynes's abilities and his dislike of Peters, Hilprecht urged their reconciliation out of concern for Haynes. Peters, too, felt "a sense of responsibility—and participation, also, which I can not shake off."[42]

Haynes's distress bolstered his reputation. Although the people at home never ranked field archaeology with philological scholarship, they did come to value its heroic nature and to appreciate more fully its importance. Haynes, said Hilprecht, was now "the most experienced Babylonian explorer living," "the best expert in Babyl[onian] excavation." Hilprecht recalled Layard's dismissal of Nippur's prospects: "What the famous Layard was incapable of doing, he [Haynes] had done for many years with striking success." "He alone of all of us—nobody excepted—has saved this expedition from ruin in the field."[43]

Back at home, mindful of his achievements, the BEF was also mindful of the stress that events had placed on Haynes. After some indecision, it gave in to his dutiful request to stay on the site for 1895–96. But the administrators also searched for one or two others to join him. Initially unable to locate suitable young explorers, the BEF persevered. It had to find companions for Haynes. The sooner the Americans put more men in Nippur, the better they would feel about Meyer's death. Moreover, if Haynes trained assistants for a period, he could return home while they carried on. The BEF need not accept Haynes's statements of conventional obligation to shoulder on at Nippur. The BEF could order his return while aides stayed, and the expedition would not lose momentum.

In the spring of 1895 Haynes worried, hyperbolically it seems, about the minor but incessant tribal fighting. When the Ottomans replaced his unscrupulous Ottoman commissioner, they relieved Haynes's fears. Yet he was still leery about his—or anyone else's—staying beyond April 1896, the end of the 1895–96 season. At home Pepper and Clark pressed to get colleagues for Haynes to permit the dig to go on.[44]

It was not easy. David Lyon, the premier Assyriologist at Harvard, recommended one young scholar who was rejected because he might not be able to command the Arab workers, being "very small and very young in appearance." After many failed efforts, Sir Flinders Petrie, the Egyptologist whom Stevenson had interested in Penn, recommended a young Scotsman.

John Duncan was in his early twenties. He had worked with Petrie in Egypt and was to begin a doctorate in biblical archaeology at Aberdeen that coming fall. After Pepper wrote Petrie for suggestions, Petrie learned that Duncan would put aside his studies to join Haynes. Three weeks later, on 7 September, Pepper offered Duncan the job, sight unseen. Pepper disclosed the hardships of Nippur, including the story of Meyer, and asked Duncan to cable a response. By the end of the month Duncan had agreed and was being nudged to pack up and leave quickly.[45]

In addition, because Hilprecht could not get a second coworker for Haynes, Pepper asked Duncan to procure this assistant himself. Duncan did so. A young architect, Valentine Geere, thus joined the expedition. Duncan himself appears not to have met him. Duncan had communicated by mail with Geere, who "has been well spoken of by his employer in Southampton." Running around London shopping for his extensive kit, Duncan was flushed with his new position. He made various observations to the BEF on how to deal with Arabs. In a month he had spent some time in the British

Museum "in acquiring cuneiform . . . [and] in trying to decipher tablets." Soon, however, although the trip was subject to the usual but still apparently unexpected and frustrating delays, Duncan and Geere were on their way.[46]

As the two Britishers journeyed to Nippur, Haynes worried about their arrival. The "turbulent, treacherous semi-savages" distressed him, though by now he was an experienced negotiator. He fretted that the mail would not go through because of "the general condition of pillage and murder" around Nippur. The government was "supine," and "its petty officials in league with . . . robbers, which make the latter more desperate and fearless." Haynes wrote that the bandits would cross the desert to attack his camp, "this very pit, and pest ridden slough of inter-tribal feud and treasonable intrigue, blood-shed, and murder."[47]

In December, from Nippur, Haynes argued against sending him relief. "There have recently arisen conditions of which it is unwise for me to write . . . which forbid one to attempt to remain here after my departure." Duncan and Geere could not stay in Nippur with this "covetous, treacherous, and bloody throng around us." "No one but myself knows or can know what it has cost in mental and physical wear and waste to accomplish what has been accomplished." Other matters about which it was "unwise to write" would make "a temporary withdrawal" expedient. "Read between the lines and trust to my discretion & knowledge."[48]

As Duncan and Geere drew closer, Haynes grew more determined that they should not come. By early February the novices were stranded in Baghdad because of flooding. At Nippur Haynes had ordered boats for himself and the expedition's belongings. As soon as the boats arrived, "I must quietly and speedily depart from these blood reeking coasts of this iniquitous land, the realm of the thieving Arab, etc., etc."

A week later Haynes's boats had not arrived, but Duncan and Geere had. As soon as they sketched a little, Haynes said, "we shall hasten from this scene of feud and turmoil." When the boats came, they would be loaded with "their cargo of ancient and modern freight: of living men and the bones of [the] dead." Sorry to leave when efficient assistance was at hand, Haynes said it was best to go, though inappropriate "to relate the most potent reasons." "We must be away from Niffer." By 19 March Duncan and Geere were returning to London; they had been at Nippur for four days. "The reasons . . . you may infer," wrote Haynes after the little party reached Hillah. "All the reasons and arguments hitherto advanced are potent," but beyond them was "a single principle of evil . . . etc., etc., etc."[49]

Duncan and Geere, on the one side, and the BEF, on the other, were distraught. From Haynes's two-month-old letters and brief but more recent cables, Pepper and Clark concluded that he had become "nervous and needlessly alarmed." "Prepared to face . . . risk[s]," Duncan thought matters seemed "slightly unintelligible" and Haynes's reasoning "slightly contradictory." When the three men reached Baghdad, the BEF made a last plea to Haynes to keep the expedition in the field. But he was the authority, and said "*No.*" Although Duncan and Geere wanted to stay, Haynes was adamant about departing himself and insisted that the two others do likewise.[50]

Even before he knew the worst, Pepper wrote Petrie that it would be a "serious blow to us" if Duncan did not remain at Nippur. Pepper also hoped that Duncan and Geere would release the BEF from its twelve-month commitment because of the "total miscarriage" of the plan. When Petrie replied, he too wondered about the "mysterious fiasco" and "crossquestion[ed]" Duncan when he got to England in May. The Egyptologist could not hide his annoyance at what had happened. The Americans could only ask Duncan, "Why did you not disobey all our directions?" The "key to the business," said Petrie, was that Haynes "has been left too long in solitary and wearing circumstances." "It becomes difficult not to be over much affected by small matters . . . and . . . as uneasy in . . . mind as Mr. Haynes appears to have become." Pepper tried to maintain a measure of the BEF's honor. "Dreadfully sorry" about the end of the third dig, Pepper wrote Clark that "I do not think Duncan did right." Yet he also told Clark to regard Petrie's letter as "strictly confidential": "show to no one."[51]

As Haynes made his way home, Clark could not close his books. Comfortable young men, Geere and Duncan had spent more on their outfits and travel than the BEF had anticipated. The Americans had also broken the contract by forcing the two to return to Britain. Now the BEF had to settle up. After much bickering, the twenty-three-year-old Duncan wrote to the millionaire banker Clark. "I need scarcely remind you that you are really bound . . . for one year's salary, expenses, and sustenance." Duncan had earlier offered better terms "of my own good will." Because of the BEF's dallying over money, he withdrew his offer. Not without merit, Duncan argued that all the problems were "the result of the bungling of your own committee." He would await a prompt reply from Clark before "placing the matter in the hands of a solicitor." With a final insult Duncan said of the BEF, "I cannot characterise their conduct as gentlemanly altogether." Soon thereafter, the Americans paid up. Despite its many successes in obtaining tablets and in excavating the ziggurat, the third campaign had ended in embarrassment.[52]

4

HILPRECHT'S TRIUMPHS, 1897–1902

I N THE SUMMER of 1898, in the middle of final preparations for a
fourth expedition, Pepper died at fifty-five while vacationing in California. His precipitous decline confirmed for his supporters his predic-
tions about how he would sacrifice himself for his projects. His death also
evoked an outpouring of grief when his friends dedicated the new home for
antiquities a year later. The University Museum was a striking architectural
achievement and a glittering sign that the United States would continue in
the forefront of high culture, as measured by the assemblage of rare objects
from around the globe. In a structure housing the ruins of lost worlds, Pepper's friends recalled the words that he used to encourage them: "You and
I must pass away, but these things shall last."[1]

Although the plans for the expedition were momentarily halted, the
Clark brothers ensured that the exploration would go on. Even with its
humiliating climax, the third campaign had gone so well that everyone
agreed that Haynes's work must be suitably wrapped up. A fourth expedition, even if it was not the last one, would systematically clarify all the
previous efforts. Assisting the Clarks was Sara Stevenson, who put aside her
mourning to push for a summary of the undertaking.

Pepper's death simplified the domestic politics of the expedition. The
Clarks were friends of Charles Harrison; both families were made up of
wealthy industrialists. Although the brothers were concerned about the
"autonomy" of the museum and its enterprises, they also dealt practically
with Harrison. He found it easier to compromise with the museum without
Pepper, and became a prominent partner in the organization of the fourth
expedition.

On the other hand, the personal animosity between Harrison and the
"Pepper faction" in the museum increased. After Pepper's death Stevenson
took up the cudgels for the former provost. Harrison soon became her bête
noire but when the museum's board of managers officially handed the
building over to Harrison at its dedication, the balance of power had swung
in favor of the university. Thereafter the museum and its personnel would
be a trial to university officials, remaining independent enough to give them
regular headaches. But the threat posed during Pepper's time had vanished.[2]

Hilprecht figured in the machinations. His servility to Harrison reached
new depths. The documents do not reveal how Harrison received Hilprecht's gush, which wove flattery and self-promotion together in equal pro-

portions. Hilprecht also consistently saw that his future was with Pennsylvania. His loyalty belonged to the institution's managers—to Pepper when he was provost, to Harrison when he took over, and still more to Harrison after Pepper died.

For much of this time Hilprecht was loyal from a distance. He had begun journeying to Constantinople in the early 1890s. From 1896 to 1903 he was there for an average of six months a year and also vacationed in Germany, at a second home in Jena.[3] Nonetheless, Hilprecht looked out for Penn and for himself. He told Harrison he was one among those of Penn's professors "who will shun no work, no sacrifice of time and health, if it be for you and our University, which fills my whole heart and mind." It would always be his "*first* duty to be at the service of my Provost." He would be "faithful to your person" "to my last breath." It was, Hilprecht said, "a genuine *pleasure* to breathe and work under you."[4]

Expressions of commitment to Harrison competed with descriptions of the many honors Europeans had accorded him. Hilprecht announced that his own studies were one of "the memorable events in the history of Assyriology" and that he had made the Near Eastern side of the museum the "first in the world." In his own person, he told Harrison, he represented "three ordinary professors' work and positions," "enough for a giant." In Philadelphia, he was so busy even on Sundays that he "*could not go once* to church." In the Turkish capital his deeds were superhuman. At one point he was so exhausted from his grueling labor cataloguing tablets that he reported he was taking a four- to six-week vacation, first with Prince Rupprecht of Bavaria and then with the sister of the king of Denmark.[5]

Hilprecht's stint with the Ottomans had made it unavoidable, he asserted, for the Assyriologists of the British Museum, of the Louvre, and even of Berlin to esteem the United States. The respect for Pennsylvania in Constantinople was enormous, Hilprecht said. It allowed him to combat the evil influence of Paul Haupt of Johns Hopkins, whom Hilprecht believed was still trying to undermine him all over Europe, and of Peters, whom Hilprecht contended was also weakening his position.[6]

Hilprecht's chief victory was securing the lion's share of the finds from the American expedition. The Turks had given the antiquities to him "as personal gifts of the Sultan," while, he said, the Germans had to pay and the French got nothing. Hilprecht of course "presented" the material, his "personal presents," to the University. As the sultan repeatedly "bestowed magnificent gifts" on Hilprecht, he noted that his donation to the university after one division was minimally valued at fifty to sixty thousand dollars. By the end of 1898, in his annual report, he wrote only that he "presented most of them [the finds] to the University of Pennsylvania."[7]

Hilprecht's obsequiousness to Harrison (or to the office of the provost, or to those in power) made him Harrison's man in the museum as the conflict

evolved between Harrison and Pepper and, later, Stevenson. Harrison, Hilprecht said, had to make the museum an integrated part of the university,
"a subdivision of the large ship steered by you." He intrigued with Harrison
to elect "University men" to the museum's board of managers. Hilprecht
consulted with other institutions on how the museum could be brought
into line, "controlled by the University."

When Pepper died, Hilprecht confided to Harrison that the former provost had been "richly gifted," but "his lack of concentration and his personal ambition" had led him to an early grave. He had valued Pepper, Hilprecht said, even though he had "suffered" and "differed radically from" the
means Pepper had used. But now, Hilprecht concluded, "the unification of
all the departments of the University is . . . completed, and I pray from all
my heart, that our Lord may keep and protect you, *our* head."[8]

When Sara Stevenson assumed the defense of the museum's interests,
Hilprecht strengthened his ties to Harrison. One major problem with the
museum's organization, he commented, was the lack of professionalism of
its curatorial staff. If the museum did not come under the rule of the university, amateurs might dominate the curators. Stevenson, for Hilprecht, exemplified this evil. "Modern science," he said, demanded an earned doctorate
in an academic field. Speaking "as an expert," he related that Stevenson's
view of archaeology was "a miscarriage among scientific men." Every curator should pass muster for appointment to a Penn professorship. The museum staff must join the graduate school. Otherwise, he said, the museum
had "*no right of existence.*"[9] Unification would prevent the "secret" cabals
against the university led by people like Stevenson. It would stop "liberal"
or "broadminded" nonprofessionals from allowing any scholar to use the
museum's resources. If the museum gained prominence "as the herald of
higher, popular education," it would come at a cost to Penn's "expensive
property." The material in the museum had to be exclusively maintained to
increase the honor of the university among a smaller but more critical group
of individuals.[10] Stevenson threatened modern scholarship with quaint Victorian ideas of uplift. Academics like Hilprecht harbored fewer illusions
about the universal value of learning.

To bring the museum into line with the university, Hilprecht advocated
that the curators have a "dean" who would report to the board of managers
but who would be responsible to the provost. In the first instance, Hilprecht
urged, the dean would approve all foreign scholars who wanted to work in
the museum's collections. Although Harrison did not want the title "Dean"
used, he liked this plan, but Stevenson scotched the effort. There were, she
said, only a few curators, and her designation as such was merely "honorary." To make one of this group the leader of the others would be invidious,
foolish, and unnecessary.[11]

It is likely that Hilprecht hoped to be dean. But in addition to demanding power over who could use the tablets, Hilprecht wanted the dean to oversee the books that the museum would print. He once again grasped how the academic world was going to work. At the same time, he embroiled himself in a controversy over publications, a controversy to which there was no easy solution.

Hilprecht advanced a clear and intelligent position. Prestige in the ancient Near Eastern field, he believed, depended on the control of choice finds. Although the university could be generous with most of what it had excavated, Penn had to be even more circumspect with the "literary" documents than Hilprecht had originally advised in 1889. He advocated restricting scholars' use of the material at the museum itself. Penn would rise in prominence as it carefully assured the "publication" of these cuneiform tablets—the reproduction of photographs of the actual tablets and enhanced drawings of the writing accompanied by transliterations of the Akkadian, translations, and commentary. All such scholarship carrying the imprint of the museum should also carry that of the university. Appropriate professors would vet these publications to guarantee that they met impeccable standards.

Hilprecht added a set of self-interested notions. He wanted personally to approve books under university sponsorship that dealt with cuneiform. Additionally, his name must appear as a principal author of all such works. Hilprecht's view was not so outrageous as it may seem and was common among senior international scholars of the Near East. The Babylonian publications of the university would be texts, translations of texts, or discussions of the work at Nippur. Hilprecht was curator of the material and, theoretically, had examined all of it, even if other scholars expended more energy in picking out a particular group of documents for study. These scholars would be students of Hilprecht's, or academics whose entrance to the museum he had favored. He had, after all, been involved in each of the expeditions. Consequently, the title page of any books on Nippur should recognize his status.[12]

Hilprecht's stature as professor of Assyriology and curator did allow him to dominate the volumes on Mesopotamia that Pennsylvania published. Although his juniors chafed under his authoritarian headship, his demands were more or less justified.

A difficult problem arose because of the finances of publication. A benefactor to the museum provided a sum to publish Hilprecht's writings on Mesopotamia. Hilprecht and museum officials wanted to use this money to bring out works by other authors. Harrison wanted the money earmarked for Hilprecht alone. But the university did not want to pay for other publications that did not come from the master; it wanted the museum to raise more money for such tomes.[13] Harrison wished the museum to remain in his grip yet hoped that it would generate independent resources to benefit Penn. For a time Hilprecht was caught between his desire to have his publishing empire grow as rapidly as possible and his need to kowtow to Harrison. This was not a pleasant situation for Hilprecht. Low-level friction continued for years, the two sides squabbling over who would get credit for a book and who would pay for its production.

The hardest dilemma came in determining the quality of work. Here Hilprecht's connection to Peters and Haynes haunted him. Peters returned from Nippur in 1891. Because the museum had not formed a publications committee, the BEF authorized Peters to write an account of the two campaigns and to print it any way he could. Peters's two-volume book, *Nippur; or, Explorations and Adventures on the Euphrates*, appeared in 1897. Although by later standards the book was completed in a reasonable amount of time, the BEF lamented the delay through the mid-1890s, and Peters apologized for procrastinating. In 1896 he sought a university subvention and imprint for his still-unfinished manuscript. The BEF rejected his request. In 1897, however, G. P. Putnam's Sons in New York brought out his work. Immediately before *Nippur* appeared, the BEF changed its mind and demanded that Peters publish the volumes under its auspices. Too late did the BEF realize that Peters would do an excellent job.[14]

Peters had taken many opportunities to mock Hilprecht and thought the German something of a fool. Yet Peters also recognized his abilities. On the other hand, Hilprecht hated Peters and was not so much above the battle; he sensed that Peters joked about him but had to puzzle out the truth of the jokes. He thought Peters a malign force, arrayed against him and Penn. Peters always "schemed" for his own benefit instead of working for "the cause," said Hilprecht. Before Peters's book came off the press, the postponements enraged Hilprecht because they would "allow our great monumental work spoiled by [an] outside influence" not committed to publicizing the exploration.[15]

Then, suddenly, Peters threatened a major publication that Hilprecht would neither shape nor share. Hilprecht was dismayed. He feared that Peters would (legitimately) emphasize his leadership from 1888 to 1891 to the exclusion of Hilprecht's. Additionally, the New Yorker's book would not only be the premier account of the first two expeditions. Peters knew Haynes's work on the third dig and, Hilprecht worried, would include in his volumes everything Haynes had learned. That is, Peters promised an up-to-date version of accomplishment that Hilprecht could not control.

Hilprecht's agitation led him into a long and tasteless involvement with Putnam's. He encouraged the firm to publish two books—the two-volume account by Peters of the first two campaigns, and another book by Haynes on the third. Hilprecht's difficulties started here, for what he had to offer Putnam's was a wretched manuscript that the BEF had bullied Haynes into preparing after he came back from Nippur in 1896. While waiting to return there, Haynes worked over his meager letters and reports written from Nippur. He broke them down into a series of topics that had come up frequently in the correspondence—Arab wars, workers, Joseph Meyer, and so on. Haynes then collated the materials on each of these topics, making a chapter of each. The result was poorly written and more or less empty of insight.[16] Haynes did not have the wherewithal to write a book. Hilprecht thus shamelessly attempted to hook Haynes's manuscript on to Peters's more substantial endeavor. Moreover, Hilprecht demanded that Putnam's not use Peters as a consultant for Haynes's effort. After Putnam's refused to publish Haynes, Hilprecht arranged for the *Sunday School Times* to print the narrative as edited by Hilprecht. But this plan, too, fell through. Haynes's writing needed more than editing. When Peters's *Nippur* appeared, Hilprecht withdrew his support for Haynes. Hilprecht admitted that the manuscript had neither literary nor scientific value and that Peters had taken "the cream."[17]

Hilprecht's self-promotion compromised his zeal for *Wissenschaft*, as he himself realized. In pushing for Haynes to lead a fourth campaign, Hilprecht also found his professional ideals and personal desires in conflict.

The organizers of the fourth dig assumed that Haynes should again go to Nippur. This was, however, a bad way to survey the results of the exploration. While Haynes's stock had risen from 1893 to 1896, the failed attempt to publish his manuscript had again underlined his shortcomings. Hilprecht and the BEF (and most pointedly Peters, when he was associated with it) had hoped that Haynes would bring home useful field notes after the third dig. At least the BEF could fruitfully interrogate him. But Haynes had only copies of his frustrating letters and could tell the BEF nothing helpful. Many photographs of Nippur existed but none allowed reconstruction of the various cities that had occupied the site. No one really knew exactly where Haynes had found his treasures. Hilprecht thought that bombarding Haynes with instructions for the fourth campaign would help. This strategy was poor too, for without being on the site no one could really figure out what Haynes ought to do to wrap up the expedition.[18]

With Hilprecht unwilling to go to Babylonia, the BEF had to give Haynes his head. Even his instructions soon became a minor matter as the Clarks and Harrison faced a critical decision in which they would disregard principle for expediency to get Haynes back to the Castle.

After the Clarks and Harrison took over the organization of the fourth expedition, they secured two assistants for Haynes. Valentine Geere from

Southampton, England, had been John Duncan's sidekick in the belated attempt to assist Haynes in 1895–96. But Geere had not been so obstreperous as Duncan when their trip to Nippur ended after four days. Haynes rejected Duncan, but liked Geere. Geere had also excavated with Petrie in Egypt between 1896 and 1898. His reputation was high.[19] In addition, the BEF sought out Clarence S. Fisher, a graduate of the Penn architectural program and a young man whom many worthies recommended. His early stint at Nippur turned out to be the first phase of a long and distinguished career as a Near Eastern field archaeologist. His appointment suggested that the BEF was now not interested only in recovering objects in the Near East. The Americans also wanted to learn about the history of urban settlements, and hoped architects could teach them.[20]

With these two assistants, Clark and Harrison had overcome the most significant problem that had disturbed the earlier campaign—companionship for Haynes. But this solution proved irrelevant as they simultaneously negotiated what for them was a far more serious crisis: Haynes's request to bring his new wife.

Forming a picture of Cassandria Artella Haynes is difficult. The lore of the Haynes family depicted her as a "gold digger," apparently because she later left her husband, but we must also remember that the thick and ponderous Haynes was no prize. Some material evidences her willful aggressiveness. But she also wrote a gracious letter to the BEF buttressing Haynes's request and urging that she could provide human comfort to aid her husband's exertions in the desert.[21]

Because the solitude of the explorer had been such a pervasive concern, Clark and Harrison felt that they *must* consent to the couple's wish. They might lose John's services if they did not. But they acceded uneasily and with a bad conscience. Now the politicians of the expedition, they made adjustments that their own convictions and the views of their subordinates told them were wrong.

Fisher and Geere thought it unusual that a woman should be in the field. Peters and Hilprecht, who agreed on almost nothing, shared a distrust for the female presence. All the men involved allowed that they strove to be fair about the issue. They nonetheless worried, especially because of the frail nature of a woman's health and the rigors of desert life. Hilprecht wished "in *his & her* interest" that Cassandria stay behind, and registered "a last warning voice" before the couple left the United States. Consulted by Clark, Peters said this "very risky matter" wanted long consideration. "Her personal equation, her temperament, training, physique, and her effect on him need to be carefully studied." Later, after the BEF had capitulated, Peters protested that Haynes's wife might hurt the expedition.[22]

As matters turned out, the worries of Hilprecht and Peters, who had each developed an antipathy to the field and desired not to be at Nippur, proved misplaced. The two Hayneses, Fisher, and Geere met in Marseilles at the end of October 1898. This time they took a less arduous sea voyage and traveled the Mediterranean to the coast of Egypt, through the Suez Canal, down the Red Sea, and around the Gulf of Aden to the Persian Gulf. Another ship took them from Basra up the Euphrates to Baghdad just before Christmas. Here they waited for more than a month to get Ottoman permission to dig again at Nippur. Four days before the permission came at the end of January 1899, Geere came down with "pleur-pneumonia." Fisher stayed to nurse him. The Hayneses left for Nippur. Geere's condition improved only slowly. Although his Baghdad doctor finally permitted him to go on the expedition, he was not to begin work until the autumn, after the summer season. In the meantime, after seeing Geere through the worst of his illness, Fisher quit altogether and left for the United States, for reasons that remain unclear. When he reached England, he was persuaded to go back to Babylonia. By October 1900, he was again in Baghdad and accompanied Geere to Nippur.[23] The fragile female had been alone with her husband on the dig for eight and a half months, including the hard summer season. During this time the two young men had screwed up their courage and health to make the trip. Peters and Hilprecht worried from a civilized distance.

John and Cassandria created an eccentric society of two at Nippur.[24] Cassandria protected her husband's reputation. Every day she took down notes on the work of the camp. They became the basis for the brief and uninformative weekly reports that John dispatched and that the BEF now anticipated with seasoned resignation. Cassandria also quickly picked up some of the practical, if narrow, knowledge that John had of Mesopotamian history and freely expressed her own views in her notes. While she jealously guarded John's fame, she did not mind her distaff side with the great man himself, though there is little record of what John, a newlywed at age fifty, made of his Near Eastern honeymoon. The two did join forces in poking malicious fun at the orders and stinginess of the Clarks and Harrison, in denigrating the abilities of both Peters and Hilprecht, and in complaining of the commitment of Geere and Fisher.

When the young men arrived in October, they were housed with the Hayneses in the renovated and expanded Castle. Cassandria treated them to "a table" that everyone who came to Nippur commented positively about and complimented her on. Yet the architects were also struck by the hostility directed at them and by a puzzling domestic scene. John and Cassandria were pitted as much against each other as against the newcomers. From November 1899 to March 1900 the director's chief duty was as much to appease his wife and to mediate disputes between her and the young men as to run the expedition.

Geere kept a diary of his time at Nippur.[25] Although he was not an unbiased narrator, he was obviously frustrated by and uncomprehending of

Fig. 3 Cassandria Haynes at Nippur

the emotional storm around him. Sorting out his feelings at the end of 1899, he wrote that Cassandria was a shrew with an "infernal temper," and John "a grossly incompetent bungler, a tyrannical pedant and hypocritical humbug." Most of all, Geere thought that the expedition was in disarray. There was, he thought, no intelligent direction and no coherent planning for the job the architects were to do. "Oh, for a Petrie here!" he lamented.

In mid-January the luck of the expedition changed. From an area that had been called "Tablet Hill" even back in 1889, which Hilprecht at that time thought might house a library, Haynes began to extract "a great quantity" of tablets. Soon he was calling it a "library" (in quotation marks); then the number of tablets grew so great that it became *Library* (underlined, but no quotation marks). Haynes concluded from the position of the tablets in the excavated rooms that "documents" had been stored there and that rooms or racks above the ground floor had collapsed, dumping their shelves of "books" in a pile. By the end of February Haynes had cleared the library. After so many letters had demanded portable antiquities, the new trove of inscribed pieces thrilled Haynes. On 2 March he capped his triumphs by finding a jar filled with different sorts of tablets, a set of exceptional museum pieces that someone had collected thousands of years ago. Even Geere was aware that the discovery of the library altered the fortunes of the expedition, although the skills and leadership of the Hayneses still depressed him.

Things changed for the better for Geere. Before the expedition had left, some concerned fund-raisers had pertinently observed, even demanded, that someone with intellectual authority oversee the results of the exploration. Peters was long gone. Haynes was not equipped to make sense of what he had dug up; Geere was only the latest person to note Haynes's lack of mental acuity. Hilprecht interpreted the demand of the donors as a threat to replace him, but actually they were attacking his unwillingness to visit the field. Fearful that he might lose control over the finds, he "meditated over the question" and decided he would "go to Nippur."[26] Hilprecht delayed as much as was seemly. "What if I should die in Babylonia[?]" he asked Harrison. Who would bring some kind of order to the BEF's cuneiform collections, "stored for years in the cellar"?[27] Nonetheless, in early March 1900 he arrived at the site for the first time in eleven years. With the power of the BEF behind him, he took command. Hilprecht remained for ten weeks, until the fourth expedition ended in mid-May 1900.

In some ways Hilprecht's work at Nippur was the high point of his contribution to the American enterprise.[28] For the past few years he had been suspect of the hunt for tablets, although that was still the organizers' main goal. Hilprecht had not responded much when Haynes developed an interest in the plans of the various cities that had occupied the site. Nevertheless, a German expedition that had recently gotten underway at Babylon stirred

Hilprecht. He now wanted to synthesize what Peters and Haynes had been doing "architecturally" for the last twelve years. Geere was impressed. Hilprecht changed the tone of the dig. He was a "Petrie-an" person, "strong, enthusiastic, energetic."[29]

Although he filled his diary with remarks about John Haynes's boorish and unyielding incompetence, Hilprecht did not publicly blame Peters and Haynes. He reported, as he should have, that Haynes agreed with his assessment of how the Americans had torn up the site. Hilprecht forgave Haynes but "personally" would have quit had the BEF ordered him to excavate in an inappropriate way. Moreover, Cassandria had been a bad influence. "Discrepancies" in John's "honest efforts" derived from trying to "please his wife." She was "the real cause of many misunderstandings and unwise actions." More fundamentally, said Hilprecht, Haynes had searched destructively for tablets. Away in Constantinople, Hilprecht said, he had not known of Haynes's instructions. Yet Haynes must have misconstrued the orders from the BEF in Philadelphia. Tablets were important, but John should have judiciously selected, say, a thousand of them for research and publication. Hilprecht and his assistants would carefully husband these, while other scholars and institutions could use the thousands of less important finds.

Hilprecht had to save the rest of the work in the field from disaster. He helped Fisher and Geere prepare a series of reports that analyzed how the ancient townsfolk had built and rebuilt Nippur. In the mind's eye a complex vision of city growth—Nippur's architectural history over three or four millennia—replaced the reality of the confusion produced by more than a decade of digging great trenches in the mounds.

Much was pretense in Hilprecht's letters home. He had no experience as an excavator or as an architect. Ten weeks of cogitation could not undo the ten years of tunneling that Peters and Haynes had undertaken at the behest of the BEF. Yet Hilprecht did have an intelligent sense of what was significant. He also was devoted to the German archaeologists who had developed a "horizontal" and architectural orientation in their excavation at nearby Babylon. In the spring of 1900, at least, he inspired Fisher and Geere to a productivity they had not displayed before Hilprecht came.

Hilprecht's repeated statements about his titanic workload revealed his level of self-regard. Without his eighteen-hour days and sleepless nights, he reiterated, he could not have reformed the expedition. The Hayneses and the architects quarreled, but he brought orderly discussion out of the tiffs. He changed the chemistry among the four and mediated their conflicts. Both sides, he said, liked and trusted him, whatever undercurrent of hostility might remain. Hilprecht intimated, too, that though the group badly needed his direction and leadership, all were helping the expedition. Now and then he even found a good word for Cassandria, the "amerikanische Drohne" whom Hilprecht disliked and whom he subtly disparaged.[30]

Cassandria, Hilprecht wrote, was "always ready" to make the explorers comfortable in the Castle. The Castle itself was now a "perfect little paradise." Hilprecht jocularly invited the BEF to vacation there. Had he known the desert was such a holiday spot, "I surely would have taken Mrs. Hilprecht with me, instead of forcing her into a long separation." In her absence from him, his wife had "suffered as much . . . as any member of our staff." On the other side, although Mrs. Haynes did well in running the Castle, she had not acted "as a true lady" in having the BEF pay her traveling and living expenses.[31] Hilprecht deprecated her insecure snobbery, evidenced in her eagerness to entertain prominent visitors, as "echt amerikanisher."[32] He sometimes reflected that Cassandria should have provided fewer amenities at Nippur, rather than more. Overall, an exploration had no place for a woman. Only *Wissenschaft* justified expenditures in Mesopotamia. Science wanted "determined . . . well-trained and equipped men." "*Specialists, nothing but specialists are needed now.*" Thus, Hilprecht gave up his notions of using Nippur "as a winter resort for delicate people" and of having his wife accompany him.

Hilprecht did not report to the BEF the central personnel problem he faced: the suicidal homosexual yearnings Fisher had for Geere. The male bonding that one might expect to develop in the desert had made for an intense relationship between Haynes and Joseph Meyer, broken only by Meyer's death. Now, four years later, some such bond existed between Fisher and Geere. Intellectually talented, Fisher was nonetheless a slight young man, dependent on his mother and shy and unable to speak in public.[33] He had been sent to the desert to become a man; Nippur did begin the making of his career but also permitted him to display other aspects of his character.

Meeting for separate tête-à-têtes with Geere, Fisher, and the Hayneses, Hilprecht learned on his arrival that Fisher had written poetry to Geere, kissed him, and on several occasions threatened to kill himself, either to gain attention or in despair that his affection was not reciprocated. With what abandonment of propriety did Hilprecht write in his journal that John and Cassandria had told him that Fisher was widely known as a "cocksucker"?[34]

Geere was himself lazy and, apparently, did little to ward off Fisher's advances. But he was also unable to lift Fisher's depression over his unrequited love. The two shared the same room and often slept late in the mornings and, at least before Hilprecht arrived, whiled away the days playing chess. They worked harder after Hilprecht arrived, but his psychiatric counseling had a limited effect. Surveying his archaeological team toward the end of the dig, Hilprecht lamented in the privacy of his diary that "a German scholar" such as he had to associate with four such Americans; he wished for the day that he would again be "on German soil."[35]

Hilprecht's real feelings about the merits of this expedition were complex. The Americans assumed that the fourth campaign would be a summing-up. After his ten weeks at Nippur and his training of the architects, Hilprecht claimed that he had rescued the project. His visit had become "a fundamental factor" in "the history of civilization." In the international race with the Germans at Babylon, the University of Pennsylvania had prevailed. Hilprecht had discredited Haynes's leadership and now argued against anyone's staying in the field after he officially closed the books on the fourth expedition in May. The great work was done, and the junior explorers could accomplish little more.

Yet Hilprecht also outlined the requirements for a large and expensive fifth expedition. Haynes would continue as business manager. After some retooling in the history of architecture, Fisher and Geere would return to Nippur with far greater abilities. In addition, another young architect would accompany them, and to head the group of three youngsters would be Penn's professor of architecture. Over everyone would be Hilprecht himself, having supreme authority and answering only to the BEF. Such an elaborate new expedition revealed that Hilprecht thought that the BEF had much to achieve at Nippur. But he probably believed that Penn would not consider the inordinately expensive excavation. In truth Hilprecht did not want to go back but did not want anyone else there either.[36] Like Haynes on the third dig, Hilprecht now found a way to return home without being replaced.

Hilprecht's wife was seriously ill at the time in Germany (and would die there in 1902). In a flourish of scientific commitment Hilprecht told Clark that the comforts and climate of Nippur would surely benefit his spouse, but that he could not think of taking her to the desert. The aim of any expedition had to be scientific only. He would sacrifice his wife in the name of science. At the same time (I am persuaded) Hilprecht believed that the BEF would not fund his proposed expensive new dig. He thus proclaimed the great results of the fourth campaign. Because these were so flimsy in "architectural" terms, he once more emphasized the tablets when he embarked for the United States. He stressed the remarkable finds that Haynes had termed "the library."

Hilprecht sailed back to America at the height of his fame and influence. The newspapers touted his heroism in leading the dangerous expeditions for the past ten years. Who was Hilprecht to disabuse them? He was himself voluble with self-praise about the discovery of the library, and people took him at his word. The Clark brothers established a research professorhip with Hilprecht as the first incumbent. The trustees of the university "gratefully accepted" Hilprecht's gift of that part of the library that the sultan had granted him as a "personal favor." He drafted an official letter in which he was given a five-year leave of absence to catalogue tablets and to conduct research at the new museum and in Constantinople. No pushover, Harrison changed the "five" to "three" before granting the benefit.[37] In any event Harrison relieved Hilprecht of all instructional obligations except those he might wish to undertake. The university provided him with a minister-scholar assistant, Albert Clay, a talented young man who had done his degree with the master. Additional aides took up teaching and menial curatorial duties.[38] As Hilprecht put it, the obligation of "constant planning" for the digs and "the exposures to the dangerous climates with the absence of every convenience of life" had diminished his productivity. Now he had welcome relief.[39] The trustees finally invested control of the Nippur finds in Hilprecht's person. He had responsibility for publishing them "for his lifetime." No more quarrels would occur about the chain of command in the production of Nippur books.

The public success at the turn of the century prompted a generous subscription for a fifth expedition. The BEF wanted Hilprecht at its head.[40]

PART TWO

FROM BABYLONIA TO

THE AMERICAN ANCIENT NEAR EAST

Fig. 4 Friedrich Delitzsch

Fig. 5 Hermann Hilprecht

Fig. 6 Albert Clay

Fig. 7 Paul Haupt

Fig. 8 John Peters

Fig. 9 George Andrew Reisner (*center*)

Fig. 10 James Henry Breasted

Fig. 11 William Foxwell Albright

5

THE ORGANIZATION OF KNOWLEDGE

BY THE TURN of the century, course offerings at various schools besides the major centers attested to a sustained interest in the languages and ancient history of the Near East. Columbia, Princeton, Union Theological Seminary, and Hebrew Union College (the first successful Jewish seminary) were among the most well established institutions committed to the field. But instructors could also be found at such schools as the University of Missouri, Drew Seminary in New Jersey, Colgate in New York, the University of Cincinnati, and Vanderbilt in Tennessee.[1]

Perhaps more important than the expanding number of courses was the growth in journals and academic organizations. The Society of Biblical Archaeology published its *Proceedings* from 1878, joining the venerable *Journal of the American Oriental Society*, which had been printed since the 1840s. In 1880 a group of scholars started the Society of Biblical Literature (SBL) and issued the *Journal of Biblical Literature and Exegesis*.[2] In 1884 William Rainey Harper introduced *Hebraica* (later the *American Journal of Semitic Languages and Literatures* and, still later, the *Journal of Near Eastern Studies*).

New groups fostered exploration. In 1879 Charles Eliot Norton of Harvard founded the Archaeological Institute of America (AIA). A prodigious figure in the genteel world of the academic humanities, Norton intended chiefly to recover Greco-Roman art. But he also promoted archaeological work in the Near East; the AIA had sponsored William Hayes Ward's original reconnaissance in Babylonia, the Wolfe Expedition.[3] In 1895 the SBL proposed a school for study and research somewhere in Palestine, modeled on Norton's American School for Classical Study in Athens. In 1900, with the aid of the SBL, a "corporation" of universities created the American School of Oriental Research (ASOR) in Jerusalem, and a similar school was later established in Baghdad.[4]

The institutions outside the control of a single university demonstrated the complex bureaucratic arrangements necessary in Near Eastern studies. ASOR funded an "annual professor" to study in the Near East. It struggled not just to make American efforts more coherent but also to provide research money that individual schools might not have available. Well-organized disciplines, such as history, philosophy, and chemistry, were becoming the standard way of guiding teaching and research. In this framework, university departments, with an agreed number of academic employees, were primary, professional associations secondary. Departments were more difficult to establish for the Orientalist, and structures of association external to them became more significant.

Four schools in addition to Pennsylvania—Harvard, Johns Hopkins, Yale, and Chicago—dominated the field. Various developments at the end of the nineteenth century and in the first decade of the twentieth led to thriving programs at these universities. Their individual histories and the histories of their failed competitors exemplified the administrative complications at work in building the ancient Near East.

For most of the nineteenth century, Harvard and its divinity school stood to the side of the burgeoning scholarly study of the Bible in the United States. Orthodox institutions of theology commanded the landscape, although Harvard was the single "liberal" institution against which other schools defined themselves. Supreme among them was the Andover Theological Seminary in Massachusetts. At midcentury this institution had educated a majority of the Bible scholars in the United States. In 1880 Andover or Andover students had trained more than half of the thirty-two chartered members of the SBL. By the end of the century, however, a revolution had occurred in higher education. As universities grew at unprecedented rates, theologians gave up conservative views and divinity schools themselves collapsed across the country as centers for advanced instruction.[5] Andover liberalized its program in the 1890s and then merged with Harvard in 1908.

In this new climate, Harvard propelled itself into a leading position in ancient Near Eastern studies. The field became a catchment area for scholars who previously might have taught at divinity schools but who now wanted both to keep their faith and to be acceptable to the modern world. George Foote Moore and Joseph Henry Thayer gave instruction in the biblical languages at Andover. When that school went into its death throes, they moved to the Harvard Divinity School. Their leader was Crawford Toy, professor of Hebrew and Oriental languages, whom Harvard's president, Eliot, had called to a job after the famous Scot, Robertson Smith, had turned him down. Through force of numbers, these three men provided Harvard with a reputation for cautious yet au courant work in the higher criticism of the Bible.[6]

This constellation of critics was joined by David Gordon Lyon, who specialized in Akkadian at Harvard College and gave the university its early prominence in Near Eastern studies. We have already met him advising Penn. He had studied in the same Leipzig seminar that had educated Hilprecht and Haupt, but Lyon was an American and had begun teaching in his country earlier, in 1882. This distinction and his *Assyrian Manual* (1886) made Lyon known as "the Father of Assyriology" in the United States. Although he was more a Cambridge gentleman than an original scholar, Lyon spoke influentially for Harvard and for the ancient Near East.

Perhaps the staff alone would have pushed Cambridge to the front ranks. But after he failed to hire Robertson Smith, Eliot continued to look for ways to build. In 1887 and 1888 Harvard planned an expedition that, like so many others, came to nothing. Acknowledging Penn's leadership in field-work, Lyon collected money for objects and a museum from 1889 on, but the going was slow. As Charles Eliot Norton's role testified, Harvard was primarily committed to Greece and Rome and their aesthetic heritage, which Norton saw developing in Italian Renaissance culture.[7] Neither the "savages" of anthropology nor the Hebrews of the ancient Near East loosened the purse strings of Brahmin gentiles.[8] Lyon became curator of material initially housed in a room of another museum. He purchased some Nippur objects from John Peters and persuaded the New York Jewish philanthropist Jacob Schiff, who had Harvard connections, to pay for anything of "real value."[9] In time, Schiff and his friends became the mainstay for the study of the Bible lands in Cambridge; for a season Eliot's modicum of support promised to overcome a studied Harvard disinclination to invest in Semitic scholarship. By 1903, with Eliot's friendly encouragement, Schiff had underwritten a building. But when the Harvard Semitic Museum was dedicated, Lyon, a Harvard University loyalist, worried with Hilprecht that the Semitic Museum might be independent of Harvard. Lyon and Schiff had a successful and cordial connection, but the museum never achieved major importance, and the donor was often unhappy.[10]

Over the years Schiff struggled to get "Boston Christian[s]" to participate in funding the study of the ancient Israelites in Cambridge. He irritatedly resisted the school's attempts to make such study, in terms of dollars, "a Jewish enterprise." Despite Lyon's efforts in behalf of Schiff and the field of Semitics, Boston Protestant culture was wary of "Hebrew learning." Moreover, the lure of Harvard was so great that Schiff (and to a lesser extent his New York associates) inevitably footed the bills in Cambridge, no matter what the gentile response.[11]

Schiff's museum needed antiquities, and thus an expedition. In an intricately connected series of events Harvard co-opted the University of California and then cooperated with the Boston Museum of Fine Arts to get into the field. For a moment it looked as if Harvard would overcome what appears in retrospect to be an almost reflexive anti-Semitism.

In the 1890s Phoebe Apperson Hearst, a San Francisco widow of great wealth, started to underwrite cultural endeavors. Curious about antiquities, she was befriended by William Pepper and Sara Yorke Stevenson. After Pepper gave Hearst a thorough medical examination in 1891, he became her personal physician, often from afar. Hearst then helped pay for antiquities and archaeological-anthropological explorations through Pepper's American Exploration Society. Pepper had formed the society to get funds for the museum at Penn that would allow it to function autonomously. Hearst was soon a major benefactor. Although she independently desired to aid the newly founded California University in Berkeley, Pepper had also catalyzed her energies around his aims, now only half-channeled toward the University of Pennsylvania.

Beginning in the early 1890s, the university in California itself had imaginatively aimed to make a mark in the ancient Near East, and vied with Pepper for Hearst's attention. In 1898 Hearst agreed to sponsor a joint California-Pennsylvania dig in Egypt; the University Museum now had the opportunity to be first on the ground not only in Mesopotamia but also in Egypt. Then Pepper died at Hearst's estate in California. Stevenson took over the organization of the East Coast aspect of this initial American Egyptian expedition. Immediately, Stevenson and Hearst argued. As a result of Stevenson's "interference," Hearst decided that the proceeds of the exploration should benefit Berkeley alone. Stevenson announced Hearst's "separation" from Penn. Hearst later browbeat the officials at the museum who had succeeded Pepper to give to Berkeley some of the antiquities that had been earlier obtained through her financing.[12]

For more than five years, Hearst underwrote the first United States dig in Egypt and the annual appointments of distant archaeologists as "Hearst Lecturers" at the University of California. In time the Hearst exploration became part of "a great scheme of anthropological research" connected to other excavations and a proposed museum in California. This complex enterprise was riven with the same sorts of tensions that had plagued earlier endeavors. New World anthropologists and Old World archaeologists squabbled. Administrators worried about the role of a museum. Patron and clients misunderstood one another. Yet the dramatic West Coast coup not only briefly shifted the geographic locus of ancient Near Eastern studies in the United States, but also made Egypt a part of the American ancient Near East.[13] Then, in 1904–5, Hearst cut much of her aid to California. Faced with economic pressure, the university in turn chose to fund the scholars who could be counted on to undertake teaching responsibilities at home, the anthropologists. Concentrating on money and instruction, Berkeley short-circuited its entrée into Near Eastern studies and its museum culture. Harvard and the Boston Museum of Fine Arts stepped in to rescue the work of the archaeologists in Egypt. California did not recapture the field, and the hegemony of the East Coast in this area of scholarship was for a time preserved.[14]

Schiff wanted Harvard to dig at Samaria in Palestine, in conformity with his Old Testament orientation. Egypt was too far from the homeland of the Jews, whose early history Schiff hoped a Cambridge excavation would honor.[15] With the explorers on the ground in Egypt and with this new push for Palestine, a more complicated program was worked out that included the Museum of Fine Arts in Boston. An American museum without formal links to a university was now going to sponsor excavation. A new actor was being added to the complexities of scholarship. The two institutions re-organized the California Egyptian undertaking and expanded its sphere to Palestine; the Boston museum and Harvard would share the proceeds. But the Bostonians and Cantabrigians could not get a firman for Palestine. They maintained the explorers in the field, but had to stay in Egypt, where Berke-ley had been. While Schiff cooled his heels, the money for Egypt principally came from Gardiner Martin Lane, a gentile partner in Lee, Higginson, and Company of Boston. The Boston museum got the finds; Harvard undertook the scholarly publication.[16]

Overall, Egypt trailed Mesopotamia in the United States conception of the Near East. The greater popularity of Egypt's imperial relics and museum-goers' fascination with mummies ultimately could not rival the scholarly lure of the Bible connections to Mesopotamia. Yet this first East Coast pledge to Egypt, to some extent produced by the desire of proper Bostonians to stay away from Jews, had an important consequence. The excavation ensured that the land of the pharaohs would be a core region in the Ameri-can ancient Near East.

To head the Egyptian campaign, Harvard's Eliot made an inspired deci-sion. George Andrew Reisner had received a Ph.D. in Semitics from Harvard in 1893 and had then studied Assyriology in Germany. He briefly taught at Harvard and published some cuneiform texts. Lyon pushed his work as an Assyriologist.[17] But Egyptology captured Reisner. He left Harvard to work in the Cairo Museum, eager to get excavating experience. Anticipating a break-through for an American dig, he convinced Hearst to explore in Egypt with himself as field director. Reisner reinforced Hearst's prejudices against Sara Stevenson and the American Exploration Society, and began excavating for California at the end of 1899.[18]

Reisner had a flair for spadework and in time became the most respected archaeologist of his generation. California had lost out when it discontinued his employment. In 1905 Harvard made him an assistant professor, and he assumed direction of the Harvard-Boston Expedition of the Gizeh Pyramids. "A settled university position," Reisner wrote Eliot, offered opportunities for research that "compensate[d] for the time given in instruction."[19]

Digging in Egypt was in some ways more civilized than in Babylonia. Getting permission to explore was easier in a land more under the sway of the British and French than was Mesopotamia. Dealing with officials was not a strain. Living conditions were not arduous, and the natives were friendly. Although he displayed the same attitudes as other Westerners, Reisner was better off than his peers in Babylonia. The locals were "a hope-lessly primitive people," and with them Reisner took "the place . . . of a father . . . to look after them generally." Yet Egyptian authorities took "very few of our objects," "the booty."[20]

At the same time, exploration in Egypt was subject to just as much psychological infighting as it was in Babylonia. Reisner fought with his assistant, Albert M. Lythgoe. Lythgoe then quit working for Boston and Harvard because he disagreed with the museum's "aesthetic" approach to collecting material. He did not like being Reisner's underling and wanted his own place in the sun. After taking a position with the Metropolitan Museum in New York City, he tried to steal Reisner's workers and initiated quarrels between the New York and Boston museums for treasures.[21] Meanwhile, administrators at Harvard and the Boston museum continued to attract Protestant funding for Reisner's non-Semitic archaeology in Egypt.

At the end of 1907 the firman for Palestine came through, and Harvard went back to its orignial plan involving Schiff's money. After a slow start, Reisner moved to Samaria in 1909, and his work confirmed his position as the greatest excavator of his day. But Palestine was only a secondary field of operation for him. Even before Eliot retired in 1909, Harvard's practical priority was Egypt, and the regime of A. Lawrence Lowell, Eliot's successor and well known as an anti-Semite, reinforced this emphasis. At the end of 1914 Schiff finally gave up on Harvard because of "the lukewarm support." Lowell complained that prospective donors shied away from the Near East—he meant gentile donors to Palestinian endeavors—because Harvard so clearly expected that they "raise or give money." Semitic studies languished at the institution, although Cambridge's reputation in the ancient Near East did not suffer.[22] Reisner only occasionally taught at home. Yet from Egypt he simultaneously maintained Harvard's status in the Near East and its distance from the Semitic lands of the area.

At Johns Hopkins, Daniel Coit Gilman promoted Near Eastern studies in a way that avoided the combination of Jewish aspirations and well-bred anti-Semitism that defined Harvard's efforts. Gilman was connected early on with William Dwight Whitney through Yale. Though barely an Orientalist, Gilman was the longstanding treasurer of the American Oriental Society and a tireless promoter of academic organizations. After a brief stint as head of the University of California (before its Egyptian dig), he reached the high point of his career as the first president of Johns Hopkins. Ancient Near Eastern studies combined science and religion in just the sort of scholarly way Gilman thought appropriate to the new universities in the United States.[23] In addition to hiring Paul Haupt, Gilman solidified the link with the Smithsonian Institution in nearby Washington, D.C., at least to secure space for antiquities. Gilman thought that the Smithsonian would function as Johns Hopkins's museum, and Haupt hoped that the federal government would underwrite Baltimore's endeavors in the Near East.[24]

Gilman and Haupt marginally succeeded in their aims. Johns Hopkins's key contact at the Smithsonian was Cyrus Adler, who had curatorial duties at the museum and was eventually employed as the institution's librarian. He went on to become a major figure in Jewish academic circles. Adler was Haupt's first doctoral student and an academic entrepreneur right out of graduate school.[25] His real value to Johns Hopkins was as a member of a circle at the Smithsonian in the 1880s and 1890s devoted to its assistant secretary, the naturalist George Brown Goode.

Goode wrote extensively on the role of museums in cultural life and had enlarged ideas about how the Smithsonian might educate the public about the flowering of human societies. Like other advanced thinkers with his kind of expertise, Goode envisioned a new sort of museum: it would display anthropological and archaeological concepts, not just an assortment of eccentric objects. The study of Native American cultures was well defined in scholarly Washington through the work of the Bureau of American Ethnology. Goode and his friends wanted to link "Indian" study with other geographically or temporally distant cultures. Goode did not want to divide the Old World (archaeology) and the New World (anthropology) as much as did many other students of the new human sciences. Ethnology for him encompassed the historic (archaeological) and prehistoric (anthropological) evidence for studying culture.[26]

Adler hoped that the Smithsonian would embrace Goode's ethnology. In addition to Native American studies, the institution would assist Near Eastern archaeology. Haupt's "Oriental Seminary" would have a repository for antiquities and the wherewithal for expeditions to obtain them. The two institutions did jointly sponsor an Assyrian collection at the Smithsonian and planned to make casts of *all* Assyrian and Babylonian tablets in the United States.[27] Haupt became the honorary curator of the Collection of Oriental Antiquities. Adler voiced Haupt's ideas at the Smithsonian when Haupt tried to overturn the BEF's claims in Babylonia in 1887 and 1888. In 1889, Johns Hopkins installed an Assyrian exhibition in the Smithsonian to honor the presidential inaugural of Benjamin Harrison. In 1890, Adler unsuccessfully tried to associate the AOS formally with the Smithsonian, and thus the federal government. In 1892, Haupt entertained a much more novel idea that would get Hopkins to Babylonia. He proposed a homeland for Russian Jews in Mesopotamia. This undertaking would relieve pressure on the United States to receive these immigrants and, as part of the enterprise, the Smithsonian would finance a preliminary expedition, choosing sites and doing exploratory work.[28]

The plans of Johns Hopkins and Haupt came to naught when Goode's career was sidetracked. In 1887 he was passed over when the Smithsonian chose a new secretary. Although Goode retained some influence, the new secretary, George Langley, was a physicist devoted to aeronautics; he had priorities different from those of Goode. When Goode died in 1896, the institution took a different direction without his leadership in ethnology. Haupt never received the benefits he thought an affiliation with the Smithsonian would bring. Peters, Hilprecht, and the BEF were greatly relieved.[29]

At the same time, Gilman's choice of Haupt was not mistaken. He became the preeminent Assyriologist in America and, in his seminary, the outstanding trainer of graduate students from the 1880s to the 1920s. Like Hilprecht, Haupt at first despised the United States. He was twenty-four when he arrived in Baltimore. A year later he told Gilman that Johns Hopkins was not a university but "only a polytechnic school." With "great reluctance" Haupt asked for a significant salary increase. He could not live in the United States "as I have been accustomed" and do the work that "six [professors in] chairs" would do in Germany. In any event, said Haupt, scholars such as he were *unbezahlbar*—they had no price. At age twenty-seven, when he negotiated a permanent position at Johns Hopkins and reduced his "elementary" instruction, one of his demands centered on the pension Hopkins would provide in forty years or so.[30] By the time he was thirty he did no undergraduate teaching.

In his first years in the United States, Haupt retained a position at Göttingen and spent some months of each year in Germany. Unlike Hilprecht, however, Haupt made peace with his adopted land, recognizing that American scholarship might one day overtake that of Germany. He was forcefully present in the United States until his death in 1926. Hilprecht so disdained America that he avoided most of his colleagues and ignored their professional aspirations. In contrast, Haupt was unusually active in the AOS, and each year its journal printed multiple essays from his hand. He urged his students on the society, and the society and its magazine on them.[31]

Finally, Haupt's scholarly writings were of paramount interest to the field. He was best known as the editor of "the polychrome Bible," *The Sacred Books of the Old Testament*, in the 1890s. In this endeavor Haupt assembled scholars from Germany, Britain, and the United States to do critical editions of Old Testament books. The volumes would show, in different colors, the various documents that higher critics had found interwoven in the biblical text. Haupt also published the first complete collection of tablet fragments pertaining to the Akkadian epic of the ancient hero Gilgamesh. This epic tale was pieced together in the 1870s and 1880s. It contained a story of a flood and was the central literary work Assyriologists could point to as evidence of Mesopotamian literary culture. Haupt's work on the Gilgamesh texts and his interest in the higher criticism figured crucially in two areas that defined ancient Near Eastern scholarship at the turn of the century.

Harvard triumphed because of the intellectual capital it had accumulated in the premodern period of American academic life. Johns Hopkins, a new school, triumphed because Gilman had fortuitously selected a major talent in the field. Yale benefited from yet another approach that, surprisingly, had it origins in Manhattan.

William Hayes Ward of New York City had led the exploratory Wolfe Expedition that antedated Penn's campaigns. He collected Babylonian seals, stones inscribed with a design that left an impression on clay and that served as signatures on cuneiform documents. Ward bought seals for many collectors, including Harvard.[32] His biggest customer, however, was the New York financial giant, J. P. Morgan, the premier influence at the Metropolitan.[33] In New York, Ward also purchased tablets through dealers for Columbia University,[34] but Columbia's presidents Seth Low and later, more significantly, Nicholas Murray Butler could not compete with Morgan. Butler and his professor of Semitics, Richard Gottheil, informally assembled groups of Jewish donors to purchase antiquities for the university. But Harvard had snapped up New York's own Jacob Schiff and his Jewish friends,[35] and Morgan's purse was unmatched. Butler attempted to extract money from Morgan himself, but the financier was stingy.[36] He concentrated on expanding his personal collection, which ultimately became the Morgan Library. Ward briskly bought for Morgan and over time became one of a group of scholars and intermediaries who were parasites on Morgan's penchant for the rare antiquity. They provided expertise and did the legwork for the financier. In return, the scholars furthered their own careers and pretended to wealth they did not have.[37] Some of Ward's seals formed the basis of the Morgan Library holdings, to which were added old Mesopotamian objects and cuneiform tablets.[38]

Morgan's own motivations were complex. Old Egypt fascinated him and, as a devout Christian, he knew that scholars of the Old Testament were exploring the ancient East. Like Edward Clark in Philadelphia, Morgan found the Orient alluring, although his attraction to it and to the deciphering of its documents was abstract. He wanted to acquire things and had the resources to persuade others to help him. At the same time, Morgan was patriotically concerned with bringing the accoutrements of elite European culture to the United States. He believed that his collections would aid American scholarship. By obtaining objects, Morgan was, in his own mind, a personal conduit to a morally elevated life in the United States.[39]

Shortly after the turn of the century he paid Albert Clay, whom Penn had hired to assist Hilprecht as he rose in eminence, to come to the city to catalogue and publish Morgan's tablets.[40] Commuting from his assistant professorship in Philadelphia, Clay was favored in New York. Although the extant documents do not speak to this issue, he likely ingratiated himself with Morgan because of a long fight with Hilprecht. In 1909, William Laffan died; he had been the editor of the *New York Sun* and one of the brokers Morgan used to purchase Near Eastern antiquities. Morgan had recently

received an honorary degree from Yale and at the end of the year commem-
orated Laffan; Morgan suddenly offered Yale a thousand shares of U.S. Steel
stock to create the Laffan Professorship of Assyriology and to make Clay the
first incumbent. This benefaction surprised Yale's president, Arthur Twining Hadley; one of Morgan's functionaries had to correct Hadley's note of
thanks by reminding him that the financier's first name was John and not
James.[41]

In New Haven, Clay received Morgan money to buy tablets as part of the
professorship.[42] From 1910 to 1920 Clay indefatigably purchased material
from dealers who, in turn, had gotten tablets from illicit Arab excavations.
He created an Assyriological treasure, the world-famous Yale Babylonian
Collection.

Morgan's commitment to his own library and then his munificence to
Yale had a side effect. Columbia could not reach the top ranks in the field,
although Schiff's loyalty to Harvard probably played a role in this as well.
John Prince, who was on the first Nippur Expedition and who with Gottheil
formed the core of Near Eastern studies at Columbia, lamented the impact
of Morgan in New York. "[T]he Morgan Library tentacles" stretched out to
all the antiquities that got to the city. Columbia scrambled to raise money
for even a portion of them. Once in the Morgan Library, "they are dead to
the Assyriological world until Clay chooses to come down from New
Haven."[43]

In the early 1920s Columbia's situation altered. James Buchanan Nies, a
friend of Clay's and a wealthy collector of antiquities and Orientalist literature, had received a doctorate from Columbia in 1888. He decided to leave
his library and twelve-thousand-piece collection to the institution, along
with a trust fund to publish the material. Four months before he died, however, Nies changed his will, apparently because Columbia refused to hold
the collection separately and call it "The James B. Nies Babylonian Collection." Instead, Clay took custody of the objects. At Nies's death the tablets
and the money to publish them went to Yale as the Nies Collection.[44] It was
strike three for Columbia.

The Yale Babylonian Collection elevated New Haven's status dramatically. Part of the reason for the sudden jump in its reputation was that
scholarship had become enfeebled there after William Rainey Harper left
in 1891 for the presidency of the new University of Chicago. In the late
1890s Yale had appointed Reisner as professor of Assyriolgy to bolster its
fortunes, but he decided instead to excavate in Egypt.[45] Thus, in the twenty
years before Clay arrived, the ancient Near East was a minor aspect of study
in New Haven. At the same time, Harper's position at Chicago guaranteed
that such scholarship at that institution would not languish. Harper turned
at once to making the "scientific" study of the Near Orient preeminent at
Chicago.[46]

He had his troubles almost immediately, for he brought his younger brother there after the BEF's disastrous first campaign. Frank Harper proved a meddlesome protégé.[47] He did, however, through disciplined effort, make a mark over the years by diligently copying texts in the British Museum. His eulogist reported that Frank Harper's "was pre-eminently the mind of a chronicler."[48]

The older brother persuaded a wealthy donor, Caroline Haskell, to contribute one hundred thousand dollars for a museum building that was completed in 1896. Chicago was poised to enter fieldwork. When disputes within the new museum prevented immediate progress, Rainey Harper agreed to chair a consortium of individuals and institutions outside Chicago to sponsor an expedition. Ward and Haupt were members, as was Peters, who had long since returned to New York. The Smithsonian was to get the finds. This consortium confirmed Hilprecht's suspicions about a conspiracy led by Peters to oust Penn from Assyriological primacy, but showed that Johns Hopkins could not count on the Smithsonian either. Moreover, the inter-institutional group demonstrated that the Harpers were having trouble at Chicago itself. The committee chose Ur, corroborating Hilprecht's and Haupt's judgment that it was a desirable site for a dig and would bring prestige to ancient Near Eastern studies in America.

The Ur Committee revealed how much scholars wished for the glory of exploration and how difficult it was for a single school to raise money for a campaign. The wish and the difficulty propelled varied interests to overcome a deep and thinly veiled antagonism and to cooperate.

The Ur Committee appointed Edgar James Banks its field director. Banks had studied with Lyon at Harvard, but after some now long-forgotten quarrel with him took his Ph.D. in Germany. The hostility between Banks and Lyon made the Smithsonian the choice for housing the finds, instead of the Semitic Museum at Harvard.[49] The Committee also left the fund-raising to Banks. He got twelve thousand dollars in pledges, three thousand of that amount from John D. Rockefeller, who had financed the University of Chicago with far greater sums. Then Banks waited for three and a half years in Constantinople, unable to get a firman.

In 1903 Harper's institution got more money from Rockefeller for Near Eastern exploration under the aegis of a new Oriental Exploration Fund at the University of Chicago. Frank Harper, one of its three scientific directors, headed its Babylonian section. He was charged with organizing the first expedition.[50] The Ur Committee was disbanded and its funds dispersed. Rainey Harper himself went to Constantinople to request the firman for the Chicago fund, and the younger Harper made Banks the field director of the new expedition. The Harpers instructed him to take up whatever firman came through first, the original one for Ur, which had been changed to Bismya (a little-known tell), or Chicago's for Sankera (or Larsa).

In September 1903, Banks got the firman for Bismya and excavated in the 1904 season. Bismya was relatively close to Nippur, and although Banks operated on a smaller scale, the same problems afflicted him. He had to bribe crooked Turkish officials; vermin, heat, and sand made life nasty; feuding Arabs all disliked the Americans; and cranky administrators at home demanded more than Banks could deliver. He also showed as little skill at excavation as had Peters and Haynes, but toward the end of his first season, Banks too claimed to have discovered a library of tablets.[51]

At the start of the next season Banks was accused of stealing antiquities, and he resigned. Chicago carried on briefly without him but soon closed down the campaign. Hilprecht was overjoyed.[52] Some material found its way back to Chicago, but the aborted expedition hardly influenced Assyriology, and it increased the difficulty for Westerners in obtaining permits.[53] It was claimed that German diplomatic influence in Turkey made it difficult for any non-Germans to excavate in Mesopotamia, but the Germans themselves had trouble getting firmans.[54] Hilprecht additionally did what he could to protect Penn and himself by dishing all other efforts.

Stolen documents distracted the Americans. Illegally exported antiquities were just the items that would shortly put Yale in the spotlight when it gained from such acquisitions. Receiving stolen property was fine, but the direct and public accusation of robbery was damning. Americans could benefit from Arab thievery but could not engage in it themselves and get caught. Banks went on to make his living as an important dealer to private collectors and smaller institutions all over the East Coast and Midwest. Clay purchased antiquities for Morgan and Yale from Banks. He told Clay that he knew he had "a corner on the market" of some sorts of antiquities, but, Banks said, he was unfairly accused of "holding up the price."[55]

In the first decade of the century, however, things were much tougher for Banks and for Chicago as well. Banks claimed that Frank Harper had ordered him to smuggle antiquities from Babylonia, a charge that has the ring of truth to it if only because the practice was so common. Once Banks was found out, however, Harper—true to type—turned on him and did what he could to ruin Banks's career. Banks was unable to lecture at Chicago, and Harper sabotaged his attempts to get a job at the University of California, still eager to be a player in the ancient Near East. Seeking redress, Banks was then accused of trying to "blackmail" Chicago.[56] He faded from the academic scene.

Banks's story is hard to reconstruct because so much documentation is missing. His correspondence with Rockefeller about the Bismya expedition has been destroyed, and material in the president's files at the University of Chicago was "withdrawn."[57] But neither Frank Harper nor Chicago got off easily. Harper wanted to start up the expedition again as soon as possible, but in addition to whatever Ottoman sensibilities were at issue, Hilprecht opposed Chicago. He had, apparently, had a hand in Banks's humiliation and would not use his good offices to secure an extension of Chicago's firman.[58] After the debacle, Harper constantly tried to get Chicago back into Mesopotamia. In promoting Yale's interests in an expedition in 1909–10, Clay had stayed away from Ur because Harper was still pestering the Turkish government. Rockefeller's son, John D. Rockefeller, Jr., increasingly decided on the family's gifts; at the end of 1910, he pulled the rug out from under Harper when the family decided to abandon Near Eastern exploration. As the Rockefellers' chief advisor put it, "The University['s] . . . agents were dishonorable. . . . The cupidity of our own . . . is certain to get us into hot water. . . . We can retire from the field with a clear conscience."[59]

The Chicago scandal had helped delay the firman for Reisner's expedition to Samaria. Hilprecht reported from Constantinople that the Turks had canceled all firmans and that he was aiding "in framing the new laws of excavations."[60] In 1907 Frank Harper was gleefully told that Harvard had not gotten to Palestine: "[I]n spite of the fact that the president of the United States [Teddy Roosevelt] is a Harvard man, the pull they have has not yet brought them a firman."[61] The Americans, said Reisner himself, would have to give up the "old method" of dealing with the Turks. The United States could no longer sign contracts "with the intention of evading them" and "winning the consent" to evasion through bribery. Indeed, Harvard's Eliot proposed that his university formally state that it would deal honestly with the Ottomans. Harvard would be "a pioneer in making archaeological explorations on this principle."[62]

In Chicago the failure of the Banks Expedition killed Frank Harper's hopes of becoming the Hilprecht of the Haskell Oriental Institute. It also ruined Chicago's credit in the field and set back Oriental studies there for some years. Luckily, Rainey Harper had invested in another young scholar who would resurrect Orientalism at the university: James Henry Breasted.[63]

Breasted had done graduate work at Yale in the early 1890s under Rainey Harper, who had then sent him off to Berlin to receive a doctorate in Egyptology. Harper, whose recognition of Breasted's gifts only made his younger brother's mediocrity more obvious, promised Breasted a position at his new university. He obtained the first teaching appointment in Egyptology in the United States, not counting Hilprecht's brief title in the subject. Breasted and Reisner defined the area, one in epigraphy, the other in fieldwork. But although Breasted's forte was decipherment, he did not work out of a study. He roughed it in Egypt, copying inscriptions. His five-volume *Ancient Records of Egypt* appeared in 1906–7. Although Breasted continued the sort of study in Egypt whose outcome was the *Ancient Records*, he turned to wide-ranging cultural and intellectual history. At first he specialized in Egypt, but in *Ancient Times: A History of the Ancient World* (1916), Breasted wrote a narrative of civilization from the Paleolithic era to the fall of Rome. In addition to being an erudite scholar, he had a gift for intelligent synthesis. The book made him famous: the sense educated Americans had of the pre-classical era came from him.

Chicago's troubles in the wake of the Bismya expedition were partly produced by personal conflicts between Frank Harper and Breasted, who had known one another since Rainey Harper's days at Yale. Breasted directed the Egyptian section of the Oriental Expedition Fund. Although Frank Harper got the bulk of the first Rockefeller money, he developed an almost pathologically hostile relationship with Breasted. On the other side, Breasted was uniquely absorbed in whatever was at the center of his career at any given time, and he was difficult to work with.

Initially Frank Harper's family connection protected him, as it always had, even after Rainey Harper died in 1905.[64] Despite Breasted's unblemished record in his Egyptian work in the first decade of the century, Frank Harper starved Breasted of Rockefeller money. The younger brother wanted it to finance the now tainted Mesopotamian endeavor. Harper's hatred of Breasted and then the Rockefellers' distaste for the consequences of the Bismya Expedition led the family to refuse to finance scholarship not just in Mesoptamia but also in Egypt.[65]

Breasted held on, and Frank Harper died in 1914. Soon thereafter, Breasted published *Ancient Times*, which Mrs. John D. Rockefeller, Jr., read to her children. Breasted used her note of appreciation to reopen his slight acquaintance with her husband. They came to have, if not an intimate friendship, at least a courtly relationship that gave Breasted advantages and that displayed his popularizing articulateness. When World War I ended and the Near East was again thrown open to scholarship, Breasted presented his maturing ideas about ancient Near Eastern studies to the financier.[66]

In 1919 Rockefeller responded by granting Breasted one hundred thousand dollars over a ten-year period to bring to birth an Oriental Institute at Chicago, "a laboratory for the study of the rise and development of civilization."[67] Even in 1919 this amount of money was not a stupendously large gift. But over the years, with Rockefeller's blessing, Breasted received more money from Rockefeller, from the Rockefeller Foundation, and from other individuals. Breasted died in 1935 in the midst of the Great Depression, and his institute limped along with diminished funding. But by that time the enterprise, originally housed in the old Haskell Museum, had relocated to a handsome new building and put together an operation that set the standard in the field.[68]

In spite of his commitment to Egypt, Breasted made the institute a premier place to study Mesopotamia. He accommodated field archaeology in Assyria and Babylonia. He also contrived an Akkadian dictionary project that Semiticists had contemplated for years. In the late 1880s and early 1890s Paul Haupt had assembled a small group in Baltimore to study the language by examining all the extant texts, using what I have called the contextual method of linguistics. Although the Johns Hopkins team devoted at least four years to their goal, a lack of funding undermined it.[69] With his administrative skills and a larger staff, Breasted applied the method "scientifically." A company of experts collated all the appearances of every word in Akkadian cuneiform. From its inception in 1921, the dictionary gave Chicago a staff and a reputation in Assyriology as well as in Egyptology.

California's entrance into the field had been aborted. But Chicago's rise to preeminence in the ancient Near East meant that the East Coast schools no longer held a monopoly. And just as Breasted shifted the locus of United States scholarship from the East Coast toward the Midwest, so he shifted the locus of the American ancient Near East. Because of its connection to nineteenth-century Old Testament studies, Palestine—as was the case with Harvard's work in Samaria—played an important role in the American conception of the Near Orient. But Palestine was too closely attached to sectarian religion, and Mesopotamia—the focus of Assyriology—emerged as the centerpiece of American concerns. Assyria was crucial to scholarly understanding of the Old Testament, and in the nineteenth century it had pushed aside ancient India as the focus of scholarship in the AOS. Indeed, India came to occupy its own geographical and scholarly region that was not even construed as a part of the American ancient Near East. Unlike Palestine, Assyria was not so close to the Judeo-Christian world as to be tainted by accusations that its study was subservient to spiritual preconceptions. Then Breasted came along. He did not move the center to Egypt. But with the aid of California and then Harvard, he shifted the focus from the Semitic lands to the Semitic lands and Egypt. By 1920 "the ancient Near East" meant—most of all—Egypt, Palestine, and Mesopotamia.

In addition to his fund-raising skills and generous breadth of interests, Breasted early on had a brilliant vision of how scholars should study the ancient Near East. The priority, he said, was not language so much as culture, not teaching languages but recovering lost civilizations.[70] The institute should be "an equipped research laboratory" dedicated to this idea.[71] Breasted drew on the philosophical thought of John Dewey, who had taught at Chicago until the turn of the century and who had left his imprint in many ways. Breasted had also collaborated with the European historian James Harvey Robinson, who believed that modern history should be written in such a way as to serve the present and future. Dewey conceived of the human sciences, history included, as similar in experimental ideal to the natural sciences. The human sciences should use relevant data from the past to resolve the problems of the present by means of careful theorizing and empirical testing. This was, Dewey said, "the method of intelligence" that enabled scholars to construct a good and just society.

Breasted had the same sort of model in mind for his institute. Controlled and organized effort would recover the ancient past. This past was a critical transitional step to the progressive present, but also had to be understood on its own terms as clearly and realistically as possible. What Breasted called "the Origins of Civilization" was its own science. It fit in between paleontology and anthropology (the study of the evolution of animals, physical humans, and the primitive races) on the one hand and history and sociology (the study of later civilized societies) on the other. Places such as the Oriental Institute would specially house this unique discipline.[72]

To this end, the Oriental Institute would gather professionals, many already teachers on the university staff. Some, like Breasted himself, would have minimal teaching duties. Other scholars would simply have contracts with the institute. The job was research and, through an apprenticeship system, the training of graduate students, the researchers' successors. Breasted would fund archaeological excavation in the Near East, as well as epigraphical work, and would coordinate and plan academic strategy. The institute would have public exhibits, but the objects were not primarily for display. They were rather assembled in "a kind of historical laboratory" that secured *"all the available evidence of every kind and character."*[73]

Breasted had come from reduced circumstances. With the help of a relative he had entered the scholarly world only after he had given up careers as a prescription druggist and as a minister. In his early years at Chicago he had sweated for an income that would give him a respectable social status. *Ancient Times* was designed to earn money. But his scholarship also drove Breasted. The institute typified a new way of life available to able academics. Breasted received substantial remuneration for his efforts but was almost never bothered by the requirements of undergraduate teaching. In 1925 the university relieved him of teaching duties altogether. Instead, he spent his time in Egypt on his epigraphy. When he was in the United States, the institute claimed his attention. Even so, he had a hard time recognizing that his self-promotion and lack of presence at the university could in any way contribute to a trace of feeling against him at Chicago.[74] In addition to his other accomplishments, Breasted became a genial academic statesman, preaching the benefits of scholarly humanism for the modern world. For him the pursuit of high ideals joined the claims of self-interest.

When Pepper established ancient Near Eastern studies at Pennsylvania, he thought a museum essential, and museums were essential to the actual organization of Near Eastern studies from Pepper's era to Breasted's era. Their place, however, altered over time and was tied to complex issues of scholarly organization.

At the turn of the century, the standard departmental structure of learning aggregated small numbers of professors. Even well-defined fields to which large numbers of students gravitated rarely had more than half a dozen staff members. A university would expend funds for comparatively inexpensive academics in an area such as American history, but this was not true for ancient Near East studies. Orientalism was in some respects a hobby of the leisured and scholarly classes. A research agenda dominated its study, teaching was minimal, and students were few.[75] Universities paid scholars not to instruct but to work in the field or in libraries. The upkeep of Near Eastern studies was costly, and trustees had to be convinced of the significance of the subject.

Creating individual chairs for outstanding professors in recherché domains was cheapest. The agglutination of such professors into administrative units remained problematic. Typically, wide-ranging programs of research and (marginally) of instruction, less fixed and secure than departments, were the norm, although such programs varied widely. Oriental studies might bring together scholars of China and Japan as well as those who specialized in the Near East. Semitic studies might narrow the focus in space but extend it in time. A student of cuneiform might sit (later) beside one of Arab nationalism.

Museums were in some ways a natural choice as the intellectual and bureaucratic home for those who had a regular connection with them. Both fledging anthropologists and archaeologists at Penn were linked to the museum there. But as anthropologists located themselves in departments, these scholars more easily dismissed museums as adjuncts to anthropology than did archaeologists. Archaeologists never mustered the administrative clout to form departments. Perhaps they spent too much time in the field, or perhaps they never mastered the requisite bureaucratic and social skills. Peters, who had left the university system, and Haynes, a dullard who never held a professorship, exemplified the leadership "dirt archaeologists" had at the turn of the century. Edgar Banks was never academically employed after the Bismya affair. George Reisner, a towering figure, was uninvolved with the Harvard administration and rarely in Cambridge.

Archaeologists did need the large sums of money that wealthy donors could contribute and a spot to hold the treasures that were excavated. Field workers consequently looked to museums for survival, and the institutions did provide minimal sustenance. The wealthy had to have archaeologists to bring cultural aspirations to fruition, and both groups had a certain disdain for the scholarly study associated with professors in departments.

Indeed, although they are not central to the story, a number of museums unattached to academic institutions entered the picture at the end of the nineteenth century. These museums supported expeditions, scholarly endeavors, and explorers and (later) archaeologists. The Brooklyn Museum received the bequest of Charles Wilbour, an amateur traveler, collector, and aficionado of Egyptological material who had died in 1896. In the first decade of the century the wealthy Theodore M. Davis funded Howard Carter's early explorations in Egypt's Valley of the Kings. Principally a patron, Davis had participated in Carter's digging as a sort of sport. Partly to advertise their successes, he donated many of the finds to the Museum of Fine Arts in Boston and the Metropolitan Museum in New York, giving them an investment in Egyptology.[76] Boston's arrangement with Harvard and Reisner underscored this investment. The Metropolitan was additionally acquiring Babylonian material through the activity of J. P. Morgan, although he later shifted his attention to his own museum, the Morgan Library.

The Boston and New York museums stepped up their dedication to Egypt (and the fighting between themselves) not only because of this investment but also because it had become impossible to dig in Mesopotamia. The most notable work exclusively organized by a museum was carried out by Herbert Winlock (and indirectly financed by Morgan). A Harvard product who dug for the Metropolitan in Egypt beginning in 1906, Winlock was another talented excavator. But he was ill positioned to negotiate the departmental politics of the American university in favor of archaeology.

The wealthy liked their connection to museums, and so did explorers whose links to universities were tenuous. But museums without a university bond never took a primary role in the field of ancient Near Eastern studies. The centrality of the American university to intellectual life meant that unaffiliated museums were ancillary to the universities in the production of knowledge. They became more tied to the aesthetic and popular demands made by the museumgoing public.[77] These museums carried on the long tradition of interest in ancient Egypt that had started with mummies and later culminated with the tombs of kings. In the nineteenth century, well-to-do amateurs outside the collegiate system unsuccessfully tried to turn American curiosity about Egypt in a more learned direction. Unmoved by the Bible, this idiosyncratic collection of individuals reflected the lure that a grand old empire had for a more secular audience. Egypt had for a long time been prominent in literary circles somewhat distant from the clerical order of the traditonal American colleges. The ancient Near East into which Reisner and Breasted had recently integrated Egypt was of academic manufacture.

The museum culture of places like the Metropolitan and the Boston Museum of fine arts thus contributed to an old disjunction. A more popular (and less religous) emphasis on Egypt contrasted with a more studious (and Judeo-Christian) concentration on Mesopotamia. Here was an added reason for the academic-intellectual ascendancy of Assyriology over Egyptology. Egyptological finds were associated early on with the Brooklyn, Boston, and Metropolitan museums, and not with a university or a museum connected to a university. Morgan promoted Assyriology when he decided to establish his Babylonian Collection at Yale and not at the Morgan Library. But this same propensity for Egyptological interests to drift to museums that were driven by their need to secure a following outside the academy had other consequences. Egypt was far more an item of upper-middle-class taste than was Assyria. The esteem in the university for Mesopotamia over Egypt was counterbalanced outside the university by the preference among cultivated people for Egypt.

Crucial as it was, the marriage of museums to universities was not easy. Penn's case was perhaps extreme: the university had to break the museum, which nonetheless remained unruly. But the pattern was similar everywhere.

Sometimes universities gave formal museum affiliations to other academics as well as to archaeologists. When the museums did function as a locus of activity, the results were ambiguous. In a museum administrators might identically categorize a field-worker, an epigrapher, and a scholar of contemporary Latin American peoples with no written language at all. In other cases, bureaucrats housed archaeologists wherever it was convenient—for example, in departments of classics or programs of religious studies. When archaeologists were put into anthropology departments, anthropologists persistently attempted to reduce archaeology to their own discipline.

At Penn, by 1910, the museum had come under the headship of an anthropologist, George Gordon, who was not friendly to Near Eastern archaeology. But Gordon was old-fashioned in believing that anthropologists should have a connection to museums: displaying "contemporary primitives" was for him still an important anthropological function. While anthropologists at Penn were trying to sever their museum connections, Gordon's power kept them uneasily under the sway of the museum. Archaeologists stayed because they had no other place to go.

Harvard's Semitic Museum was a much smaller and more particularistic affair than was the University Museum. Nonetheless, it had the same sort of troubled liaison with its guardian, Harvard University, as did the museum at Penn. Moreover, Near Eastern archaeologists at Harvard were, like those at Penn, stranded at the Semitic Museum while epigraphers in Cambridge moved to departments of languages. Archaeologists often remained stepchildren, with the Semitic Museum their only haven.

In Baltimore, the failure of the collaboration between Johns Hopkins and the Smithsonian meant that Johns Hopkins had no program in archaeology through the 1920s. Throughout this period Haupt pressed for exploration; without it his ancient Near Eastern studies program had a limited focus on literary issues that even his renown could not hide. When Baltimore did develop a distinguished record of digging in the Near East, Johns Hopkins carried on its own tradition of using other institutions. Funded by many schools, ASOR in Jerusalem by that time had many of the characteristics of Chicago's Oriental Institute; ASOR became the vehicle for Johns Hopkins's aspirations.

Of the five institutions of the first rank, only Yale had no museum link. Consequently, however, Albert Clay was nervous about the institution's status. He hungered for excavation and an archaeological dimension to ancient Near Eastern studies in New Haven. Even before he left Penn, Clay was trying to orchestrate an expedition that he would lead and that would free him from Hilprecht. But in the first years of the century, as I have suggested, German influence in Constantinople increased. The Turks looked to the Reich to protect them from English and Russian plans to dismantle the Ottoman Empire. German power in the Near Orient grew until the outbreak of World War I in 1914, when the Turks allied with the central powers, Germany and Austria-Hungary. In this political climate only the Germans, and they with difficulty, dug in Mesopotamia, although Hilprecht still spoke with authority for American interests, or at least those of Pennsylvania. At the time Clay went to Yale, he hoped that Morgan would pay for an expedition and that his overriding international financial power would obtain a firman over German objections.

Both Clay and Morgan's intermediaries recognized that Hilprecht could thwart their efforts. "If Hilprecht maintains his attitude," a Morgan associate wrote to Clay, "it will be necessary to retaliate. Please put the necessary material in my reach."[78] Clay's appointment at Yale may have been consolation for the inability of the Morgan people to get this expedition off the ground. But no evidence suggests that measures were taken against Hilprecht, and Clay in New Haven continued to press for an expedition.

Nothing worked, and World War I interrupted all archaeology. After the war Clay tried again, this time hoping that Clarence Fisher, Hilprecht's onetime assistant in Nippur and now the one experienced archaeologist eager to work in Bible lands, would dig for New Haven. Clay was so anxious that he even went to John D. Rockefeller, Jr., for funds, just as Rockefeller was deserting Chicago.[79] Nothing came of these attempts, just as Yale also languished in the related area of Egyptology into the 1920s, after Clay's death.

Yale perceived its situation as desperate. The victory of the Allies in the war meant that it would now be easier to dig in the Near East. The sale of tablets, however, was more strictly regulated, and the prices were higher. If New Haven were to maintain its position, its experts reasoned, Yale had to excavate rather than purchase.[80] Matters were complicated by competition with classicists. The students of the Greece and Rome of late antiquity encouraged Yale's archaeological efforts elswhere. Not until 1957–58 did New

Haven explorers dig in Babylonia, and their share of the tablets amounted to only about three hundred pieces.[81] Yale suffered in Near Eastern archaeology, but the Babylonian Collection assured New Haven a position in the ancient Near East. Although Yale had a more specialized, epigraphically oriented program, it succeeded without exploration and without a museum.

When Breasted founded his institute thirty years after Pepper's University Museum, the conception of a museum had changed but was still ambiguous. Both Pepper and Breasted believed in a humane American social science in which the study of the ancient Near East played a role. Such a science would discover the best that was thought and said; it would show how the best had been created and transmitted through the ages, and how it could be preserved and enlarged. A building housing the remains of past cultures was critical to this conception, but for Pepper a museum was a more public institution. It would exhibit the semisacred history of cultural progress to an educated group beyond the academy. Despite popularizing the civilizations of the past, Breasted separated the popular and the academic in a way Pepper did not. Like the anthropologists, Breasted disdained the exemplification of culture. Instead, the museum was primarily the repository for the material on which scholars worked, and so was renamed an institute.[82]

As an entity for housing scholars, the Oriental Institute was not clearly better than a museum. The institution attracted students in all the Oriental languages from the university itself, as well as research fellows who had no other academic connection. Nonteaching researchers who did not study languages at all might also be on the staff. Many of the people who did fieldwork under Chicago's auspices had never taught at the school, and indeed may never have been in Chicago prior to their appointment to excavate abroad. They brought prestige to the university and required some sort of position, which the institute gave.

Though they were secondary, like the non-university museums, divinity schools played a role in the story. Penn and Johns Hopkins each lacked a seminary; nevertheless, their triumphs in the field, while not extraordinary, were distinctive, at least in contrast with the efforts of Yale, Harvard, and Chicago. The connection of the ancient Near East to Bible studies meant that Protestant schools of theology initially competed with universities in promoting what became the ancient Near East. In the 1880s Francis Brown of Union Theological Seminary in New York City was an early force in Assyriology and had declined to go to Johns Hopkins before Haupt was appointed there. Hilprecht had, with misgivings, decided not to go to the Hartford Theological Seminary. As independent divinity schools (such as Andover) decayed, they became less important in the field of ancient Near

Eastern studies. The intellectual space they occupied in the academy shrank. Nonetheless, a university-based school of theology remained a useful adjunct for the field, at least in the start-up phase. Yale's first rank in Orientalism in the nineteenth century was assisted by the repute of its divinity school. As ancient Near Eastern studies developed, Harvard benefited when more-conservative seminaries collapsed and its own liberal divinity school survived, as I have indicated. Rainey Harper's plans for Chicago linked the fate of Near Eastern studies there with the divinity school, which would also be integral to the university. Without the aid of theology, Johns Hopkins and Penn (and to a lesser extent Columbia) relied on Jews and Germans to forward their claims effectively. More cosmopolitan than Harvard and Yale, these schools, ironically, were led to the quasi-religious scholarly pursuits of the ancient Near East by non-Protestants and foreigners.

Money, in addition to what a university would normally put up for scholarship, was imperative for Near Eastern studies. University administrators and individual professorial entrepreneurs who staked claims in the ancient world stretched out hands to wealthy donors: Peters to Clark; Pepper to Hearst; Harvard to Jacob Schiff and Gardiner Lane; Breasted to Rockefeller. Morgan blessed Clay and Yale, and his indifference hurt Columbia. Phoebe Hearst's withdrawal of money nipped in the bud California's entrance into the field. The generosity of wealthy amateur Egyptologists would have had a different effect had they targeted universities and not museums. Even the exception, Johns Hopkins, hoped to get the support of the federal government through the Smithsonian. Fieldwork halfway across the world was expensive, whether to obtain art or inscriptions or material evidence. Large sums of private money had been necessary to the growth of the American university and museums in the last quarter of the nineteenth century. The study of the ancient Near East called for even more funds. The quest for knowledge flourished as a pet project of post–Civil War industrialists, eager to identify themselves with cultural endeavors.[83]

As important as money and administrative structures was a divide that had a bureaucratic dimension but was fundamentally a difference of ideas. The burgeoning of the study of the ancient world complicates generalizations about the decline of religion in the twentieth-century American academy. A substantial number of influential scholars in the field were incompletely secularized Jews or committed Christians with ministerial leanings.

In making the scholarly understanding of the Old Testament more sophisticated, archaeology was for a time a friend of those who disputed the higher criticism. The Bible could not be dismissed on the basis of internal literary inconsistencies. Rather, scholars analyzed it in conjunction with external material evidence. This evidence compelled a complex interpretation of ancient civilizations in which the Bible stories gained credit. Old records went from having the status of absolute truth to being mere fables, and then to being regarded as more or less accurate accounts of some events, the old-time equivalent of history.[84] As one authority has noted, for many scholars archaeology brought to an end the destructive period of higher criticism and ushered in a period of reconstruction.[85]

Had these scholars been organized into departments, it is a nice question whether they could have escaped the annoyed scrutiny of their peers. Academics were not so much forsaking religious commitment as devaluing its worth in the university. Heterogeneously grouped on different campuses, small in number in any event, and without the administrative prominence and strength that went with departmental status, the religiously inclined among the Orientalists were left alone.

In extreme cases they did gather in a field that came to be called biblical archaeology. Those academics inclined to biblical archaeology were in the tradition of those who had first conjectured about the Orient in the middle of the nineteenth century.[86] John Henry Haynes wrote from Nippur that "the Christian faith suffers no violence, but is rather strengthened by the . . . fragments of early history." [87] The point of all nonbiblical evidence was to confirm the Bible. As one of this group of learned men at Pennsylvania lamented, one of the university's problems was that it did not have "the corollary" of oriental studies, a divinity school.[88] For these people Scripture was given preference as evidence. On some questions biblical authority had to be acceded to. The reason for this was plain: as committed believers, the biblical archaeologists made their faith contingent on certain historical truths expressed in the Bible. Scholarship served these truths.[89] The biblical archaeologist was thus awkwardly positioned in respect to the historical reasoning that the higher criticism had brought into being. Many of the faithful ignored the issues. Other believers developed various strategies to ease the tension between faith and their scholarly consciences.

For some the role of archaeology was not to corroborate the historical story of the Bible. Nor did they think that the supernatural purport of the narrative was at issue. Rather, as the multiauthored *Authority and Archaeology* put it in 1899, Bible and archaeology—literary evidence and material evidence—together told what had happened during the Bible era. It was assumed that this history would not undermine religious truths, but scholarship was not judged against these truths.[90] Some faithful academics even accepted that the higher criticism ruled out supernatural explanations in the history the erudite wrote. But such a viewpoint did not rule out faith. It only meant that "empirical history" did not encompass the Christian life.[91]

Study of the ancient Near East did not coincide with biblical archaeology, nor were all students of the ancient Near East religious. For purposes of analysis, the field of comparative religion represented the antithetic area of inquiry within Orientalism. In contrast to biblical archaeology, comparative religion shared the growing secularism of twentieth-century intellectuals.

Comparative religion was a stopping place favored by liberal Protestants and Jews or by scholars with interests further from Palestine—at first Indologists, later Egyptologists. The field was the "scientific"—meaning somewhat detached, impartial, yet sympathetic—study of something innate in the individual or group psyche of human beings. Worshippers in various cultures all tried, and all in finite or incomplete ways, to comprehend some fundamental reality. The comparative religionist neutrally outlined these attempts.[92]

Such an ideological stance allowed its protagonists to remove themselves from the Bible and from sectarian battles. The higher criticism could be accepted without pain. Yet scholars of comparative religion maintained spiritual beliefs. Some believed that religious theorizing slowly progressed, so that, for example, monotheism was better, more true, than polytheism. Jews liked comparative religion because, in a Christian culture, it elevated Judaism to equal rank with Christianity. Comparative religion also spoke to the ecumenical longings of men like John Peters. One reason for the antagonism of Haupt and Hilprecht was this silent clash. Hilprecht remained an ardent and believing Lutheran; Haupt was an ecumenical Christian. Hilprecht could find an enemy to evangelical Protestantism in Haupt. Haupt could see sectarian battles as an enemy of scholarship.[93]

Although comparative religionists may have implicitly liked the Judeo-Christian heritage or sensibility, they often studied comparative civilization. Their religious proclivities withered further—or rather, faith was transferred from a faraway supernatural to a nearer but spiritualized hierarchy of human civilizations. Of ultimate concern to men like the Egyptologist Breasted was humankind's evolving upward journey. Breasted was in one sense a nonbeliever. Somewhat exotic in Oriental studies, he accepted the pragmatic worldliness of the wider American academy. The higher criticism entailed for him that religion was no longer credible. But it would be fairer to say that his "humanism" had slowly replaced a theological affirmation.

Scholars were not so much confused on this issue as they were in agreement that some problems should not be thought about. Secular academics never really tested their own nonreligious ideas. The biblical archaeologists, too, turned their eyes away from the conflict between the historian and the believer that the higher criticism had made prominent.[94] A gentlemen's consensus dictated that in their work professionals, believers and nonbelievers alike, would ignore deep questions of religion.[95]

6

THE PETERS-HILPRECHT CONTROVERSY,

1903–1910

HILPRECHT'S first wife died at their home in Germany in 1902, but a year later Hilprecht advantageously married the heiress Sallie Crozer Robinson. The second Mrs. Hilprecht was the daughter of Samuel Crozer, who had made a fortune in iron and steel, coal, railroads, and textiles. A philanthropist, Crozer had endowed the Crozer Theological Seminary as testimony to his interest in the doctrines of American Baptists. His wife had translated books by German authors into English, and their daughter was an accomplished linguist with an international perspective and a love of Germany. In her mid-forties, Sallie Crozer Robinson was a widow who was prominent in cultural circles. She gave her new, younger husband an impregnable social base and entrée into cosmopolitan society.[1]

Hilprecht was flushed with his marital conquest. On a European tour on the eve of his wedding he reported to the BEF that he had had twenty requests to speak in Germany. They included a Berlin performance attended by "princes and ministers, officers of the army and navy . . . and the high dignitaries of the church." He quoted newspaper reports on the "thundering applause" for the "brilliant" lectures by the "celebrated explorer." The Germans, he wrote, had begged him to take a university position "in the land of my birth."[2]

The growth of Hilprecht's eminence was the worst enemy for this "Columbus of archaeology," as one newspaper called him. On several occasions he bragged about plans for a fifth expedition in which he would lead "six or eight white men" on the grand excavation he had argued for at the turn of the century.[3]

Would he return to Nippur? At the end of 1902 he boasted that he was ready to set out.[4] The press quoted Hilprecht as saying that the bride and groom would spend the summer of 1903 in Europe. Then he would make his way without Mrs. Hilprecht to Nippur. "I do not think it proper to subject her to the discomfort and danger."[5] Hilprecht proposed that his newly appointed assistant professor, the Reverend Albert Clay, would go also. After Hilprecht had "initiate[d]" Clay, the master would leave, spending most of his time at Jena working on the documents. Lesser helpers would do the teaching at home.[6]

In addition to ensuring public recognition for Penn and its museum, Hilprecht had given the university real scholarly benefits. Despite the fracas over publishing, he set a high standard for printing cuneiform texts. An acute reader of the tablets, he introduced a careful and beautiful cuneiform script in his publications. He imparted his skills to students who, in increasing numbers, enrolled in the graduate program.[7]

Nonetheless, Hilprecht's inability to get along with his students and his peers made another expedition and much else impossible. First, the conflict over publishing the tablets intensified. Hilprecht oversaw access to the tablets and decided how they would be presented to a wider audience.[8] His greed for preferment, however, was impossible to satiate, and no one could curb his heavy-handed dealings with underlings. He wrote about Clay's book, *Business Documents of . . . Nippur* (1898), that he had spent "3 months [,] 10–12 hours per day . . . correcting and strengthening it, as if it was my own." Clay did not appreciate the ministrations: Hilprecht wanted "to absorb and make my work look like another of his." From his semi-protected position as assistant professor, Clay fought bitterly for a modicum of independence. But Hilprecht "had taken the heart out of Clay, who is greatly depressed."[9] In any event, Hilprecht had motivated Clay to go to New York and eventually to New Haven.

Clay was not alone. Herman Ranke, who took over menial curatorial duties, had similar problems with his publication of *Early Babylonian Personal Names . . .* (1905). So too did a visiting foreign scholar, David Myhrman, who eventually published *Hymns and Prayers to Babylonian Gods . . .* (1911).[10] Clarence Fisher, one of the two architects of the fourth expedition and a careful and intelligent archaeologist of increasing ability, was not permitted to use the Nippur records because the professor needed "all the notes for his own work for some time to come." Fisher finally made other arrangements for the publication of his book on the buildings of Nippur after Hilprecht asserted that no funds were available and that he would have to give the subject "personal study" for "several years" before publishing.[11] Fisher's book, in particular, represented a departure in the analysis of Nippur. The German had a personal antipathy to Fisher. It is difficult not to conclude that Hilprecht stood in the younger man's way because he feared that the book would give Fisher an independent reputation.

In each case the pattern with Hilprecht's students was the same. Young men worked with him and served him loyally as he unlocked for them the secrets of the ancient Near East. But all came to grief because they were unwilling, each in his own way, to make the sacrifices needed to win Hilprecht's full favor. All were then subjected to Hilprecht's academic wrath as he did what he could to destroy them. Myhrman, who went through a particularly ghastly episode with the professor, put it best. Hilprecht had great prestige. "When he says . . . bad things . . . , people . . . sit up and take notice." It was hard for outsiders to grasp "what a *queer* person" Hilprecht was.[12]

Hilprecht did little better with his colleagues. Morris Jastrow, Jr., a professor of Semitic languages, had little connection to the museum and no experience as a field archaeologist, nor did he work on the actual cuneiform tablets. Nonetheless, Jastrow was an intelligent and assiduous Assyriologist, and he applied his skills in Semitic languages to all the published texts. He was a well-known scholar both of the Old Testament and of Assyrian literature.

Animosity between Jastrow and Hilprecht went back to the 1880s, when Hilprecht had received the job as professor of Assyriology that Jastrow thought was his. Although Jastrow was soon named professor of Semitics, their rivalry was intense through the 1890s. Under a controlled exterior, Jastrow had a self-righteous academic intelligence that would have been insulted by Hilprecht's contempt for anyone who had never entered the tablet room. Hilprecht knew that Jastrow was a Jew uncommitted to the ancient Near East's role as a servant of Bible studies.[13]

The son of an influential rabbi, Jastrow had repudiated his father's Judaism by choosing an academic career over the rabbinate. Jastrow did want a connection with his community, but he was also stepping outside it to the secular Christian world. He distanced himself from the religious affiliations that often touched Assyriology.[14] A student of comparative religion, Jastrow wrote from a perspective in which the various religions of the ancient Near East all mirrored imperfect human attempts to grasp the theological truths of existence.[15] He may have privileged the monotheism that Judaism expounded, yet his ideas had something in common with John Peters's belief that the Bible, while expressing moral truths, perhaps did not uniquely reveal the supernatural. Jastrow also sympathized with Sara Stevenson's reverence for ancient Egyptian religious practices, which implied Stevenson's tolerant sympathies.[16] Jastrow, however, found an even closer intellectual kinsman in Professor Friedrich Delitzsch of Berlin, formerly of Leipzig.

Delitzsch was the world's most influential Assyriologist. In the late 1870s and the 1880s his seminar at Leipzig had awarded doctorates to almost every Assyriologist in America—including Banks, Frank Harper, Haupt, Hilprecht, Jastrow, and Lyon. Peters had also studied with Delitzsch. Delitzsch's students trained the Americans he had not.

Delitzsch fired a major controversy in his published 1902 lecture, *Babel und Bibel*.[17] He began by eloquently setting out *the* intellectual issue animating students of Assyria and Babylonia:

> What is the object of these labors in distant, inhospitable, and dangerous lands? To what end this costly work of rummaging in mounds many thousands

of years old, of digging deep into the earth in places where no gold or silver is to be found? Why this rivalry among nations for . . . securing . . . these desolate hills . . . ? . . . there is one answer . . . *the Bible*.[18]

Delitzsch made several points about the study of Old Testament lands and Judeo-Christian religions. The Bible version of the world, he wrote, was not compatible with the world of natural science. That meant, however, only that science and religion occupied two separate realms. At bottom the peculiar revelatory feeling carried in every breast defined religion. All people grasped this emotion, but they did so imperfectly and symbolized it in their own history and legends. Religious ideas furnished the human mind. The Judeo-Christian ideal codified in the Bible had earlier analogues in Babylonia. The literatures of ancient people all fallibly mirrored the same sorts of truths. If there was an evolutionary component to religion, Jewish monotheism might be ethically higher than Babylonian polytheism. In any case Delitzsch argued that Babylonia was the progenitor of Christianity. This "pan-Babylonian" thesis, embraced by many scholars, found the sources for Western civilization in Mesopotamia and elevated the intellectual importance of Assyriology. But Delitzsch hinted further that in some respects ancient Near Eastern religion was morally superior. Not only was everything Babylonian, but Babylonian was better. The genesis of civilization in the ancient East and its migration from there might not entail religious progress.

The ideas Delitzsch expounded in 1902 led to a celebrated international discussion. At the end of that year Jastrow captained the effort to bring him to the United States.[19] After Jastrow had almost completed the arrangements, Hilprecht, who had originally gotten to the United States on a recommendation from Delitzsch,[20] forbade the invitation. In 1903, on his grand speaking tour in Germany, Hilprecht urged that Christian truths were only revealed in the Bible and that Assyriology provided historical evidence for the Bible. The "greatest men of science," he wrote home, "all now cling to me as the representative of the other view." After Jastrow had moved heaven and earth to get Delitzsch, Hilprecht told Harrison: "The University of Pa. may praise itself happy that I had the courage to veto Delitzsch. . . . He would have ruined our reputation forever." "I do not go to America," said Delitzsch, "because of Hilprecht."[21]

This academic spat showed a growing disparity between scholars oriented to the Bible and those with less sectarian visions, a disparity fraught with emotion. Religious disagreement was not the only issue. Hilprecht's assistant, Clay, for example, was a Lutheran minister who imbibed his mentor's biblical commitments, although, like other religious types, he eventually fought Hilprecht. Yet as one of Jastrow's friends put it, the "pietistic," certainly overseas, inclined toward Hilprecht,[22] and his enemies included all the religious liberals and the secularists.

The disagreement with Jastrow exemplified Hilprecht's troubles in getting on not merely with his peers at Penn but with those outside the university. This problem was confirmed when *Explorations in Bible Lands*, a volume edited by Hilprecht, appeared in 1903. This book attempted a more popular history of Near Eastern archaeology. Hilprecht narrated the story of nineteenth-century exploration in Mesopotamia in an outstanding and detailed treatise. But, according to many, *Explorations in Bible Lands* lacked proportion. A half-dozen other experts surveyed scholarly advances as they pertained to ancient times. Essays covered Palestine, Egypt, Arabia, and Anatolia (the land of the Hittites). Hilprecht's own article on Mesopotamia, however, took up three-quarters of the text. Of these nearly six hundred pages on the decipherment of cuneiform and the excavations culminating with Layard and the later English, French, and German exploration, half were devoted to Nippur. Layard's spectacular work got forty pages, Penn's seven times as much. But the contributions of Harper, Meyer, Fisher, and other lesser figures almost vanished. Peters and Haynes were contemptuously deprecated. In his version Hilprecht became the guiding star of Near Eastern exploration.

Within a brief time the irritation that many had long felt for Hilprecht erupted into a scandal that energized Orientalists for almost ten years. Although they debated Hilprecht's scholarship and methods, the heart of the conflict was his personality, his lust for fame, and his pandering to what he thought people in power wanted. Americans were angered that someone whose loyalties were German should garner all the glory from the single expedition that the United States had sent to Mesopotamia. Moreover, Hilprecht put this glory to work for narrow religious beliefs. Frank Harper at Chicago stated it well: Hilprecht took credit for all that was good and blamed his colleagues for all the mistakes.[23] Harvard's George Foote Moore wrote that it was a book "no American can read without being ashamed."[24] Of course Hilprecht's colleagues unanimously proclaimed that "personal feeling" had nothing to do with the confrontation; its essence was "the reputation of American scholarship" and "a proper scientific method."[25]

As the Americans dropped the reticence conventional in their private communications, Hilprecht's faults became clear. He was "a bag of wind," a "humbug," a man of "exaggerated conceit" and "vanity"; his "egotism" and "desire for cheap notoriety" were "well-nigh miraculous."[26]

Explorations in Bible Lands and other overlapping publications contended that Hilprecht had discovered a great temple library at Nippur comparable to what Layard had dug up at Nineveh. But many people knew that Haynes had uncovered the tablets at the end of the fourth dig. Hilprecht had arrived only after Haynes had excavated the documents. Moreover, scholars who had used the material reported that crates of tablets still lay packed in the basement of the museum after their long trip to Philadelphia via Constantinople and Nippur. Haynes, who could not read cuneiform, had proclaimed the library in 1900, and Hilprecht had echoed this finding. But how could he make such an assertion in print if no one had examined the documents? One of the complaints of Hilprecht's juniors was that he insisted on the phrase "Temple Library" in their publications when they preferred less contentious titles.[27]

Explorations in Bible Lands had photographs of some of the "books" in the library and various other important finds. Yet, as it turned out, several of the illustrative tablets had been unearthed in prior explorations, or purchased in Baghdad in 1888 when the Americans did not know what they would dig up. Finally, when Hilprecht's enemies investigated, they learned that some of the artifacts were not in the museum, but were rather the private property of the professor. Some material was at his home in Jena. How had this appropriation taken place?

Gossip spread through the small academic community in 1903 and 1904. Scholarly meetings discussed the deficiencies of Hilprecht's "methods." The attacks were all the more virulent because Hilprecht had, by and large, avoided the conferences of his American peers and, consequently, was not on friendly terms with his fellows.[28] Chief among Hilprecht's accusers was John Peters, but an even more vindictive voice was that of Jastrow, who kept in touch with Hilprecht's erstwhile students. Hilprecht had threatened the museum's prerogatives by taking artifacts and aggrandizing publishing projects, and Stevenson, now president of the museum's board, allied herself with Jastrow and Peters.

Hilprecht defended himself in various ways. He pointed out that a footnote in his book had testified that the finds of the fourth dig "have not as yet been unpacked."[29] Having made such a statement, he could not have implied that the illustrative tablets were from the fourth expedition. Only a careless reader would infer that Hilprecht had uncovered the illustrations in 1900.

Hilprecht argued that his book, designed for a popular audience, was not scholarly. A certain looseness in the presentation of evidence was permissible. Although the objects purchased from dealers had not been found on the fourth campaign, Hilprecht argued that they might well have come from Nippur, and in any case typified the material that was from Nippur.

His convoluted reasoning on this point is difficult to accept. Hilprecht's footnote was significant but not exonerating. As many careful and intelligent readers pointed out, they studied Hilprecht's book and pictures and came away believing that Hilprecht had found the tablets in the Temple Library on the fourth dig. But Hilprecht did not originally intend to deceive.

He believed that he had discovered a library, if discovery had anything to do with the intelligent appraisal of the character of the tablets in 1900. Everything else was minor.

In the late 1890s Hilprecht had repeatedly stated that he had presented to the BEF most of the treasures Turkish authorities had given to him. In 1902, when he became Clark Professor, the Trustees thanked him for his gifts. When Hilprecht noted these facts during the dispute, Peters rebutted that the gift of the tablets to the excavator was an Ottoman formality. Everyone knew that Western explorers negotiated with Turkish officials for a share of what had been dug up; the Ottomans then made "gifts" to the archaeologists, said Peters, and these gifts went to the institution sponsoring the expeditions. In truth, however, Hilprecht's relation to the Turkish museum had differed. His work there had resulted in personal ties. Although he had turned over "far the greatest number" of the finds to the BEF, he had freely admitted that he had kept some, and believed they were his to keep.

Peters's amour propre did not allow him to distinguish his connection with the Turks from that of Hilprecht. As head of the museum, Stevenson had better grounds for her outrage.[30] The BEF had in the first instance promised the university that Penn would get *all* the finds and that they would be placed in the "fireproof building" that eventually became the museum. Hilprecht had participated in this arrangement and had disregarded the Philadelphians' moral compact. Some of his antiquities, too, had gone through customs as property of the BEF.

Hilprecht may have been obligated to turn over all the material, but at the same time he was not the only one to get specimens; everyone connected with the digs had samples. Moreover, although the twenty-five hundred tablets that eventually rested in Jena were more than samples, the meaning of "ownership" was obscure. The Americans had initially devised various strategies, illegal under Ottoman law, to get tablets back to the United States. The Turks were surely one group that could claim the objects. The Americans never considered at all the rights of the Arabs who lived in and around Nippur, yet one could argue that the material was theirs. Why did lawful possession of the tablets become an overriding issue of virtue only when they reached the United States?[31]

Yet Hilprecht could not escape the obloquy that his taking the finds brought. The failed Chicago expedition under Edgar Banks had necessitated that Americans take the moral high ground about the rightful ownership of artifacts. Americans, moreover, were disgusted that significant objects stayed in Hilprecht's house in Germany. Scholars were aroused because Hilprecht treated the Nippur finds as if they were his, restricting their use to those upon whom he smiled.

As president of the museum, Stevenson wanted both to vindicate its authority and to put Hilprecht in his place. But she also wanted to avoid washing the institution's dirty laundry in public. She advised Hilprecht to emend his work in an academic magazine, clarifying the link between his illustrative finds and the Temple Library. Such a minor correction would embarrass Hilprecht but would get everyone off the hook with a minimum of attention. "No one would have been the wiser," and the matter would have been settled "without scandal or friction." She wanted a "modus vivendi," the matter "adjusted . . . with perfect dignity." She also suggested that in his will Hilprecht leave the disputed items to the museum. Hilprecht told Stevenson that his wife had made a similar suggestion. He promised to take it under advisement, and at his death the museum did inherit some of his material.[32] At the time, however, Hilprecht stuck to his guns: he never promised the museum the property and insisted that his illustrations were from the Temple Library.[33]

Was there such a library? Hilprecht was fairly close. Later scholarship maintained that the American expedition had come across a collection of buildings in which substantial numbers of tablets were found, perhaps a scribal quarter. Even so, however, Hilprecht had not discovered it. He had examined samples of the tablets that Haynes had left out for him, but something like seventeen thousand documents in over one hundred boxes had been crated and sent back to the United States, most from the third and fourth digs. Hilprecht testified that he had opened each of these boxes and examined and cleaned all the tablets when they reached Constantinople for the divisions. Fisher, who in 1900 had packed some of the material at Nippur and unloaded it in the United States, said time and again that many boxes reached Philadelphia just as they had been shipped from Babylonia. Fisher was the more credible witness here: one can imagine negotiations in the Turkish capital where selected boxes would be opened and where others, unopened, would be consigned to the BEF or the Constantinople museum.[34]

In any case many crates remained unopened in America, and the evidence presented for a library was meager. Yet Albert Clay, who had often worked on the Nippur documents when Hilprecht was in Constantinople, warned Hilprecht's critics that they could not sustain the charge of "no library." Hilprecht had not *proved* there was a library, but the hoard of tablets that Haynes gathered from a single place signified something extraordinary. Perhaps, as Peters allowed, they simply had to wait and see what investigation of the sealed boxes would show.[35]

Part of the problem had to do with the definition of *library*, a term meaningful in early-twentieth-century English but hard to apply to this long-dead civilization. Jastrow, whose animosity to Hilprecht ran deep, took the extreme view that except for Layard's discovery, ancient Mesopotamian cities had no libraries. Hilprecht's European defenders, however, urged the significance of a cache of documents, whatever it was called. They believed

Hilprecht would show the literary or cultural nature of a good portion of the tablets and demonstrate that they were not business records or bricks with conventional inscriptions. Hilprecht focused on the library, where his claims were strongest. His detractors would not abandon the questions of the methods of presentation and the ownership of the antiquities.

From the middle of 1903, when *Explorations in Bible Lands* came out, Hilprecht's enemies denigrated his probity at every opportunity. In private correspondence, in scholarly discussions, and in book reviews and essays his detractors went after him. The success of Hilprecht's foes can be first measured by the fifth campaign's receding into the distance and, in the end, never taking place. Energies were otherwise occupied.

In 1904 ownership of the tablets became a moral problem for the museum. Stevenson met with Hilprecht to avoid a public confrontation. It was at this meeting that she intimated the resolution that would have left Hilprecht only mildly humiliated and limited only the inheritance of the objects. When Hilprecht refused this compromise, the museum formed a committee to settle the property matter. Stevenson wanted to strip Hilprecht of his curatorship. By this time, however, the decision depended on people who were also university trustees. They thwarted the museum's attempt to punish him.

In early 1905 Peters, from New York, publicly complained to the trustees in Philadelphia. At Hilprecht's request, after some shilly-shallying, they investigated the charges. This investigation, which occurred in March and April 1905, was known as "the Peters-Hilprecht Controversy."

Peters was still ministering at St. Michael's in New York. In addition to him, John Prince, who had dropped out of the first expedition when he took ill, and who was now a professor of Assyriology at Columbia, gave evidence against Hilprecht. Frank Harper, the co-Assyriologist of the first expedition who was now teaching at Chicago, refused to testify for Hilprecht, intimating his animosity. Hilprecht's old rival, Paul Haupt of Johns Hopkins, disparagingly reviewed Hilprecht's efforts, although he declined to participate in the hearings. Finally, the Assyriologists at Penn joined to speak against Hilprecht—Jastrow, Clay, Fisher, and Ranke.

William Hayes Ward, who had led the first surveying expedition in 1885, thought Hilprecht had slighted Haynes. Haynes himself, however, was "mentally unbalanced," according to Ward and, in any case, now in a sanatorium and unable to speak for himself. The desert had broken Haynes's health. Hilprecht's adversaries used Ward's good offices for the next best thing. They induced Cassandria Haynes also to testify, although she no longer lived with her husband.[36]

Just as the inquiry got underway, Stevenson and her friends on the board of managers severed their connection with the museum. Her worst fear was realized. As she put it, the managers had to finance the museum but were forbidden to govern it.[37] Harrison's worst fears were realized also: the museum broke with the university before the world. Although, in the new order created after Stevenson's resignation, the museum would be more beholden to Harrison, he paid the price of public embarrassment. Newspapers up and down the East Coast debated Assyriology as if it instanced sexual scandal. And so, at last, were Hilprecht's fears realized: Peters, Prince, Harper, and Haupt were sabotaging ancient Near Eastern studies at Penn.

An insoluble problem faced Harrison. Universities were fragile institutions based not so much on contractual obligations as on collegial relationships premised on mutual trust, decorum, and politeness among gentlemen. Colleges had no way of reprimanding a difficult professor. Hilprecht may have deserved punishment, but American higher education had no mechanism to maintain standards of civility. A major crisis faced the institution. If its own investigation did not find the professor innocent, Penn would in all likelihood be forced to dismiss him. Was this an appropriate penalty for a scholar who had served the Babylonian expedition at least as well as Peters and Haynes, and whose skill as a decipherer was uncontested? Hilprecht's fall would also cast doubt on the worth of the expedition itself when everyone believed in the value of the exploration, and most believed in the existence of one of its chief prizes, the library. At stake, said one of Hilprecht's defenders among the trustees, was not just the value of these costly excavations, but "the fair name of the University."[38]

Harrison had little room to maneuver. His enemies thought the university was set on "stupid," "tortuous" "folly." Peters wrote that he could not grasp the "inwardness" of the administrators' position.[39] Yet all the critics were insensitive to the provost's plight. He tried to avoid an open battle, hoping the tempest would blow over or that Hilprecht would appease his detractors. When Harrison could no longer circumvent a confrontation, he cleared Hilprecht. Were the accusations against him justified, they would jeopardize the work the museum had done in the past twenty years. A finding of no confidence in Hilprecht might have punished him too severely for obnoxiousness and scholarly missteps, and such a finding was certainly too harsh for the university itself.

In one of many ironies, Hilprecht depended on amateurs whom he regularly disparaged. He precipitated the attack in his meeting with Stevenson: he refused a nonexpert's (and a woman's) advice about his departure from "strict methods" and about the need for his utterances to have "unimpeachable authority."[40] Nevertheless, the hearings themselves pitted an array of experts against the businessmen, lawyers, and men of affairs who made up Penn's trustees. Some were astute. Before the hearings Hilprecht met at length with Levering Jones, a tough Philadelphia lawyer who was one of the trustees. Jones took steps to "strengthen our position" and said the appraisal of Hilprecht had to be "non strictarian."[41] Others were dull and easily manipulated: Clay referred to Stevenson's successor as president of the museum (Samuel Houston, a Hilprecht supporter), as "the ass."[42]

The trustees thought the scholars "were making a mountain out of a mole hill." On the other side, through "ignorance of the scientific conditions, & reluctance to blame a man who had been a good advertising card for the Univ. & whose new surroundings are wealthy," the trustees were led "into a quagmire."[43] With no standing to evaluate learned methods or the ancient Near East, the group decided in Hilprecht's favor. In the quagmire, the trustees concluded there was a library; the tablets Hilprecht said were his indeed were; and the charge of "*literary dishonesty*" (in regard to his illustrations) was "entirely unsubstantiated."[44]

Penn undoubtedly hoped that after the hearings the controversy would fade away. Perhaps it would have, had not the professor's enemies fought on. Peters called the findings a "whitewash." Hilprecht's Orientalist peers continued a drumbeat of accusations: more essays in journals, more formal papers at scholarly get-togethers, more letters. Jastrow was particularly unrelenting. He got in contact with his Orientalist friend in New York, Richard Gottheil—another Delitzsch student and the Semiticist on whom Nicholas Murray Butler relied to attract Jewish donors to Columbia. Jastrow had Gottheil organize opposition to Hilprecht outside Philadelphia.[45] Hilprecht thought that publication of the hearings would satiate critics. To that end he edited *The So-Called Peters-Hilprecht Controversy*, a transcript of the twenty-five hours of testimony and accompanying documentation. But to no avail.

After Penn absolved him, Hilprecht was damaged goods. He rightly saw that Peters and Jastrow meant to do him "serious and permanent injury."[46] But he refused to give an inch, though his life was consumed with the effort to bear up under the assault. Hilprecht had become "*morally corrupt*," Jastrow wrote. More important, he noted that Hilprecht's "mind has become affected."[47] Hilprecht was not merely ineffectual; he was a burden to the administration that had saved him. Harrison's strategy did not contain the damage but instead sent the war into a new phase.

In 1906, sixteen Orientalists representing Harvard, Yale, Columbia, Johns Hopkins, and Chicago asked Hilprecht to clear up the "imputations" on "the integrity of American scholarship." When Hilprecht did not satisfy them, the *American Journal of Semitic Languages and Literature* printed their complaint. Their leader, Harvard's Charles R. Lanman, an influential Indologist student of William Dwight Whitney, sympathized both with Hilprecht and with his peers. Lanman told Hilprecht that neither the existence of the library nor Hilprecht's role in its discovery was at stake. Rather, Lanman said that Hilprecht knew the "real issue" and must confront it "without evasion." Hilprecht's readers "naturally received an impression" that Hilprecht had dug up his illustrative tablets at Nippur. Hilprecht was "morally

bound to make honorable amends for . . . letting such an impression prevail." Lanman did not assume that Hilprecht had wanted "to deceive or
mislead the greater public, still less your colleagues." "I fancy that in the
excitement of the situation you allowed loose statements to be printed
which made a great sensation, perhaps far greater than you could foresee;
and that, once placed in a more or less compromising position, you found
it harder and harder to withdraw."

Hilprecht's friends would like to have him "reinstated in their respect and
fellowship." Could he not, asked Lanman, "dropping all voluminous tech-
nicalities," make a brief statement to the effect that he had laid himself open
to criticism and regretted the failure not to have made such an admission
earlier? Then, said Lanman, the fraternity could "dismiss the matter from
our minds." But, he finished, nothing short of that would "reinstate you in
the good opinion of men whose opinion, for my part, I should value the
most if I were in your place."

Hilprecht "seriously regret[ted]" that only such a statement would reinstate him. He would not apologize.[48]

Hilprecht's benefactor Edward Clark, from early in the controversy,
thought that "pressing" Hilprecht to publish his findings was the best action
to take. Both Harrison and new museum board president Houston—"the
ass"—agreed and urged Hilprecht to disseminate his research. At first Hilprecht said he would publish the tablets within ten years. That was far too
long a period. Houston wrote time and again that "it is to your best interest,
and the best interest of the University, to get the contents of the unopened
boxes labelled." Then Hilprecht should get "competent scholars to hammer
them [volumes of research] out as fast as can be done with accuracy." Harrison added that it was "most important" "to go on with the cataloguing" and
"to get our publications out."[49]

From the perspective of these laymen, Hilprecht's vindication would
come from proof of the existence of the library. Hilprecht adopted this idea,
instead of thoughtful confession, as the key to his "reinstatement." The
actuality, however, proved difficult to realize.

Over a hundred boxes of tablets from various campaigns lay in the basement of the museum. Organization was minimal. Finds that Haynes, for
example, had found extraordinary might be boxed separately, but basically
the antiquities were packed by campaign. The tablets themselves were not
in good condition. Officials had opened some boxes, shifted around their
contents, and repackaged them in Constantinople. As far as I can discover,
however, most items were not repackaged when they passed through the
Ottoman capital. But in Nippur the Americans did not anticipate the hazards of shipment to the United States. Occasionally tablets arrived in Philadelphia crushed into hundreds of pieces. When fragments were large

enough to be repaired, the process was difficult and time-consuming. Some-times one piece of a document in Philadelphia would later have its "join" found in Constantinople. If tablets survived the voyage, they were subject to other dangers: dampness and the packing materials might combine to cause a tablet to decompose chemically, or materials might cling to the clay and necessitate a complicated and sometimes destructive cleaning. After un-packing, cleaning, and repair, Albert Clay reported, the documents were "gradually going to pieces," laid out in the damp museum cellar.[50]

Hilprecht often did not have time to examine them. At his best a careful interpreter of cuneiform, Hilprecht knew his vocation required hours in the study. Others might undertake the onerous curatorial duties of preparing and cataloguing material. Yet Hilprecht still had responsibility for oversight, a job made harder by his contretemps with his staff and his fear of losing control of the publication of the tablets. Additionally, many commitments kept Hilprecht from the cloister. He frequently traveled to Constantinople to work in the Turkish museum. He spent some of this time appropriately, relating the American objects to those remaining in Turkey, but Hilprecht was often at his home in Jena, Germany. When in the United States, he had an active social life. To maintain his scholarly position he cultivated that part of the Philadelphia elite friendly to the Crozer family.[51] Hilprecht pro-tested that various serious ailments kept him from the tablet room. At one point he asked for a three-month leave of absence. His health had been "greatly undermined" by the "unprovoked attacks" and the "extraordinary labor" of preparing *The So-Called Peters-Hilprecht Controversy*.[52]

Overall, Hilprecht pushed forward with researches that had to go slowly at best. He desperately needed to justify *Explorations in Bible Lands*, but the task was difficult. His enemies pressed him, and his style of living detracted from his scholarship.

In 1906, Hilprecht printed *Mathematical, Metrological, and Chronological Texts from the Temple Library of Nippur*, which first attempted to demon-strate the existence of a library. The documents, however, fell short of the sort of "literary" tablets that Hilprecht needed to vanquish his adversaries. Then, in 1910, with great fanfare, he published a text that told of the flood: *The Earliest Version of the Babylonian Deluge Story and the Temple Library of Nippur*.[53]

Ever since George Smith discovered tablets in the 1870s that were "an-cestors" of the Old Testament story of Noah, Babylonian analogues to the Bible signified the public triumphs of ancient Near Eastern studies. The "Babel and Bible" fight was about grasping the connections among similar stories. Did such stories confirm the Old Testament? Or show that Babylo-nian culture generated the essence of the Old Testament? Or merely demon-strate that all ancient cultures had common myths?

Hilprecht claimed that the fragment of the deluge epic he published was the most ancient such document yet recovered. To have discovered the object was a triumph, and it had just the kind of literary character needed to establish claims for the library. Moreover, the age of the tablet and its peculiar rendering of Noah's story, Hilprecht asserted, confirmed traditional views of the origins of the first five books of the Bible. One of Hilprecht's friends touted the publication as "destined to usher in a new period in the history of religion."[54] Hilprecht himself kept in close touch with Harrison over this little volume and made available a great number of copies "for clergymen and college presidents." Harrison was more interested in the response of the professoriate, and Hilprecht dispatched excerpts of academic praise to the provost's office. Harrison was "glad to see any . . . letters, especially from scholars abroad." Hilprecht eagerly obliged Harrison, but in truth the praise from Europe was more or less perfunctory. Academics had received Hilprecht's essay but had not seriously attended to it.[55]

In the United States, Hilprecht's foes were more assiduous. This time George Barton, a professor at Bryn Mawr College, delivered the initial blow, deprecating Hilprecht's techniques of decipherment and the importance of what he had found. Barton, who shared Hilprecht's religious convictions and was thus a credible opponent, joined Hilprecht's old enemies—Clay, Jastrow, and Haupt. As Hilprecht put it, the "dogs are barking again very loudly."[56] In his defense he explicitly questioned the knowledge and competence of his accusers, "though they profess to teach cuneiform inscriptions."

In learned gatherings and again in the newspapers Barton and his friends argued that Hilprecht's tablet was less old than he claimed, that his translation was dubious, and that the document's meaning for Bible studies was minimal. As Clay put it in preparing for the American Oriental Society meeting of 1910, "We are cooking up an indigestible mess for his Serene Highness, the Deluge hero."[57] Hilprecht's critics also said, later, that this tablet was not found on the fourth campaign; it was not from the library, in respect to which Hilprecht could at least gain some credit.[58]

The issue in this round of the controversy was the importance of a specific object. Hilprecht had staked much on it because it could make his case for the library and disarm critics. Yet his self-promotion about this tablet would prove unjustified. The altercation, however, almost immediately ended as he simultaneously faced another crisis.

Early in 1910, a dramatic change was taking place in Hilprecht's fortunes at the museum. With Hilprecht's blessing,[59] Harrison had appointed George B. Gordon as "director" of the museum. Gordon was a Harvard-trained anthropologist who had formerly been a curator of American ethnology. More important, he was Harrison's choice, devoted, first, to molding the museum to university policies. Second, Gordon in the museum

mimicked Harrison's policies in the university: the new director wanted
clear authority over his institution. He would curtail the rights of the museum's Board and break the independent power of the curators. As an anthropologist, Gordon could be expected to contend with the archaeologists
on disciplinary issues, but this does not seem to have been paramount in his
thinking. Rather, there is evidence that he was one of the group that wanted
to oust Hilprecht on personal grounds.[60]

In any event he soon crossed swords with Hilprecht and his supporters.
The imperious curator now found himself on the wrong side of disputes
involving his autonomy and Gordon's desire to shape the institution as a
part of the university. It is hard not to receive the impression that Gordon
had the general consent of the provost. As soon as Gordon took over, he
removed members of Hilprecht's clerical staff, took over some of his space,
and made it more difficult for Hilprecht to do menial tasks. Both Clark
brothers had died. Gordon made it clear to the other moneyed Philadelphians who had funded Hilprecht's trips to Constantinople and his publications that they could not secure favorable treatment for the professor.[61]
These people, who had sided with the university and with Hilprecht during
the 1905 investigation when Stevenson resigned, soon found themselves in
the marginal position that had formerly been hers. Hilprecht tried mightily
to reassert his authority, but power in the museum had shifted. He could
not command helpers or office space.

When Gordon had been on the job only two months, Hilprecht was so
thwarted that he used his ultimate weapon on Harrison. Just as he published
his tablet on the Flood, he announced that the work on the library had
stopped "owing to the repeated interference on the part of Dr. Gordon." "I
have ceased going to the Museum and shall cease going there," he concluded, until his old privileges were restored.[62]

Uncharacteristically, Harrison did not resolve the quarrel. He prevailed
on Hilprecht to ask for privileges and upon Gordon to bestow them. The
provost took the high ground. He would not be "the friendly judge" between them but rather reminded them of common obligations. One of the
"great trusts" of the university was "to uncover what has been forgotten in
the history of the race." Both men had to see that the "organization [had to
be] made more and more perfect" and that "there must be friendly and
harmonious co-working and co-operation."[63]

Harrison's words papered matters over for one month. Then Gordon
began to check on Hilprecht's comings and goings, and observed that he was
only in the museum for, on the average, two hours a day. He told Hilprecht
that he (and the assistant curator) were expected to be in the museum during its hours of operation and that he should spend more time cataloguing
tablets. Hilprecht ignored this order but claimed that a detective was watch-
ing him. He was being treated as "an ordinary day laborer or a criminal."[64]

Hilprecht saw the handwriting on the wall. Toward the end of April he was presented with the *Hilprecht Anniversary Volume*,[65] a collection of essays by scholars to commemorate his fiftieth birthday and the twenty-fifth anniversary of his receipt of a doctorate. A festive occasion was filled with forboding. The book was printed in Germany, and of the ten organizers and thirty-one contributors, not one was an American faculty member in Hilprecht's field.

Immediately after the celebration Hilprecht left abruptly for Germany, begging the trustees' pardon and asking for leave until November 1910. The Constantinople museum, he reported, demanded his emergency services in its administrative reorganization.[66] But a trip might also secure European assistance against the complaints about his tablet on the Flood. The sudden departure also suggested that he had learned of Gordon's plan to clean and organize the boxes of tablets from the Nippur campaigns still in the museum basement. By leaving with the keys to the basement rooms, Hilprecht may have intended to sidetrack Gordon and to come back to a different situation six months later.

The tactic did not deter the director. He changed some locks and made duplicate keys. In June he announced that he had been "devoting much time to unpacking and cleaning the tablets contained in the boxes and excavated at Nippur." In October, Gordon reported that during the summer he had cleaned and mended material in ten out of more than one hundred crates. At the same time he noted that "exposure to the atmosphere" had caused "the complete demoliton of tablets" that had "already gone to pieces."[67] Hilprecht learned in Europe that this final indignity had occurred. He made a fatal error and submitted his resignation, effective at the beginning of 1911.

On his return in the autumn he had some friends, including the president of the board (who had appropriate keys), accompany him on his first visit to his old quarters.[68] He then reported to the university trustees that someone had broken into his office and, in addition, destroyed material that would have enabled him to sort out the tablets. Hilprecht hoped the report would explain his resignation but also compel the trustees to turn it down and punish Gordon. Following receipt of this report, board president Houston also resigned.[69]

Once again the trustees dutifully investigated. Two of their conclusions were well-grounded. First, from the evidence at their disposal, they confirmed that in the spring of 1910 many of the tablets were in poor condition. Second, from everything they could determine, Hilprecht had not marked the individual boxes in such a way as to locate where at Nippur groups of tablets had been extracted. At least Gordon had lost no information in the uncrating. This conclusion was consistent with what was known about Haynes's excavating and packing techniques.

The trustees relied not on their meager knowledge of the Nippur finds but on the testimony of Hilprecht's helpers and of Clay and Fisher, who had expert knowledge of the tablets. Of course, both men hated Hilprecht, and the trustees neither accepted nor rejected Fisher's claim that no one had repacked the tablets when they passed through Constantinople. The trustees did accept the statements of everyone that the boxes were not significantly marked. It is hard to believe that the people doing Hilprecht's chores would have been unaware of such markings, or that they would have dissembled about them, or that such markings would have escaped their attention.

It is much more likely that Hilprecht lied or, to put a face on it that corresponds to his actual state of mind, convinced himself that Gordon had not only violated his rights but also destroyed information on the boxes and in the packing material. Hilprecht wanted to discredit Gordon and restore his own power at the museum. Proof that Gordon had mistreated the boxes would justify any difficulties in demonstrating the existence of the library or delays in the publication of tablets. At this stage of the Peters-Hilprecht controversy, one can see the operation of a mind that was not merely self-aggrandizing but had lost some of its empirical moorings. The scandal was destroying Hilprecht.

At the same time that Hilprecht protested to the trustees, Hugo Radau, a German student who had maintained good relations with the professor, circulated a letter among European scholars. Radau told the Europeans of the "outrage." He asked them to write to the trustees, demanding punishment for the guilty and a reconsideration of their action "in accepting the resignation of Professor Hilprecht."[70]

Harrison, nonetheless, would not give Hilprecht his job back. The strategy of 1905 had failed; the case had not blown over. Hilprecht had continued to be an albatross. His antics had at last warranted the personal charges that were the essence of the criticism against him. So far as Harrison was concerned, Hilprecht—through Radau—had slandered the university, dishonestly and misleadingly reporting what had gone on at the museum.

This was the second time since 1905 that some museum personnel were united against Harrison. But now Hilprecht, in refusing to play an appropriate role in Harrison's bureaucratic system, was on the side of the museum people (like Stevenson) who could not stand the discipline of the university.

The dispute showed the growing power of American academic professionalism. In his defense Hilprecht (and Radau) mustered a host of Europeans—English, German, Finnish, French, Italian, Swedish, Danish, Austrian, Hungarian, Czech—to condemn the trustees and to urge his reinstatement. But, as happened with the *Hilprecht Anniversary Volume*, no Americans joined this effort. To the extent that Hilprecht mobilized United

States citizens in his favor, they were religious leaders—members of the Lutheran, Presbyterian, and Reformed clergy. From time to time he was also supported by Bible scholars at lesser-known schools of divinity. But none of these communities was any longer crucial in ancient Near Eastern circles. Radau recognized that "competent scholars" could influence the trustees,[71] but Hilprecht's clique did not see that the meaning of "competent scholars" was changing. Penn might have responded to American scholars, but not to Europeans only. It might heed the wishes of academics but not those of a religious and theological group. (Hilprecht's European advocates were religiously conservative, while Friedrich Delitzsch and his liberal confreres would not assist him.)

There were, said the trustees, "certain situations in which an institution of learning must be content to forego [sic] the services even of the most eminent scholar." The charges against Penn that Hilprecht had helped publicize would make it "impossible" for the university to regain confidence in him. Nothing could make "his connection with the University either useful to it or agreeable to him." The restoration of his relationship to the university "is not for an instant to be thought of." Hilprecht had not asked for reappointment, but if he did, the trustees would now find themselves "compelled to refuse it."

7

ARCHAEOLOGY AND OBJECTIVITY

T OWARD THE END of the nineteenth century explorers in the Near
East recognized that the site of a city might contain the accumulated
debris of many successive periods of occupation. The main goal of
exploration shifted from discovering antiquities to learning about changes
in ancient towns. Evidence of different periods might be contiguous if
change had been gradual. If change had been cataclysmic, however, traces of
destruction, say by water or fire, might separate material attesting to obviously different styles of living. Adventurers began to see the places as the
remains of towns often rebuilt. Especially in Mesopotamia, continual construction had raised artificial hills from the flat plain.

Explorers called their repeatedly built-upon sites *stratified*, after the same
phenomenon in the formation of the rock of the earth's surface. What is
now a truism only slowly came to practical clarity in the minds of excavators: what was lower down in a site had to be earlier than what was higher
up. If scholar-diggers could examine a Near Eastern mound or a tell strati-
graphically, they had a key to understanding chronological growth; the
lower remains would be older. Explorers could document the way human
habitation altered if they could properly interpret the varied data that the
ages had stored up. As the orientation of explorers changed, they developed
a set of expert talents that came to define archaeology as a peculiar academic
field, and that were essential to a vision of humanistic scholarship that
could proudly claim objectivity.

The puzzle of extreme proportions was how to dig so that a site would
reveal its secrets. Moreover, the excavation itself was a one-shot attempt.
Explorers made the evidence unusable as they worked; they got no second
chance. The actual stratigraphy was complex. Ancient peoples did not start
on level ground and regularly rebuild on top of older, decayed houses, leaving behind neatly differentiated rubbish. Talking about such a collection of
buildings might be useful, as it is here, for illustrative or teaching purposes.[1]
But the topography of the land was irregular, rarely level, with hills and
hollows to which deposits had accommodated. The trash from everyday life
accumulated slowly underfoot while the inhabitants of ancient towns went
about their daily business. Shards of pottery, broken water jars, and other
common utensils were trodden into the soil. The razing of a town might
leave sudden accretions, bringing to what was then the ground level clay

from roofs, wooden supports, and walls, as well as whatever was inside dwellings. In ancient times, if cities were rebuilt, or even if selected houses were destroyed and built over, laborers cleared the ground. An area might have within it various dumps that mixed together the general rubbish of a certain time. Merely rebuilding on a site might disturb a pristine stratification, confusing levels. Excavators also contended with later thieves or diggers who did not value the original order of the material.

Explorers faced intriguing problems in what might be called conceptual engineering. They had to ponder the ruins and work out how to access the evidence. Then they had to interpret the evidence as it hinted at the story of a changing city. The way they dug partially determined what the evidence was. The apprenticeship system of fieldwork had a cogent rationale as soon as archaeology emerged as an academic field of study. Students could learn only by doing. One critical part of archaeological method, moreover, became the routine carrying-out of simple rules: the number of diggers to hire, the tools to use, the sort of supervision to employ, the way to dispose of dirt, and so on. Writing up one's findings as quickly as possible was also imperative. If one's peers could not learn what someone had uncovered, expeditions were almost worthless.[2]

Heinrich Schliemann initially noted that different layers of cities existed when he excavated at Troy in the 1870s. His techniques for sorting out these layers, however, were primitive and ruthless until the architect Wilhelm Dörpfeld began to assist him in 1882.[3] At the same time, Julian Pitt-Rivers gained a reputation by carefully attending to how he dug on his estate in England and by making obsessive observations and notes.[4]

Another Englishman, Sir Flinders Petrie, had developed habits of exact measurement and of skillful and complete recording. They became critical for archaeology in Egypt, Palestine, Syria, and Mesopotamia. Petrie began digging in Egypt in the early 1880s and continued for more than fifty years; indeed, he consulted there with both Schliemann and Pitt-Rivers.[5] Petrie's tenacity and high technical intelligence left the greatest imprint on archaeology. His relative ignorance of epigraphical matters and the idiosyncrasies that permitted him to be alone in the field for so long lent peculiarity to some of his findings, especially as he grew older. Yet by the 1890s he was regarded as *the* archaeological authority in the Near East. The Americans often depended on his expertise.

Nonetheless, the first Americans to dig did not use the techniques more or less common to Schliemann, Pitt-Rivers, and (more crucially) Petrie. The Americans had different aims, and their mentor was still Henry Layard. The campaigns sent out from the United States were the last ones generally based on the principle of extracting as much worthwhile material as possible from the ground. The Americans adopted the "sondage method," digging long, deep trenches to see what might turn up. John Peters thought the "scientific" point was to devise a way to hit on valuables quickly, but his fieldwork convinced him that excavating was "a lottery." One could not expect to find through academic expertise, he said, the best place to dig and come up with treasures. In southern Mesopotamia the Americans were "pioneers, path-breakers." They faced "a total inability to predicate anything as to the probable contents of different portions of the ruins," and it was hard to estimate immediately the desirability of what they did find. Hilprecht, said Peters, believed that if the Germans recommended something, "that was the only scientific method." But no method was on its face better than any other.[6] Peters did not change his mind about the goal of the enterprise or the limits of science in achieving that goal. When John Haynes left to go on the dig at the end of 1898, Peters advocated that Haynes, with his experience, be allowed to excavate more or less as he wished. He could dig broad trenches, "pie cuts," from the top to the bottom of various mounds to find out where the prizes were.[7]

Others did alter their thinking over time. In the 1880s Hilprecht thought excavating barely worthwhile. On the first Nippur dig, he paid no attention to the fieldwork.[8] Archaeology was only a poor way for Westerners to extract tablets, which he wished to procure from dealers. Monumental art never interested him, and the BEF ultimately reconciled itself to the notion that the precursors of the Assyrians had not produced such objects. By the mid-1890s Haynes was concentrating on shipping tablets back to the United States. After long field experience and becoming friends with the architect Joseph Meyer, however, he perceived matters differently.

In addition to unearthing tablets, Haynes thought that the excavation should uncover what the city of Nippur had been like in various stages of its development: "It exasperates me beyond measure to be obligated for the sake of showing immediate results to dump the excavated earth over a spot that ought to be thoroughly explored and it grieves my soul to think of abandoning the Temple Hill." The full exploration of the ziggurat was of such moment, Haynes argued, that he ought to dig according to a definite plan over a series of years. He deprecated what he called the "German" method of digging large trenches or "sections" through an entire hill to reveal various levels of occupation. Nor did he believe that one section of the ziggurat at a time should be excavated by going down stratum by stratum. He had an architect's sense of the design of the area and a vision of how the temple and its precincts might have been built and rebuilt over the centuries.

This sense of the growth of the ancient city led Haynes to some extravagant, foolish accounts of what things were like. Moreover, he still had no great insight into Mesopotamian history, and both deficiencies called forth Hilprecht's disdain. "One might picture the ancient ruler, Naram Sin," said Haynes, "walking upon the cool of the day upon his unfinished wall. . . .

Perhaps he was especially thinking of a line of guest rooms to be built for winter use. . . . The humane monarch could but think with pride of the substantial comfort in store for his countless guests, whose lips would never cease to sing his praises, while their grateful hearts would respond in deeper chords." On Haynes's letter Hilprecht wrote "schreckliche Fantasie."

Yet Haynes's feel for the job was not unsubtle. He did not simply assume that one large, sweeping excavation would reveal the entire area of the temple as it had once been. Indeed, there probably had never been a single way it had been. One had to excavate layer by layer "to distinguish the different epochs of its history, each well defined level to be thoroughly explored, sketched, photographed, and described before the excavation of any part should be carried to a lower level." Such a strategy would be "less likely to lead to confusion of strata" and would preserve evidence that "would be lost to the method of removing section by section" of a given area. Although Haynes pontificated in silly ways, he had a better grasp than did Hilprecht of the imaginative reconstruction necessary to successful field archaeology. One needed, said Haynes, "the fancy in strict accord with the laws of logic and science."[9]

By 1900, Hilprecht had joined Haynes in thinking about how the spade could promote the recovery of the cities of Nippur. Throughout the 1890s he discouraged indiscriminate collecting of tablets. Hilprecht encouraged Haynes to excavate the ziggurat, "a most important sanctuary." Its full exploration would be "one of the greatest works done for science in its present state."[10] By the turn of the century Hilprecht had also absorbed the import of the new German fieldwork in Mesopotamia and eagerly pushed the Americans to emulate it. He came to see the point of Haynes's earlier musings about ancient architecture.

The Germans had searched for places to excavate in Mesopotamia in the late 1880s and 1890s. The Americans regularly but vaguely referred to ideas about excavation that they attributed to the Germans. When the Germans got to a permanent site in 1899, at Babylon, near Nippur, they successfully tested their theories. The German leader, Robert Koldewey, was an architect interested in what Babylon looked like. The Germans inaugurated excavation in Mesopotamia as a tool for figuring out the urban contours of past civilizations. Koldewey assumed that the archaeologist should function with the mind of a city planner or architect and look at the whole design of an evolving urban site. He applied the methods of Schliemann's assistant, Dörpfeld, and the systematic enterprise of the Germans was at roughly the same level as that of Pitt-Rivers in England and Petrie in Egypt. Digging for fifteen years, Koldewey uncovered a succession of cities that had been built and rebuilt at Babylon. The most efficient and thorough examination at that time of the ancient Near East,[11] the expedition had its importance increased by growing German political clout in the region.

The German ideas were on Hilprecht's mind when he went back to Mesopotamia in 1900 and conferred with Koldewey. Hilprecht had always been
hyperbolically dissatisfied with the work of the other Americans, but when
he reached Nippur his usual jeremiad had more a truthful ring. The "utter
failure" of the architectural work at Nippur shocked him. It was "a crime,"
and the "scientific loss was very great"; "we are in detail almost a complete
failure." The job Peters and Haynes had done was no better than that of the
Arab thieves who stole tablets for the export market, or the prospectors who
looted the American goldfields. Trench after trench had been dug into the
Nippur mounds. These labors had destroyed "the historical continuity in
the strata of the different cities and completely chang[ed] the entire picture
of what Nippur actually was at its different periods of existence." He wrote
that he wept and almost broke down when he saw the "bewildering mass of
. . . trenches"; the "large confusing site of remains of wall, pieces of plat-
forms, scattered drains, collapsed sides and deep holes of removed earth and
destroyed important structures"; and the "20–60 feet rubbish heaps, gathered there by my predecessors." The "fundamental error" was that again and
again Haynes had excavated by making "perpendicular" or vertical trenches.
Both he and Peters should have excavated horizontally, peeling off period
after period, developing the layout of the whole city in its various stages of
evolution. Hilprecht would prefer to resign, he said, than to say one unfriendly word about Peters and Haynes in public. But only that determination made it impossible for him to recommend that the BEF preserve its
scientific dignity by formally denouncing the results of the digs.

Hilprecht decided instead to correct the mistakes of the past decade and
reconstruct the history of the cities that composed the mound of Nippur.
The time for digging "as a charming sport in Babylonia" was "pioneer
work," but it belonged to the nineteenth century. His young assistants,
Clarence Fisher and Valentine Geere, had little training in "architectural"
archaeology, and Haynes had not been able to instruct them. "At great inter-
vals," Hilprecht said, "incompetent men" had done "a little superficial [ar-
chitectural] work." But in his three months at Nippur, Hilprecht wrote, he
gave Fisher and Geere a crash course in applied German methods. This
intensely practical instruction involved them in interpreting the various
buildings and rebuildings of the city. Through his knowledge of the written
evidence, Hilprecht showed the two neophytes how to calculate the connection of various strata to one another. With his help they produced reports
on the design of the major features of Nippur.

Hilprecht's claims were rhetorical, but his sensibility had changed. Overall, the Americans had gone from a concern with big pieces of art to documents, and finally to ruminations on all the material remains as evidence
for the rise and fall of city life. The travel adventure had become archaeology. The Americans had not actually risen much above the tunneling and

hacking in the ruins characteristic of earlier nineteenth-century daredevils. In fact, when Edgar Banks dug at Bismya in 1904–5, his style went back to that of Layard. Nonetheless, conceptually, Peters's account of the 1889 and 1890 campaigns, *Nippur; or, Explorations and Adventures on the Euphrates* (1897), differed from Fisher's *Excavations at Nippur: The Topography and City Walls* (1905).[12]

Despite the interest of Haynes, Hilprecht, and Fisher in the German methods developing in the 1890s, the Americans did not give up Layard for Koldewey. Hilprecht complained that he and Koldewey were not jointly serving a strong German government.[13] But the "Hilprecht controversy" meant that the United States did not go back to Nippur after 1900. The delays of the Banks expedition, ultimately associated with Chicago, signaled the growing influence of Germany with the Ottoman Empire. This influence curtailed archaeological work by Americans and other foreigners. Perhaps only Hilprecht could have kept Mesopotamia open for Westerners in the fifteen years before World War I. The war and its aftermath discouraged respect for anything *deutsch*. The United States did not return to Mesopotamia until the 1920s.

In the meantime, the English in Egypt provided the model for the Americans for new digging techniques. In general the methods that Hilprecht came to grasp too late for Nippur consisted of meticulous observation and recording of what a site looked like and what the digging brought to light. The excavator had to work vertically and horizontally, and different field-workers proposed various techniques that would best reveal the shape of ancient towns. Slicing through a mound would display the diverse strata. Then, according to the theory favored in Mesopotamia, the diggers would take off each layer in succession. Workers leveled the remains carefully, analyzing them before going to an earlier level. Archaeologists convention-ally investigated a higher stratum before destroying it and proceeding to a lower one.[14] These were the German conceptions that Hilprecht, in his a priori way, deliberated on in the late 1890s and grappled with at Nippur in 1900. Yet Germany and Mesopotamia became less important to the United States after the turn of the century. Sir Flinders Petrie in Egypt became the exemplar for the Americans, and even before that time he had developed more complex methods.

Overall, Petrie thought of the tells and Egyptian sites as architectural products, as did his German peers. By digging along walls he got a sense of the whole. Town plans were critical, though Petrie then might sacrifice a stratigraphic record of various construction phases. The impulse toward horizontal digging, from a later point of view, compromised the results that Petrie's careful measuring produced. Yet at the end of the nineteenth cen-tury, on the basis of his excavations, he established the fundamental princi-ples of reasoning in the field.[15]

In a dig at Naucratis in Egypt in 1885 and then, in 1890, in a stunning excursion into Palestine at Tell el Hesy, Petrie went beyond methodical observation and a concern for strata as he excavated. At el Hesy he started digging at a point where a stream had cut into the mound, leaving successive layers visible, like the layers of a cake that had been sliced through. The objects dug out at each level were marked and kept together. After determining the height of the tell at various points, Petrie later drew a "cross section," the first pictorial stratified analysis of a Near Eastern site. Petrie's work was significant because he used the variation in pottery found in different strata to determine that he indeed was looking at different strata. Alternatively, he found that different strata were characterized by different ceramic styles.[16] The diverse styles of pottery bespoke different periods of occupation. Linking the ceramic evidence from el Hesy with parallel pottery forms he knew from Egypt (and the Aegean), he connected the chronologies of different sites.[17]

Petrie believed that pottery would change its form after repeated imitation—that is, after an artisan had copied one form, and the copy had been copied in turn a sufficient number of times. He could thus categorize objects such as wavy-handled jars in a series. It might be hard to decide which end of the series came first—whether the wavy handle had developed from a rudimentary form or had gradually changed into something vestigial. But other evidence, in Petrie's case the finding of pottery in dated tombs, might secure one or both ends of a series. Moreover, a great concentration of one sort of wavy-handled jars in a low stratum would indicate that they were older than a related sort found predominantly in a higher stratum. By applying the same method to other kinds of pottery found with the jars, Petrie could corroborate his results and lengthen his sequence backward and forward in time. If he found the same types of pottery at other sites, he could extend his analysis geographically as well as temporally.

Petrie analogized his work to comparing the furniture in successively sealed-off rooms to demonstrate which rooms were of consecutive dates.[18] But Petrie was actually doing something more intricate. He confronted different pieces of furniture and imagined "rooms" to which he could assign the pieces and give them a temporal ordering; but he sometimes assumed he had rooms so that he could organize something called "the furniture of a certain period" in them.

Petrie did not find but "constructed" two sorts of facts: different strata and different types of ceramics. From these facts he drew conclusions, first about stratified levels of occupation and then about a chronology based on the distribution of pottery.

Archaeologists conventionally distinguished *typology*, or the classification of objects—pottery—according to types, and *stratigraphy*, or the study of the relation of objects to the deposits in which they were found and the

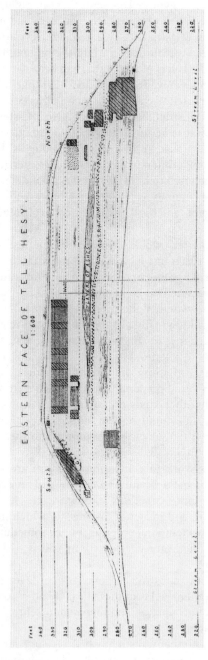

Fig. 12 Petrie's Cross Section at Tell el Hesy, 1890. This was the first attempt at a stratified diagram of a Near Eastern site.

relation of deposits to one another.[19] But these two conceptions derived from the same mental process. Petrie classified objects as what they were because he could assign them to specific strata. He made strata into what they were because of the objects that could be located there.

Working at home in London around the turn of the century, Petrie organized much of the material he had brought back. He named what he was about "sequence dating." He put his pots into a chronological order of before and after, even though he could not determine dates in the order. He additionally allowed for earlier and later times than the ceramics evidenced. Each individual time was "relative" to another. Such "seriation" enabled explorers to generate a connected narrative of the historical, temporal development of Egyptian civilization. Ultimately, they extended the chronology over the ancient East. Scholars could often correlate a relative time with an "absolute" one—for example, the time of an astronomical event that they could calculate. The archaeologists might finally reconstruct a year-by-year order for events that had occurred in the ancient world.[20]

Frederick Jones Bliss, a young American, creatively carried on Petrie's work at Tell el Hesy after Petrie went back to Egypt. Bliss had worked with Petrie, and he became a talented excavator. With any luck he would have matured into one of the doyens of American dirt archaeology. But he had dug for the London Palestine Exploration Fund and never held an academic post. Moreover, although he lived until 1937, Bliss gave up fieldwork at the turn of the century.[21]

Thus, just as the Americans were ending expeditions, which they would not resume in Mesopotamia for almost twenty years, archaeologists in Egypt and Palestine were developing ideas that went beyond what even Hilprecht had adumbrated. Following the Germans, he had, essentially, hypothesized about the relevance of the recovery of ancient architecture for the study of Nippur. By 1900 Petrie had practiced this "horizontal" sort of archaeology and made it the basis for a more complex chronological organization of ancient history.

The Americans ultimately absorbed Petrie's ideas but, again, Mesopotamia was not in the forefront, although Nippur's Clarence Fisher was. At the peak of his powers at the turn of the century, Petrie influenced everyone who dug in Egypt, and he attracted exploration there. With Mesopotamia effectively closed down, Egypt was soon hosting a relative explosion of archaeological work. Excavation was prompted by the institutionalization of Near Orientalist scholarship in the United States and the interest of museums in pharaonic antiquities. Explorers routinely adopted Petrie's techniques; of the Americans who dug, the most important was Harvard's George Reisner.[22] Using Petrie's ideas, Reisner consulted with him and for several years excavated with workers Petrie had trained.

Reisner gradually elaborated new techniques. For him a site was not so much a collection of artifacts, as it was for other archaeologists, but more a product of human activity. Petrie's horizontal emphasis gave way to analysis of layers of debris, a more vertical approach. Reisner concerned himself with changes in living arrangements.

Reisner introduced even more rigorous filing and recording methods than Petrie had used. He also took more photographs to detail the location of objects.[23] Even the Americans at Nippur took pictures, but these were unhelpful in the comprehension of strata. Petrie was better—indeed, often ingenious. With technical advances in filmmaking, Reisner raised photography in archaeology to an exact art. Meticulous description and measurement would enable other scholars to reconstruct what Reisner had done in the field and so put themselves in his position when he was digging. The disturbance and removal of earth destroyed a minimum of information if the recordkeeping was good enough. Reisner's alteration of Petrie's techniques converted the report of the excavation into an almost impenetrable, expert exercise: detail after detail thrust at the reader with endless, painstaking precision. As might be expected, publication was interminably delayed, which ironically worked at cross-purposes to the point of the exercise.[24]

Reisner called his advance in recording a "scientific method." He also believed that a campaign should display scientific principles in the habits of fieldwork. Training for the staff was crucial even before labor in the dirt began. Experts in various disciplines were to be present, and Reisner particularly tried to synchronize epigraphy and excavation. Good science and effective bureaucracy were, for him, the same in archaeology.[25]

For Reisner, the social organization of an expedition mirrored a military or authoritarian ethos that simultaneously served the ends of the profession and the self-interest of the archaeological leadership. Hierarchy and an officer-class mentality pervaded this peculiar professorial culture and grew as graduate student trainees—second lieutenants—became more prominent. Reisner, however, was both idiosyncratic and portentous in his lack of concern for popularization. Archaeology had depended in the past and would continue to depend in the future on the showmanship of its practitioners. Sometimes poseurs when they were bad, influential field leaders attracted needed public support and money for their enterprises, especially where Egypt was concerned. Reisner had no interest in such a role. He looked forward to the day when archaeology would be an exclusively specialist pursuit, though one funded by the museum and university public.[26]

In 1909–10 Reisner interrupted his excavation in Egypt to work in Samaria, Palestine, where Harvard's firman and Jacob Schiff's money supported him. This was the dig long delayed in Constantinople by German influence and by the theft involving the Chicago explorers. Indeed, David

Lyon of Harvard had refused to participate in the attacks on Hilprecht because he feared German hostility to Reisner's interest in Samaria. Morris Jastrow had thundered without effect that "it is better that the enterprise should fail" if it depended on a dishonest man.[27] Reisner introduced his methods in Palestine, and Clarence Fisher assisted him. Hilprecht had sent Fisher to Nippur because of the student's architectural background, and had in 1900 lectured Fisher on the importance of the German architectural archaeologists. When Hilprecht cut Fisher, Reisner took his part; like most others, Reisner disliked Hilprecht, but he was less afraid to show it than Lyon was. Reisner thought Fisher's study of Nippur "the one redeeming feature" of the Penn fieldwork; this was the book that Hilprecht had inspired but whose publication he had tried to prevent. Fisher later showed his own authoritarian streak and even broke with Reisner, though in Palestine Reisner made Fisher his "right-hand man."[28]

For a long time Fisher was the one American who had experience in Palestine and Mesopotamia. After his fight with Hilprecht, he had for a time no settled academic job and was willing to work continuously in the field. Frank Harper wanted Fisher to get Chicago back into Babylonia after the Bismya fiasco, even though Hilprecht had weighed in against him. Later, Clay tried to persuade Fisher to initiate digging for Yale in Babylonia.[29] But no one went back to Mesopotamia after Bismya. Penn reemployed Fisher after Hilprecht resigned. He stayed in Palestine and, with the added influence of Reisner, for some time moved the center of the American ancient Near East away from Mesopotamia to Egypt and the Holy Land.

Fisher also shifted thinking about practices in the field back toward the horizontal. Excavation should not proceed just by digging "pie-cuts" ("sections" or "strips") through a site to reveal the stratigraphy. The field-worker must combine this vertical approach with a horizontal one that comprehended the general outline of a site at any given time. Reisner was such a stickler for detail that he did not move so much earth as other archaeologists at the time. Some of the sense of the whole may have escaped him. As an architect, Fisher had an overriding concern with the layout of buildings and areas in a single period. He emphasized what went on at a given horizontal level, and not the vertical "debris layers" in a strip.[30] He liked to excavate areas and clear complete building units.

After World War I, Fisher's career continued in Palestine and guided nearly every American expedition there in the 1920s and 1930s. Thus was born the "Fisher-Reisner" excavating method. Although the two men were sometimes supposed to have pursued identical tacks, critics charged that Fisher's architectural approach created stratigraphic problems circumvented by Reisner.[31] Theoretically, however, the method combined, in the words of one less scientifically enamored writer, "onion peel stripping" and "cheese wedge sampling."[32]

Petrie had excavated layer by layer after having made vertical sections of a mound. But after 1900 he dug few settlements, and he focused on sites dated by the presence of inscriptions. To some extent Petrie lost his feel for stratified digging. Reisner (and even Fisher) persisted in attacking mounds this way, and had a far better practical sense of the complexities of "real" strata.[33] Both Petrie and Reisner, moreover, dug in Egypt, and left their imprint on digging farther to the east by onetime spectacular achievements. By the 1920s and 1930s a received set of techniques had grown up under Fisher's aegis, and some of Reisner's nuances were lost.[34] When the British and the Americans returned to Mesopotamia in the 1920s, this version of the Fisher-Reisner method became conventional there too.

Later, two English archaeologists, Mortimer Wheeler and Kathleen Kenyon, criticized the Fisher-Reisner method as merely continuing Petrie's constricted ideas. For them, Petrie had dug on a horizontal level without much sense of the slope of a site or the difficulties of ascertaining the different debris layers. Reisner and Fisher, it was argued, followed Petrie; they supposedly had little regard for topographical problems. Reisner, at least, was better than this critique allowed, although Wheeler and Kenyon were more sensitive to topography, and they developed methods for ascertaining it.[35] Overall, the later English digging concentrated more on vertical relationships, reaching such a state of precision that the English excavated only comparatively small areas. The Americans, with less precision and a greater interest in the horizontal, now cleared more ground.[36]

Later in the twentieth century, distinctive excavating strategies proliferated among archaeologists all over the world. It became more apparent that, after a certain point, archaeological spadework was as much a matter of style as of science. The core problem was that different things were uncovered if one dug one way rather than another, vertically rather than horizontally. Various tactics could be used to integrate judiciously each sort of earth removal. Yet one could not do both at once. Not even a preferred way of excavating could uncover all the evidence, while a nonpreferred method might uniquely preserve material. These truths were transparent to an innocent, but not grasped by the expert devotees of a method.

Critics disputed each substantive finding that Petrie made. They argued over the number of strata and so the concentration of pottery types found in a stratum. Scholars might contest the absolute age Petrie attributed to a certain period of time and even whether it was a discernible period at all. The interval between different periods was up for grabs. Even their order might be rearranged. Levels and pottery distribution were as much interpreted as given. But archaeologists did not dispute that a temporal ordering existed: some things happened earlier or later than others. The leftover artifacts evidenced this ordering. Although the evidence was fragmentary and always subject to question, archaeologists accepted that there was a correct order. Indeed, they could not dispute this supposition; it was part of the way their minds worked when confronting temporal existence. Ordering in time was *how* their brains processed material.

For many archaeologists, the attribution of what I have called "absolute time" to a stratum was crucial. Excavators found something that they could associate with a date; the usual example was a coin or an object located in a dated tomb. Ancient dating systems were based on the calculations by the old-time peoples of the movements of the heavenly bodies. Scholars with an expertise in ancient mathematics and astronomy could translate such systems into an extension of the universal calendar time used today. Founded on contemporary physics and astronomy, such "absolute" dates had the authority of today's hardest sciences. They had the greatest weight for scholars because they joined archaeology to physical science and tied human time to the natural world.[37]

Recent ruminations on the theory of measurement and the philosophy of physics have given absolute time less of a shine than it once had. Moreover, relativistically inclined humanists have argued, as I understand them, that different cultures construct the ebb and flow of lived time in ways that absolute time cannot capture. The latter itself may be a construct of certain cultures.[38] Whatever the force of such arguments, they do not weaken the premise of Petrie's invention of sequence dating. It was produced neither by culture nor by the external world, but by the way the human mind necessarily operated. Sequence dating then furnished the framework for an absolute chronology. The latter's status might be less than firm for some theorists, but it was at least such that archaeologists did not dispute that an object had just *one* such locus.

The chroniclelike history archaeologists wrote—one king after another—followed from the poverty of the evidence available. Chronology also reflected ideas with which scholars could not dispense. The establishment of temporal order (and then dates) marked the impartial nature of their practice; all competent observers accepted ordering as beyond argument.

The manner in which Petrie constructed a temporal continuum forced archaeologists to confront basic problems about the way human beings understood succession in time. At Nippur, Peters, Haynes, and Hilprecht reorganized and extended their chronology by some two thousand years. They fought the whole while, and based their insights on digging considerably less deft than that done by Petrie. Their views were also challenged. But no one could think away the principle that there was an order, from before to after, earlier to later, in the ebb and flow of Nippur's life.

Place had a role similar to that of time. In digging, spatial location (higher or lower) signaled temporal order (later or earlier). Spatial location too was beyond cavil. An object found in the earth had had an exact location. Precise recording was critical to give the provenance of an artifact, its origin or derivation. After 1900 this became the conventional wisdom. Hilprecht claimed to have found a library because of the precise location of tablets unearthed at Nippur. Yet his flippant use of unprovenanced illustrations undermined his credibility. No one knew where the items had been found.

In 1905, at the height of the Peters-Hilprecht controversy, Hilprecht argued that it was standard for Europeans to illustrate finds without regard for provenance so long as the illustrations were characteristic. To "real men of science," said Hilprecht, "the time, place, and method of acquisition of an antiquity" were "utterly irrelevant" in this sort of illustration. It was "inconceivable," he went on, "that any scholar in Europe would ever make such criticism" as the Americans had.[39]

Hilprecht, however, acutely realized the critical nature of provenance to his case. He conceded that the documents illustrating the library were not discovered on the fourth dig. But that did not show they were not from the library. Various sorts of considerations about a tablet—its color, age, handwriting, content—might prove that it had been extracted from the library mound at Nippur even though it was purchased in Baghdad.

In 1910 Hilprecht resigned from Penn over the issue of provenance. The BEF had unpacked one hundred cases from the third and fourth expeditions. Hilprecht claimed, untruthfully as far as I can make out, that the boxes contained information on where the explorers had found their contents. "The scientific data contained in these boxes personally packed by me in Constantinople in distinct layers" provided the "objective proofs for the topological situation and the actual establishment of the . . . Library in certain mounds of the ruins." When the boxes were unpacked, the data had "almost entirely been destroyed and are irretrievably lost to science." This was an "act of vandalism unparalleled in the history of archaeology."[40]

By the second decade of the century, the Nippur disputes had heightened American awareness of the point of temporal and spatial locus in research. This awareness was not enough to prevent Yale from making its mark by purchasing illegal antiquities. Yet this method of climbing into the academic stratosphere disturbed even scholars disposed to Yale. The quality of technique in excavation had risen by that time, and so too had the ethics of exploration. Everyone frowned on the purchase of unprovenanced material. Some of this criticism arose from scholarly jealousy, and obvious moral ambiguities still characterized the acquisition of material on excavations. Yet even John Peters, fond of his alma mater, objected. Such collections were made at "enormous cost," because in obtaining them so much information of importance in explaining them was destroyed. The Arab excavators and dealers, Peters claimed, got rid of as many objects as they salvaged. The thieving amateurs disregarded remains of buildings, pottery, and most fragments, all useful from an architectural point of view.[41] The result of this sort of critique was that Babylonian studies at Yale had relatively little archaeological value.

Objects existed at certain times. The discovery of such objects and the determination of their age were tasks that everyone recognized as essential. No one gainsaid that there was one correct answer to a question of where and when. The concentration on the discovery of a fundamental spatiotemporal ordering gave archaeology its reputation for objectivity. It was about fundamental, bedrock truths that scholars could dig up.

This focus had long-term effects inimical to faith, in spite of the penchant for religiosity among Orientalists. Archaeology made it more difficult to sustain the substantive, literary conclusions of the higher criticism. The evidence of the monuments and the earth claimed an equal place with the composite Old Testament sources that German savants esteemed. Yet the techniques of exploration also shifted the mindset of archaeologists away from Bible truth. Nowhere was this effect more ironic than in the history of the exploration of Palestine.

In the mid–nineteenth century, Edward Robinson had made scholarly study there intellectually viable. Interest grew during the period when there was no digging in Mesopotamia. Religious commitment propelled Palestinian archaeologists to determine the truth of Bible stories. They continued the movement that Robinson had begun.

In the Holy Land, scholars confronted, first of all, conflicts between the reports in the sacred book and the contemporary wisdom of native informants, who gave what amounted to guided tours to nineteenth-century travelers. Careful observation and measurement, as well as logical reasoning on Robinson's part, made him jettison nineteenth-century legends about Bible events. Later, actual excavations tested the traditional stories. Easiest to discredit was the local lore that archaeology could show was not congruent with a sacred tale. The Bible, for example, might say that a place was inside old city walls. Affirming the Bible, archaeological evidence might make clear the faulty nature of contemporary traditions that put the place outside where these walls once had been. Defenders of local tradition *could* argue that the archaeological evidence was misinterpreted: the city walls as properly reconstructed by archaeology might be such that the place did lie inside them.

In such disputes, measurement and spatiotemporal locus grounded informed, nonpartisan debate. Surveyors' coordinates were critical in themselves, whatever one said about the Bible.[42] As Near Eastern studies and biblical archaeology emerged as academic fields, the university rewarded and punished scholars in the area as it did men in other disciplines. Publication of results was the key to preferment, and in archaeology publication depended on the facts that belonged to a given researcher. Everyone possessed the spatiotemporal data, but the honor of discovering them could belong only to a few. In order to *be* scholars, even biblical archaeologists had to make the hunt for objects in space and time primary. By the time Reisner and Fisher were excavating, the focus was not so much on the veracity of the Bible as on exact metrology.

In the professional lives of scholars, biblical truth became secondary. The search for the sacred yielded to the determination of a network of facts that existed in the natural world. Such an emphasis eventually made it impossible for some to leap from the natural facts to the supernatural realm of belief. The religious meaning of Bible stories was a genre of disputable narrative that burdened the facts. Religious belief became, if not supernumerary, at least only personal, unrelated, for most, to the concerns of employment.

Orientalists presupposed a grid of spatiotemporal facts, yet so few facts were at their disposal that the larger story placed on the grid was significant. At first the larger story involved the religious meaning of Old Testament history. Later, scholars in effect ruled out stories with a supernatural dimension. Nonetheless, they seemed more determined to propound nonsupernatural stories that went beyond the given information. The bias toward indisputable facts in the practice of archaeology and in the self-conception of the discipline was overwhelming. Yet just as overwhelming was the zeal with which practitioners elaborated argumentatively on these facts.

It may have been impossible, even by March 1900, to tell where the Nippur library tablets or Hilprecht's illustrative objects came from. The confrontation had become so angry that even if the disputants had agreed on the location, the place might have ceased to be the compelling piece of evidence that they thought it was. Even though their altercation went beyond what the facts could establish, all the principals supposed that objects were truly located somewhere.

As one rather old-fashioned archaeologist put it, the discipline was "a technique by which facts are obtained for the construction of history and prehistory."[43] Seton Lloyd, a distinguished student of ancient Mesopotamia, wrote that the histories of that old civilization consisted of "stringing together the evidence of a series of isolated texts such as dedications, date-formulas or genealogical inscriptions, and amplifying or disguising its inadequacies with the conventional phrases used by historians to create a narrative."[44] These inadequacies led anthropologists who were more inclined to the social sciences to move archaeology in the direction of their own, more modern discipline. Up-to-date archaeologists should eschew the notion that they could use the agreed-upon facts "to form an impression and subjectively [to] paint a word picture." Rather, archaeologists had to go beyond subjective and impressionistic stories. They had to discover warranted explanations for the facts, as the modern anthropologists did. Sophisticated scholars believed that they invented theories about the past and then tested them "by excavation."[45]

Two archaeologist-philosophers used a detective story by G. K. Chesterton to illustrate this point.[46] In "The Honour of Israel Gow," Chesterton's hero, Father Brown, solves a mystery in a castle. When Brown arrives, Inspector Craven of Scotland Yard produces an inventory of clues: diamonds, some snuff, bits of metal, and candles. "By no stretch of fancy can the human mind connect together" these items, says the inspector. Father Brown immediately tells three different stories about the dead owner of the castle that link these clues. After each one, Brown's straight men ask, "Is that . . . the . . . truth?" The amatuer sleuth replies, "ten false philosophies will fit the universe; ten false theories will fit Glengyle Castle. But we want the real explanation of the castle and the universe."[47] The development of methods at the turn of the century had given the archaeologist possession of irrefutable facts, but there was no assurance that these facts would be part of a true story or warranted generalization.

Outside archaeology, two later projects in ancient near eastern studies showed how scholarship went beyond the facts in a more or less justifiable manner. The first of these was in decipherment, the second in historical synthesis. But in each of them a "true" history and warranted generalizations were still elusive. The final two chapters take up each of these projects in turn.

8

INTELLECTUAL PROPERTY

THE PETERS-HILPRECHT controversy was about a peculiar kind of property. Rightful or lawful ownership of the tablets was interesting to speculate about, and physical possession of them was not trivial. Once scholars published pictures and drawings of the tablets with translations, however, control of the artifacts was less valuable. Who received the credit for discovering the antiquities and making them available was critical. The conflict over *intellectual* property was central to the dispute. In a later act in the drama of Nippur, the role of intellectual property became clearer, although the protagonists filtered the problem of credit through talk about who actually owned the documents. In the end, the Nippur tablets became part of a complex epistemological story of decipherment that opened up the cultural history of Sumer. As scholars translated the Nippur Sumerian texts, they recovered the ancestors of the Gilgamesh poem, the Homeric writing of Mesopotamia. This recovery had repercussions for a wide audience ready to be tutored about the ancient East.

In mid-December 1910, Hilprecht delivered his yearly curatorial report, generous in its praise of others. He had served "you and this country loyally . . . however little the life-blood of one person counts in the development of a great institution." "My efforts," he continued, "were honest, but the re-sults . . . not always acceptable. You must judge me leniently when I am gone." "If only a little should remain," he concluded, "*I shall carry with me back to my own country* the conviction that my sojourn and my efforts . . . have not . . . been in vain."[1]

It looked at last as if the professor would go, and go far away, gracefully, and in January 1911 the museum returned his compliment. It unanimously approved a minute presented to Hilprecht. A lengthy and enthusiastic trib-ute expressed "profound appreciation" for Hilprecht's many services in the past and hoped that "his labors may continue for many years to come."[2] But then the authorities heard again from Hilprecht. When he had sent in his resignation the previous summer, he said, he had explicitly reserved his exclusive right to catalogue and publish the tablets. In 1902, when he was given the Clark Professorship, the university had "gratefully accept[ed]" Hilprecht's gift of the material that the Turks had personally bestowed on him. Penn, however, had "vested for his lifetime in Professor Hilprecht" the right "to determine and control the details of the scientific publications."

Hilprecht now wanted sole access to the finds and his old authority to publish them. He asked how the trustees would protect his rights.[3]

Academic bureaucracies are not morally refined instruments. They overpraise their professors because experience shows that flattery appeals to scholars. When these bureaucracies are threatened, they are not sticklers for ethical propriety. In their haste to reward Hilprecht when he brought them fame, the trustees had erred in giving the man "lifetime" prerogatives in 1902. Now, in 1911, they scrambled to locate the documents that originally committed them, and then tried to erase their mistake. In 1902, the officials now told one another, they had had "no power" to grant Hilprecht such an "individual" privilege. Although it was "a serious legal question," they "found themselves unable to recognize the existence of the rights asserted by Dr. Hilprecht"—the very rights they had granted.

Having informed Hilprecht of its decision in April 1911, the university failed to respond to his request for immediate clarification of how he could use the tablets. In the summer, with Hilprecht in Europe, the newspapers reported that he was negotiating the sale of the Nippur library to German institutions.[4] A new provost at Penn, Edgar Fahs Smith, told the press that the antiquities were "its property." Hilprecht did not own the treasures and could not sell them abroad. He "was acting as an agent of this institution [during the explorations] and his services were paid for." Penn had persuaded the Ottomans to give up the finds. Hilprecht was not operating "in his personal capacity."[5]

Scholarship played a role here in addition to Hilprecht's persuasive legal claims. His life was centered on the tablets. He could scarcely go on without them. The academic world would lose if the only person who understood the connection of the finds in Constantinople to those in the United States could not use the American documents.

Yet Hilprecht's enemies were unrelenting. Albert Clay had by this time gone to Yale, leaving no obvious successor at Penn. He wrote exultantly that the most recent events would "kill H." Hilprecht's wife had "sense enough," said Clay, to know that if Hilprecht was a further public embarrassment, "the property issue will kill them even more."[6]

Clay, who reached his academic zenith using J. P. Morgan's money to purchase property of dubious ownership, was right. Hilprecht did not push his case. He let fourteen months go by without hearing from the trustees about his request for clarification. Then he denounced the institution for "depriving me of the material available in Philadelphia for the completion and publication of my further scientific proof of the existence of the Temple Library of Nippur."[7]

For twenty-five years Hilprecht had argued that Penn must strive for almost secret possession of the finds. The argument had not fallen on deaf ears. According to its lawyer, the university now owned "certain scientific material." Hilprecht might for the present have access to a limited number of documents, as might any other outside authority, if it did "not involve expense to the University." The museum would have to curtail this access if a new professor wanted unique privileges.[8] The university, however, did not have to act on these decisions. Hilprecht wrote his denunciatory letter from Paris. His presence there and the lapse of more than a year may have convinced the trustees that they had little to fear in dropping the case. The denunciation went unanswered. At a trustees' meeting in October 1912, "upon motion" Hilprecht's letter was "ordered to be filed."[9]

As far as American universities were concerned, Hilprecht dropped off the face of the earth. He did, however, travel back and forth from Germany, and he held up his head in Philadelphia society.[10] He established "the [Frau] Hilprecht Sammlung" at the university in Jena, and controlled a considerable number of Assyriological antiquities. Finds from Nippur (and other material) that Hilprecht considered his own had gone from Constantinople to Jena. But he did no more significant writing there, or in Constantinople or Philadelphia. At the age of fifty, when he could have looked forward to fifteen years of peak scholarly activity, his career had ended. He wrote to one friend about "my life's shattered work." For a time his wife tried to get Hilprecht reinstated at Penn by promoting an investigation of some of Jastrow's underhanded behavior in 1910 that had led to the resignation. The attempt failed.[11]

When World War I broke out in Europe in August 1914, Hilprecht, in Germany, promptly wrote propaganda pieces for American newspapers. The articles put the best face on the German effort against the Allies, Britain, France, and Russia. Many upper-middle-class people on the East Coast supported the Allies from the start and became rabidly anti-German well before the United States joined the Allies in 1917. Hilprecht's newspaper writing confirmed the justice of their low esteem for him.

This war work also changed the structure of the opposition to Hilprecht. The Europeans who supported Hilprecht came from many countries. His strongest advocates in England and Germany represented the two most prestigious scholarly traditions. The wartime carnage altered that. England opposed all things German, and its scholars condemned Hilprecht and gave Penn anti-German advice as the university struggled to rebuild its staff in ancient Near Eastern studies. One Englishman wrote that Penn should "never allow any more Germans into the . . . Babylonian Department" but wished that "American Assyriologists were better scholars." Someone rejoiced that the university was rid of a "German egoist whose conceit and bad manners were all too long tolerated," but that in any event Penn should not replace him with any "intriguing Jews." Now that Penn had rid itself of Hilprecht, said another, perhaps "some clever young American could take over."[12]

Instead, Penn courted an English academic who despised the United States even more palpably than had Hilprecht. Stephen Langdon had been born and raised in the United States, but after his Assyriological training, he lived in England. He was appointed at Oxford, naturalized a British subject, and served for a time in the British armed forces in World War I. Langdon was an energetic scholar and one of only a few learned in Sumerian, the non-Semitic language whose literature predated that in the Akkadian; but the Americans overrated Langdon. Moreover, he dismissed his native land as if he were, indeed, born an Englishman. After examining tablets at the museum and dickering with Penn, Langdon stayed at Oxford. "Living as I do among the world's greatest scholars," he said, "Philadelphia came upon me as a dark cloud."[13] Failing to appoint an English equivalent to Hilprecht, Penn floundered in carrying on its tradition.

The museum did maintain its status in Near Eastern field archaeology, especially as Clarence Fisher's reputation grew. Nonetheless, the United States only got back to Babylonia later, in 1922, when, at long last, the dream of Haupt, Hilprecht, Frank Harper, and Clay was realized, and Americans went to Ur. Unfortunately for the United States, the British Museum cosponsored the venture. Although Penn had equal status, and the University Museum for a time employed the dig's director, the British Museum got the credit. The public associated (Leonard) "Woolley of Ur" with the English, particularly after Max Mallowan, another famous twentieth-century English archaeologist, joined the dig as assistant to Woolley. Mallowan's wife, however, wrote a piece of fiction that was based on her time in Mesopotamia and that assumed the preeminence of the United States and its German connection.

In this narrative "the world's greatest field archaeologist" from the University Museum led the exploration. Yet this American archaeologist had been a German spy in World War I and became a homicidal maniac in Babylonia. He murdered his wife, who was having an affair with the expedition's architect, and then his chief assistant, who discovered the killer's identity.

Other things went awry on this fictional campaign. Another archaeologist was a drug addict. The epigrapher stole the valuable gold finds. His fabricated translations of tablets were thought only surprising and slightly unorthodox. One character reported that the architect was "planning" the city he was supposed to be uncovering and that his workmen merely "hack[ed] out" walls wherever he wanted them to. The property of the murdered wife was left to the University Museum.

Such was Agatha Christie's view in *Murder in Mesopotamia*, published in 1936.[14] Before that date most of the real participants in the first American Babylonian drama had left the scene. Haynes had died in 1910, Frank Harper in 1914, Peters in 1921, Haupt in 1926. An irritable old man in Jena,

Hilprecht was a welcome target for the street boys to bombard with tomatoes. He was back in the United States when he died in 1925.[15]

Clarence Fisher, who had been with Hilprecht on the last dig in 1900, had a distinguished archaeological career that lasted far longer than Hilprecht's did. Fisher returned to Penn after Hilprecht left and was employed by the museum into the 1920s; he then left and excavated through the 1930s in Palestine. He died in Jerusalem in 1941. In 1987, however, a St. Louis newspaper informed museum officials that Fisher had died that year, and the museum received inquiries from the son of the St. Louis Clarence Fisher. Had this been the real Clarence Fisher, he would have been 109! The archaeological archivists in Philadelphia reasoned that in the chaos of the Near East at the start of World War II, a German national had taken over the dead Fisher's identity and come to the United States to make a new life.[16]

A mystery surrounding the Nippur documents had an equally long life. After the public bloodletting in 1905, Hilprecht had some significant tablets that were not in his private collection and that the museum had accessioned. It would not have been untoward for him to have taken these tablets home for study, either in Philadelphia or in Jena. Between 1912 and 1914, researchers at the museum could not find these documents, and at some point the cuneiform catalogue listed them as "missing." In 1985 some of the tablets turned up at the University of Haifa in Israel. They had been donated to Haifa by a Philadelphia art dealer living in Haifa who had acquired them in the early 1960s in a Philadelphia estate sale. Someone had attempted to remove the accession numbers, but they were still visible. Some of the other documents listed as missing are in Jena. Others have not yet been accounted for.[17]

In the years after Hilprecht's resignation and death, the tablets that remained at the university did not continue to molder in the basement of the museum, but little was done with them either. Had Hilprecht remained on the scene, we cannot know that matters would have been different. Without his leadership, accomplishments were meagre. Not until the late 1930s did scholars fully grasp the significance of Haynes's finds from 1900. It turned out that in the scribal quarter (or temple library) the Americans had excavated a lode of material central to the recovery of the Oriental culture of the earliest period. This find remained unique a century later. To understand how students justified claims almost equal to Hilprecht's boasts, we must return to George Smith at the British Museum in the early 1870s and to the recovery of the Akkadian epic of Gilgamesh.

At that time, Smith deciphered fragments pertaining to "The Chaldean [Babylonian] Account of the Deluge." In the last two decades of the nineteenth century, this discovery of an "antecedent" to the story of the Flood generated popular interest. But in those twenty years scholarship also focused on the longer tale in which the deluge narrative was embedded—what became known as the Gilgamesh epic.

The epic, in Akkadian cuneiform, had been found in several similar copies, most of which had been discovered at Nineveh. Each copy filled twelve tablets of six columns, three to each side of the tablet, with about three hundred lines to the tablet.[18] The epic related the story of the hero Gilgamesh, who apparently actually lived about 2700 B.C. Scholars believe that stories about this Sumerian king of the city of Erech (the biblical rendering of the Akkadian Uruk) were orally transmitted and circulated until at least some were written down in Sumerian about 2100 B.C. A longer Gilgamesh composition in Akkadian appears in fragmentary form in the Old Babylonian period, and the so-called standard account was written in the last half or quarter of the second millenium. In addition to the copies found at Nineveh, which date to the seventh century, other copies found elsewhere in Assyria and Babylonia were dated as late as 200 B.C. The epic was translated into several ancient Near Eastern languages and was widely known in one or another of these versions.

The epic begins with an introduction (on the first tablet). It makes known to us the king, Gilgamesh, who built the enduring walls of Erech. The narrator directs attention to Gilgamesh's lasting city. "See its wall . . . look at its brickwork." After going on a series of adventures, Gilgamesh has engraved his story "on a stone," a document to be found in a tablet box in a secret place in the wall itself. Thus, his autobiography inscribed on stone was the ultimate source of the epic. The narrator says "I will proclaim to the world the deeds of Gilgamesh," and the story is told in the third person.

At the beginning of the story Gilgamesh is unstable, living a hedonistic life. His people complain to the gods, who provide him with a friend. Enkidu makes Gilgamesh realize that life is more than women and revelry. Together they go on heroic adventures that lead Gilgamesh to think that human immortality lies in memorable achievements. But when Enkidu dies, Gilgamesh understands the irreplaceable value of human companionship. He becomes aware that the loss of loved ones is inevitable. Death appears inescapable, and great achievements are not the same as immortality. Gilgamesh changes course and desperately seeks eternal life. He goes on a long journey, including, in tablet XI, a visit to the Assyrian Noah, who tells Gilgamesh his story. By the end of his travels Gilgamesh has learned that he must die. Although the epic does not treat his death, Gilgamesh faces its possibility with sensitivity, some detachment, and even a sense of humor. Wisdom comes in recognizing that participating in one's culture, and for a king or hero contributing significantly and lastingly to its progress, is the best that humans can do. Great achievements do bring immortality of a sort, but "of a sort" is the operative phrase. Sadness tinges even successful endeavors.[19]

The end of tablet XI underscores this message. The document repeats tablet I's tribute to the magnificence of the building of the city wall, Gilgamesh's enduring legacy to Erech. The repetition illustrates what scholars call the "ring composition" of epics, the repeating of a theme that permits the narrator to close a story. The last tablet (XII), however, contradicts the rest of the epic in various ways. A number of inconsistencies suggest that tablet XII is an "inorganic appendage" "tacked on" to the epic.[20]

Although Gilgamesh had a scholarly importance in the years after Smith's discovery, enthusiasm for its ethical dimension was circumscribed. Its study took place in the context of the study of the Bible.[21] Nonetheless, as the intense Judeo-Christian commitments of Near Eastern scholars declined in the twentieth century, so did the moral appeal of many Old Testament stories. On the other hand, by the end of the twentieth century, Gilgamesh's weary struggle seemed newly significant. Having passed out of human experience during the Christian era, Gilgamesh was rediscovered in a period in which many found meaning in nonredemptive tales.

By the early twentieth century a scholarly industry was comparing Gilgamesh to various biblical stories. As this industry evolved, Gilgamesh's relation to the Bible waned. Putting the Bible aside, scholars conveyed to an educated audience beyond the academy the sense of loss and of the limited notion of human prospects that the ancient Near East had. Diminishing the worth of the epic would be unfair, but value did accrue to it in the century that saw the decline of salvific, Judeo-Christian belief among intellectuals.

Morris Jastrow emerged as one of the great learned students of the story. From the 1890s on, academics argued that the epic displayed internal contradictions. Tablet XII appeared added on; the flood story seemed a digression and interpolation, as did the introduction and its repetition in tablet XI. With these anomalies in mind Jastrow made a pathbreaking argument in 1898 that he returned to for the next twenty years and that shaped scholarship on Gilgamesh.[22] The epic, Jastrow held, was "a composite production containing a number of independent tales, loosely strung together, and all brought into connection with the favorite hero."[23] Analogizing the epic to the opening books of the Old Testament, he said that editors had created Gilgamesh from earlier disparate texts. Jastrow's evidence was the unintegrated character of the extant version and a few older but barely deciphered tablets. They hinted at earlier, different accounts.

Jastrow had one basic insight about specimens of ancient literature. Over time scribes melded originally distinct narratives into the synthetic versions that exist in the twentieth century.[24] In a related argument, Jastrow asserted that the literature of both Israel and Assyria had borrowed the story of the flood from a more primitive text.[25]

Old Testament criticism conjectured about the actual sources of the Pentateuch. A careful reading of the Bible indicated that its books were made up of older, separate documents. Scholarly ingenuity led to inferences about what the original materials were—who wrote them, where they came from, how they were assembled, and what consequences this had for Jewish and Christian inspiration. Jastrow applied the techniques of this tradition to the Mesopotamian epic and tried to demonstrate its evolution from other elements. His reasoning was both pioneering and sensitive, although the higher criticism of Gilgamesh lacked the theological importance that propelled biblical studies. Interest in the epic was bounded by the academy.

At the same time, Gilgamesh scholarship proceeded in a more intriguing way than Old Testament work that looked to Wellhausen. The texts on which the Bible was based had not survived. The reasoning of scholars about the book was hypothetical. In Iraq the excavation of more durable writing, the inscribed tablets, proceeded apace, and new tablets were translated. The discovery of new sources augmented the literary techniques of biblical criticism that Jastrow brought to Gilgamesh. The suppositions of scholars now bumped up against fresh documentation.

Making inferences was still not easy. Even in written form, one theorist noted, ancient Near Eastern literature was peculiar. A later version of a text might not be fuller than an earlier one, nor was an earlier one necessarily more authentic. Divergences in the text might reflect regional differences. Experts could not easily use newly discovered fragments to complete portions of texts they already possessed, for each period and area had its own version of the story.[26]

In the early part of the century, students had sixteen hundred fully or partially preserved lines of the thirty-five hundred lines of the standard version of the epic, and somewhat more than half the lines if they used all versions.[27] Some important episodes were missing from all accounts. In some chapters of the standard version a number of fragments could not be placed in an agreed-on sequence.[28] In working with the material, epigraphers were faced with breaks in the text and fragmentary or unreadable lines. Putting together connected fragments of one tablet or joining different fragments of two versions of a connected story was an art itself. The Akkadian language changed over the course of a thousand years. The handwriting of different scribes and the state of preservation of the individual tablets partially determined intelligibility. Scribal errors were not inconsequential, especially when some of the texts were those of apprentices or students.

The first step toward understanding the tablets was to transcribe the writing. Rawlinson's work on the Behistun cliff inscriptions made vivid the tasks that faced the early students, although here the problem was accessibility and not epigraphy. Even working from the best-preserved tablets was intellectually taxing. Maddeningly difficult, copying was critical to the training of epigraphers and, in the early days, a skill on which their prestige hinged. Transcription was itself an act of interpretation but had then to be followed by transliteration—representing the cuneiform syllable by syllable, word by word, in the corresponding characters of a standardized modern European alphabet. Then, with an ample philological commentary on the texts, the Assyriologist could begin to render them into a modern tongue.[29]

Although Jastrow himself translated the epic, he had depended on the first complete edition of the Nineveh documents that Paul Haupt had made. This was complete by the early 1890s, and many scholars followed with linguistic exegeses.[30] But scrutiny of Jastrow's ideas about the construction of the epic depended on knowledge of older documents. He supposed not just earlier versions of the standard epic, but progenitors in the most ancient Sumerian tongue of southern Babylonia. Yet knowledge of Sumerian was still in its infancy. The problems of interpreting the Semitic Akkadian cuneiform multiplied for the scholars whose concerns were working out the earliest sources of Gilgamesh in the infant science of Sumerology.

The Sumerians were the non-Semitic people of southern Mesopotamia who bequeathed their older cuneiform writing system to their Semitic successors.[31] Practically all the peoples of western Asia had borrowed cuneiform for their own records and writings. To adopt and adapt it demanded training in Sumerian, even after the time it was appropriate to speak of a distinct land of Sumer. Neighboring peoples probably imported scribes and teachers from Babylonia while native scribes traveled to Babylonia for instruction. This spread Sumerian ideas and maintained Sumerian literature long after the language ceased to be spoken or the independent kingdoms of Sumer existed. Despite this influence, Sumer, unlike other ancient Near Eastern cultures, left almost no trace of its peoples and language in the biblical, classical, or postclassical literature. The civilization vanished from human memory. Evidence for Sumer was buried, and reconstruction of the civilization came only in the nineteenth and twentieth centuries.[32]

The Sumerians began to write down their literary works by 2500 B.C. They continued to do so for perhaps a thousand years, although Sumerian was gradually being replaced by the Semitic Akkadian as the spoken language of southern Mesopotamia. When the Babylonians stopped speaking Sumerian, scribes continued its use. The language survived, Assyriologists said, much as Latin survived beyond the Middle Ages. The available Sumerian documents were copies by Semitic scribes of earlier works, dating from the first half of the second millennium.[33] Many scholars, Jastrow included, thought that the sources of the Gilgamesh epic would be found in Sumerian.

At Nineveh, Rawlinson had discovered bilingual texts in Assyrian and Sumerian. They implied the existence of this people, but their language was different from Akkadian and even more difficult. The French first made credible the existence of Sumer and its language. Rawlinson had sent copies of the bilingual texts to the French Assyriologist Jules Oppert.[34] But even before that time, scholars had doubted that the Assyrians or their older Semitic kin, the Babylonians, had invented the cuneiform script: the syllabic values of the signs went back to words for which there were no Semitic equivalents. Some cuneiform tablets from southern Mesopotamia in a non-Semitic language verified these ideas. In 1869, with the aid of the bilingual texts, Oppert concluded that both Babylonians and Sumerians lived in ancient southern Mesopotamia. Royal inscriptions about the "King of Sumer and Akkad" indicated a non-Semitic (Sumerian) civilization in addition to the well-known Semitic Babylonian (Akkadian) one.[35] Nonetheless, Sumerian literary works (from which the Assyrians had made their bilingual copies) were still only postulated; no one had yet found them.

From 1877 on, the French, under Ernest de Sarzec, excavated at Telloh, like Nippur the site of a southern Sumerian city, Lagash. This undertaking provided documentary evidence for Oppert's historical and epigraphical theories about the Sumerians and their language. Then, at the turn of the century, the British Museum published some Sumerian "unilinguals." These tablets were dated from about 2000 to 1650 B.C. They were the type of Sumerian document that the Assyrian scribes had before them a thousand years later when they prepared the bilingual texts and translations from Sumerian to Akkadian for the library of Assurbanipal at Nineveh. Another French scholar, François Thureau-Dangin, worked on this sort of material and produced the first reliable studies of Sumerian sources. Thureau-Dangin's 1905 *Inscriptions de Sumer et Akkad* was central to a long career. He established Sumerology as its own field of expertise and made the existence of Sumerian civilization and literature undeniable.[36]

Following the excavations by the French, the Nippur digs gave the United States and the rest of the world the trove of documents, the primary literary evidence on which scholars would base further knowledge of Sumer. In 1900 Haynes had shipped back to the United States a collection that, along with the one that remained in Constantinople and the one that eventually wound up in Jena, was the key to Sumerian literature. In 1900, neither Hilprecht nor anyone else knew how properly to decipher this material, or the purport of Haynes' discovery. But Jastrow had initiated the hunt for the progenitors of the Gilgamesh epic. This project exploited the Nippur tablets and led to the rediscovery of Sumerian culture.

At the end of the twentieth century, learning Sumerian was a difficult enterprise requiring an arduous apprenticeship. Although one does not want to overstate the problems, the most reliable experts warned of the uncertainty of the effort. As they put it, some passages in the texts were dubious, unintelligible, obscure, or enigmatic. The problem was the vagueness and ambiguity of the writing itself and a vocabulary, some of it technical or specialized, that scholars still could not learn contextually. Experts disagreed on some points of grammar. Moreover, some documents important to decipherment, especially the bilingual texts, were inscribed by Assyrians who treated Sumerian as a dead, literary language. The Assyrians were unaware of the finer grammatical and phonetic nuances that had governed the living tongue.[37]

In the 1950s an attempt to get acceptable translations of ten Sumerian proverbs by eight reputable scholars produced "considerable disagreement about practically all of the proverbs, and no agreement whatsoever in the case of some."[38] At the end of the century, Thorkild Jacobsen, one of the great twentieth-century scholars of the material, acknowledged that translations, "even by highly competent scholars, may diverge so much that one would never guess that they rendered the same text."[39] A French scholar, Jean Bottero, wrote of engaging himself "in the unending, arduous, and fatiguing study of the frightening cuneiform writing system." The languages were "so far removed from us, so loaded with pitfalls." The cuneiform had between four and five hundred characters "that changed in outlines from one century to another, and even became unrecognizable." Akkadian and Sumerian were as different as French and Chinese. "Their usages . . . dissipate in an abundance of dialects over a dozen centuries." "[T]here is never a question of just reading but only of deciphering."[40]

At the beginning of the twentieth century, the process that led to a modest mastery of Sumerian had just begun. Wallace Budge, the gossipy curator of the British Museum, was bureaucratically indispensible to ancient Near Eastern studies for many years. He recalled one scholar at the museum "cleaning" the tablets with a knife. The academic, said Budge, was erasing or reconstructing inscriptions to make them mean what he wanted them to. Budge noted that in the early days Hebrew biblical scholars suspected many translations of the tablets. Decipherment left room for pretense as the fraudulently erudite grasped for reputations that were almost impossible to call to account. Wild theories could easily replace exhaustive empirical study. Some authorities have urged that the competitiveness and insecurity of the field ignited the intense hatreds of the Peters-Hilprecht controversy.[41] Where outright dishonesty was not an issue, many scholars approached the Sumerian with biblical interests in mind; their interpretations could be as relevant to the Bible as to the text under the magnifying glass.[42]

With little evidence, Jastrow had reasoned that scribes had patched together the epic from earlier material. Later, having discovered an Old Babylonian Akkadian epic, he assumed a still earlier version in Sumerian. Jastrow's hunt for the composite elements and the discovery of more documents pushed the supposed origins of the first stories further and further back. The actual discovery of earlier material seemed only to give scholars grounds for presuming even earlier and less integrated texts. The search for primeval stories might be unending.[43] Jastrow's substantive ideas changed over the years, and his peers contested them, but he set the paradigm for how professors would study Gilgamesh. They would interest themselves in the way it came into being, and so in Sumerian.

Although not adept at Sumerian, Hilprecht controlled the Sumerian tablets and encouraged their study. In the first decade of the century, some of his students and preferred visitors took the first steps toward interpreting the Sumerian finds. Hugo Radau had emigrated from Germany as a young man and received a doctorate in Assyriology at Columbia in 1899; a postgraduate assistant of Hilprecht's, Radau maintained the confidence of the master. (He took a prominent role in the attempt to reinstate Hilprecht at Penn after his resignation.) In the *Hilprecht Anniversary Volume* of 1909, Radau pioneered in publishing Sumerian literature. In 1911, with Hilprecht on his way out, Radau wrote *Sumerian Hymns and Prayers*, another early work that showed his skills.[44] Yet Radau had agitated on behalf of Hilprecht, and denounced his enemies all over Europe. After the professor left, Radau had no further access to the tablets, and gave up Sumerology.[45]

Stephen Langdon, the prolific English scholar whom Penn had tried to hire, spent some time at the museum during the 1910s. He did much Sumerian deciphering, the claims for which outstripped his achievements. Langdon approached the texts with fixed ideas of the relation of the Bible— the Creation, Adam and Eve, and the Flood—to Sumerian literature. He read into the latter what he thought might corroborate the former. Nonetheless, his 1915 *Sumerian Epic of Paradise, the Flood, and the Fall of Man* found its way into handbooks and encyclopedias used by students and scholars. These tablets were not authoritatively retranslated until thirty years later, at which time it was apparent that there was nothing about the Fall or the flood in them. The paradise described was a divine one and not the human one of Adam and Eve.[46]

Edward Chiera, who took his degree just after Hilprecht left, made a better start. Chiera, a copyist of extraordinary gifts, made some pathbreaking copies of the Sumerian literary tablets.[47] Born in Italy, he emigrated when his father became minister to the First Italian Protestant Church in Philadelphia. He went to Penn from Crozer Theological Seminary and, after receiving his degree, taught at Penn for fifteen years. Although some of Chiera's work was deficient by later standards, he studied Sumerian seriously but had little impact in the 1910s and 1920s. Changing direction, he made a reputation for himself with fieldwork. Hilprecht's greatest student, Arno Poebel, did his doctoral work on Sumerian texts, but then returned to his native Germany. Poebel combined his study of the Nippur tablets with a flair for Sumerian grammar. But in 1923 he had to publish at his own expense in Germany a book that only slowly was recognized as the cornerstone of the proper understanding of the language, *Grundzuge der sumerischen Grammatik*.[48]

For more than twenty years after the Peters-Hilprecht controversy, work on the Nippur Sumerian tablets stalled. Langdon's work was poor. Radau, Chiera, and Poebel, who were better Sumerologists, were overlooked.

In 1927, at the invitation of James Breasted, Chiera did fieldwork for the University of Chicago. He later headed the Assyrian Dictionary Project at the Oriental Institute, an important position that allowed him to return to the study of Sumerian. In 1930, Chiera brought Poebel to Chicago, but in the early 1930s there was still not much known about Sumerian literature in general or, in particular, its relation to Gilgamesh.

One dimension of the problem was that the Germans, especially those who had worked on the tablets, had had their work downgraded during World War I and its aftermath. Hilprecht had limitations as a mentor but had led in publishing the documents. The Peters-Hilprecht controversy ended his career and that of his young German protégé, Hugo Radau. A more interesting case was that of Hilprecht's archenemy, Jastrow. Jastrow was a Jew who identified with his German heritage. At the start of the war in 1914, he, like Hilprecht, publicly defended German ideals and claims. Jastrow changed his mind about international affairs when the war dragged on and the United States became involved, but his initial partiality for the Germans made many suspect him.[49] When he first attacked Langdon's *Sumerian Epic of Paradise*, Jastrow's political sympathies permitted some scholars to undervalue his critique.[50]

Chiera had taken his degree with Jastrow in 1913, after Hilprecht left, but maintained relations with Hilprecht. Hilprecht's brother-in-law at the Crozer Theological Seminary financed Chiera's examination of the Sumerian texts in Constantinople that the Turks had gotten in various divisions of the Nippur finds. The seminary publicized Chiera's work and printed his *Sumerian Religious Texts* the year before Hilprecht died.[51] But for nine years after he received his doctorate, Chiera stayed at Penn as an instructor, while other, lesser figures were promoted more quickly. For some of the work that Chiera and Poebel had done, Langdon took credit. In the heat of anti-German wartime sentiment, he appropriated their discoveries; his own efforts were inferior.[52]

In 1927, Chiera, who had been a full professor at Penn for only one year, went to Chicago. When he brought Poebel to the Dictionary Project three years later, Poebel's study of Sumerian grammar got more attention. Fifteen years after the war, Chiera assembled a staff unhurt by its German associations. Under the auspices of Breasted's institute, Hilprecht's students furthered the decipherment of Sumerian. The value of the library became evident.

Poebel initiated Samuel Noah Kramer, the leader of the new generation that would unlock the Sumerian texts. Kramer was an underemployed Assyriologist with a doctorate from Penn. In 1932 Chiera brought him to the Oriental Institute as a lowly assistant researcher, and Poebel trained Kramer in his techniques of decipherment. Diligent and intelligent, Kramer was blessed with an ability to synthesize. In a career that lasted more than sixty years, Kramer sat in the tablet rooms of the museums in London, Philadelphia, Constantinople, and—in the 1950s—in Jena; he was the first explorer of Hilprecht's tablets there.

Chicago rescued Sumerology from the low ebb it had reached during World War I. But the institution lost some of its preeminence through prejudice. It refused to promote Kramer because he was a Jew, and then it terminated his employment. Later, Penn appointed him Clark Research Professor, the successor (once removed) of Hilprecht.[53]

Kramer's breakthrough on the epic came in the late 1930s and early 1940s, when he published a series of separate Gilgamesh stories translated from the Sumerian. They included tales that in various forms were taken over into the Akkadian epic, but also narratives such as "The Death of Gilgamesh" that were not in the standard text. These Sumerian tablets, dating from the period 2000–1600 B.C., were presumed to be based on originals from 2100 B.C. or earlier.[54] Like Jastrow at the end of his career and like most students in the 1930s, Kramer was convinced that a Sumerian prototype of Gilgamesh existed.[55] After his investigations, however, Kramer argued that there was no epic in Sumerian. Rather, the successors of the Sumerians had taken Gilgamesh stories and other material from the Sumerian literary tradition and woven them together into the epic. Although the ur-stories were Sumerian, the Semitic peoples added creative elements and, in addition, the pointed interest in immortality. The early Semites furnished the theme that made the story of wide interest in the first millennium and in the twentieth century.[56]

Significant for its use of the Nippur tablets, Kramer's work nonetheless left larger questions about the Akkadian epic unanswered. Kramer could not explain why the standard edition had nonintegrated interpolations and an added chapter. In the second half of the twentieth century, the learned broached this issue with the aid of several significant tablet fragments. The two most important had been acquired from dealers by Penn and Yale at about the same time earlier in the century. The so-called Pennsylvania and Yale tablets gave a connected account of some earlier portions of the epic. These tablets were Old Babylonian, from about 2000–1600 B.C., and thus about a thousand years earlier than the standard version from Nineveh. In 1920, Jastrow and Clay published these fragments of an older version of the epic, and started the scholarly reconstruction of an Old Babylonian rendering of Gilgamesh.[57]

Although the Babylonian fragments contained portions of a Gilgamesh tale far older than the Nineveh one, the extant material from the earlier version was not extensive. There was nothing from tablets VI, XI, and XII of the standard version, and only pieces of tablets I to V and VII to X. Much later in the century, after Kramer's work on the Sumerian, a host of Assyriologists contributed to Jastrow's and Clay's initial study. From fragments, they concluded that an Old Babylonian edition of the epic had the first integrated story. It had no extraneous tablet XII and no flood story, and absent were part of the standard introduction and its repetition in tablet XI. One scholar who wrote about the epic concluded that this version had a single author, the scribe or editor who, at some time, created a connected tale from the separate Sumerian narratives.[58]

The development of the epic thus occurred in three stages. First, scribes wrote down in Sumerian the Gilgamesh material and stories that in all likelihood were part of an oral tradition. Second, the Babylonians created the epic from these tales. They probably wrote directly in the more accessible Semitic cuneiform (though in an early stage of the Akkadian language's evolution). Although the epic relied on Sumerian tales, this second stage required inventive genius. Differences in culture and language separated Babylonians and Sumerians. The making of Gilgamesh required more than editing.[59] For example, the main theme of the epic, the attempt to evade mortality, was basically unrepresented in any of the Sumerian stories.[60] Finally, at some later time, a conventional account of the story on twelve tablets, including an array of nonintegral parts, was formulated. The best examples of this account dated from Nineveh.

Agreement on the fragmentary Babylonian version as the first exemplar of the epic led to a curious set of priorities in modern editions of the epic. Scholars strained to give twentieth-century readers of English, Dutch, German, and French the best sense that Assyriologists had of the real epic. Unlike versions of Homer or Virgil, for which there were definitive texts in the original languages, any text of Gilgamesh was based on a great deal of speculation. Since all the existing material amounted to only half the epic, much speculation would occur in any event. But taking the Babylonian as the first true text was ironic. The earliest story designated as the epic was the most incomplete. Fuller narratives from the Sumerian stories and the Akkadian of the standard version had to supplement the Babylonian, but they were less trustworthy as exemplars of the epic.[61]

In making this material available to the modern reader, translators and synthesizers adopted a variety of strategies. Tablet XII might be dropped, or some of it integrated in a more appropriate place. The flood story might be made less anomalous in the context of the whole work. Dismissing the conclusions of the most erudite scholars, editors of a modern Gilgamesh epic might include the introduction and its repetition. Similarly, the Sumerian story "The Death of Gilgamesh" could be worked in. Some authors thought the division into twelve tablets was critical; others did not. Some

thought scholarly translations with breaks in the text and scrupulous attention to alternative renderings mandatory. Some tried to make a place for the
Akkadian stylistic conventions, for the twenty-five-hundred-year-old equivalent of meter, puns, or wordplay.[62] Some renditions tried rhymes, others
used blank verse, others liked prose. Many modern translators could not
read the original, and in some respects the "original" was itself a fanciful
document.

One must consider this industry against the background of the standard
version, which, by conventional wisdom, had an egregious addition. Why
did the Assyrian redactors or editors or authors add a twelfth tablet? Either
they thought it belonged, or they had different ideas from ours of what a
connected story looked like and, with such ideas in mind, added tablet XII,
because they thought it belonged.[63] These ancient scholars too were trying to
present to their readers the best edition of Gilgamesh. The two thousand
years between the first Gilgamesh stories and the final Semitic cuneiform
edition were not unlike the span that separated the latter edition and the
various twentieth-century texts. Is the difference between the Sumerian and
the later Akkadian any less than that between the Akkadian and the modern
European languages? Contemporary students had a task that did not differ
from that of the Assyrian scribes—or rather, these scribes engaged in the
same work as later students: establishing the best text of the epic.

Decipherment of Sumerian and Akkadian operated on two pairs of related
beliefs that juxtaposed the created and the found. First, the erudite accepted
imaginative construction, but also assumed that what was on the tablets
dictated constraint. Scholars were permitted to make inferential leaps and to
go beyond the evidence at hand, but they were also liable to be called to
account by other evidence or by new evidence. Driving this activity was the
growing group of Orientalists. Each one was eager for preferment and so
motivated to achieve a reputation, but each was kept on his honor by the
zeal with which his brethren would attack lapses. As one of them put it,
students of the ancient Near East were "an army of eager minds, each anxious to discover the mistakes of all the others, for only so can we hope to
reach secure results."[64] Here was a collection of self-interested individuals
whose interactions transformed their relationship. The clash of private interests produced a communal good.

Pervasive cultural norms affected the more ordinary workings of this
scholarly community. The general distrust of Germans and Jews, for example, curbed the selfish tendency of individuals to seek out error: Stephen
Langdon received perhaps less criticism than he otherwise would have because an attack on him inevitably meant a defense of Germans. At different times it was believed that German or Jewish scholarship could be

discounted. Suspicions about this scholarship were, unfortunately, an aspect of the evidence.

The other pair of beliefs implicitly joining the created and the found entailed two different criteria for ascertaining truth. On the one hand, scholars behaved as if truth was what the consensus of the competent said it was. The community of investigators at any given time defined the truth. There was, in fact, no higher authority than expert opinion, and to this extent the truth was created. The opening line of the epic was what Assyriologists told us it was.

At the same time, scholars acted as if the achievements of their own time had to be measured against a larger, transtemporal community. Academics saw a history of decipherment extending back to the mid–nineteenth century, and they extrapolated that history forward. More evidence and refinements of technique had brought (and would continue to bring) progress. An indefinitely large community of scholars converged on what was true— not a created truth but a found one. The actual evidence might not suffice for asserting the meaning of a document, or the actual translations might be wrong. Truth was not what the evidence told us now, but what must be meant by the writing. The opening line of the epic was what it was, irrespective of what the Assyriologists of a certain day said.

These two notions of truth, the one created, the other found, existed uneasily together. It is significant to note, however, that the latter was universal. The most authoritative study of the development of the Gilgamesh epic postulated that scholars were dealing with the minds of editors and writers, something determinant yet elusive.[65] The twentieth-century doyen of Sumerologists remarked that all his work assumed the principle of analogy: that minds across time were crucially alike and that their intentions could be recovered by the like-minded.[66] All the epigraphers assumed that a stable meaning was expressed in the tablets and could be recovered.

Even when scholars got it wrong, they did so within limits that intimated convergence on what was correct. Langdon did not translate his *Sumerian Epic of . . . the Fall* by writing "Sing Heavenly muse of Man's first disobedience and the fruit of that forbidden tree, whose mortal taste brought death into the world and all our woe." Langdon may have approached the Sumerian texts with inappropriate biblical ideas in mind, yet his examination of the tablets in the context of the ancient Semitic literature known at the time was reasonable. In what other context would it be rational to examine them? The whole structure of knowledge at any moment nudged ancient Near Eastern studies in the right direction.

Scholars, moreover, had to presume one right answer to questions like this. Even the scoundrel with the knife in the British Museum made his tablet conform to what he wanted it to say; it could not mean just anything. Certain symbols had certain meanings. If this Orientalist wanted or needed a different meaning than the wedge-shaped marks allowed, he had to change the marks. If you want to make words say something different from what they say, you must alter the words. The rules were inescapable: unless the texts had a determinate sense, even deception was pointless. Deception was predicated on a correct answer.[67]

9

ORIENTALISTS AND THEIR CIVILIZATIONS

ENSCONCED in the university system in the second decade of the century, American students of the ancient Near East pondered more earnestly the point of their enterprise. They had to justify the significance of their recondite field and to distinquish their goals from those of their competitors, especially the Germans. They had to connect their work to the Bible studies that had nurtured them and to assimilate the range of new evidence—translated documents and material remains—that empirically sustained their labors. The result was a series of histories of civilizations that, like decipherment, inventively advanced on what was given.

By the middle of the nineteenth century, the Germans had established history as a professorial field of inquiry.[1] It gave a European elite a more detailed picture of the human past that had gradually transformed itself into the nineteenth-century present. This past had been altered through a series of events that nineteenth-century intellectuals would recognize as akin to what produced change in their own time. Historians reconstructed this past—"what essentially happened," in the words of Leopold von Ranke. According to their self-image, historians relied on the scrupulous and impartial analysis of documentary evidence. Yet they were also self-consciously modern: past times resembled the present in certain structured ways. Change was dictated by the inherent traits of the particular "race" that historians were investigating: by social authority, competition for wealth, military struggle, and comparable variables. Concerns that educated Europeans would recognize as close to their own had motivated past populations. Scholars came to see the a priori necessity of understanding the past in terms that were legitimate for the present. The higher criticism underscored this principle.

Historians usually examined the beginnings of their own kind, such as the Anglo-Saxons or the Teutons. But scholars interested in the oldest cultures were involved in telling a grander tale about the rise of Europe itself. An important piece of this history was how the classical epoch transmitted its highest values to France, Britain, and Germany. A harder part of the story was to connect the Greco-Roman world to the Judeo-Christian one. The two could be seen as opposed, and the latter rose from soil that was not even European. The Jews had somehow developed monotheism out of a mix of preclassical cultural assets; they then passed on this precious heritage in a way that survived the paganism and naturalism of the Greeks and Romans. The latter contributed politics and culture, but not religion, to the contemporary West.

The West appeared to have risen from at least two incompatible social sources whose histories were disconnected. Moreover, in the early nineteenth century, evidence for Israelite life was based on one book, the Bible. Even European intellectuals might take the biblical narrative seriously. But scholars of the ancient Hebrews did not have a range of evidence to write a history of this people whose story, in any event, rapidly led back to legends about the origins of the human race. Material about other Near Eastern cultures was virtually nonexistent. As these cultures of the ancient Near East were recovered and reconstructed, scholars simultaneously attempted to present a more comprehensive account of the evolution of the present-day West. Americans who had imbibed German professorial ideals believed that the ancient Near East fit essentially into this account. Not surprisingly, as the Americans sorted out their differences from the Germans, Bible scholarship was at the heart of many narrative projects in the United States.

Julius Wellhausen and his followers had undercut the prima facie integrity of the Bible as a source. Wellhausen's research demonstrated that it was a composite text, written by different unknown authors with different purposes. Although Wellhausen was not directly associated with the rejection of Judeo-Christian belief, he did propound a novel history of the Hebrews; it controverted the Bible's view of Moses' monotheism and the progressive development of Judaism. According to Wellhausen, the Israelite story fell into three temporal eras. The period of Moses was first, although he was not clearly a monotheist. In the second period of the prophets, the religion became monotheistic and reached its highest development. In the third period a centralized, ritualized, legal religion replaced some of the genuine spirituality of the prophetic age. Whether or not Wellhausen thought the Judeo-Christian tradition was true, he questioned its depiction in the Bible and wrote a tale of fluctuations.

For evidence, Wellhausen relied on the literary biblical sources. In the years after he published, scholars challenged his understanding by widening the base of evidence in various ways; they drew on the religious practices of contemporary "primitive" tribes, on the literature of other ancient religions, and on archaeology in Palestine, Mesopotamia, and Egypt.[2]

Wellhausen's history attacked the special quality of the Israelite experience by deconstructing the biblical record and by positing change and even decline. Wellhausen did not offer much that was positive. The German pan-Babylonians, whom Delitzsch called to public attention in the *Babel und Bibel* controversy, were less negative. They proclaimed that a proto-Semitic Babylonian culture had generated the Hebrew religion. For a time some scholars even argued that the ancient Sumerians of southern Babylonia were

Semites, denying that their non-Semitic tongue was a language at all.[3] If Sumerian were a priestly Babylonian code, there was even more ground for seeing southern Mesopotamia as the home of an ur-Semitic race. Its culture had existed in Sumer and spread to the north and west, influencing not only the Egyptians but also the Israelites.

The chief pan-Babylonians were German, but their theorizing attracted some Americans. Using a variety of ancient Near Eastern literary documents, pan-Babylonians did not merely diminish the religion of the Israelites, as had Wellhausen, but placed it in a broader perspective. Americans like Morris Jastrow interested in comparative religion found this view meritorious. The study of ancient Mesopotamia was significant itself and not subservient to the Bible.

Jastrow, however, may not have appreciated an irony here. For some pan-Babylonians, Babylonia was the cradle of Israel, and Judeo-Christianity arose from these more ancient roots. For others, pan-Babylonianism had an anti-Semitic thrust. The primacy of Babylonia denigrated Israel's achievements. When Sumerian was fully recognized as an early non-Semitic language, pan-Babylonians could see, for early-twentieth-century German civilization, an "Aryan" ancestor that bypassed Hebrew influence.[4] These developments, however, were restricted to Germany, and in the United States Albert Clay at Yale crusaded against pan-Babylonianism.

Clay had left Penn for New Haven because of his disputes with Hilprecht; he and his wife thanked his benefactor, J. P. Morgan, "everyday of our lives . . . for the change."[5] Yet Hilprecht had made his imprint on Clay. At Yale he worked out a program of study similar in structure to that of Penn. Although his students were not as successful as Hilprecht's, Clay edited a series of Yale Babylonian publications. The students contributed, and he magisterially presided, just as Hilprecht had. Taking Hilprecht's methods to an extreme, Penn epigraphers were producing copies of texts duplicating even nonessential markings on the tablets. Clay returned the effort of publication to accuracy and essentials, carrying on the beautiful and exact copying that Hilprecht had begun.[6] Clay's organizational ability lifted him and Yale to the first ranks of American Assyriology.

Clay's religious commitments led him, like Hilprecht, to interpretive excess. Clay conceptualized ideas about the ancient East to attack both pan-Babyonianism and its implicit secularism. According to the pan-Babylonianism that Hilprecht had also disliked, the Babylonians and their ancient proto-Semitic culture had influenced the Hebrew people. For Clay there was instead an independent northern Semitic empire (now the home of the West Semites, the Amorites) in Syria. In the first campaign of a long war, Clay argued for his views in *Amurru, the Home of the Northern Semites: A Study Showing that the Religion and Culture of Israel Were Not of Babylonian*

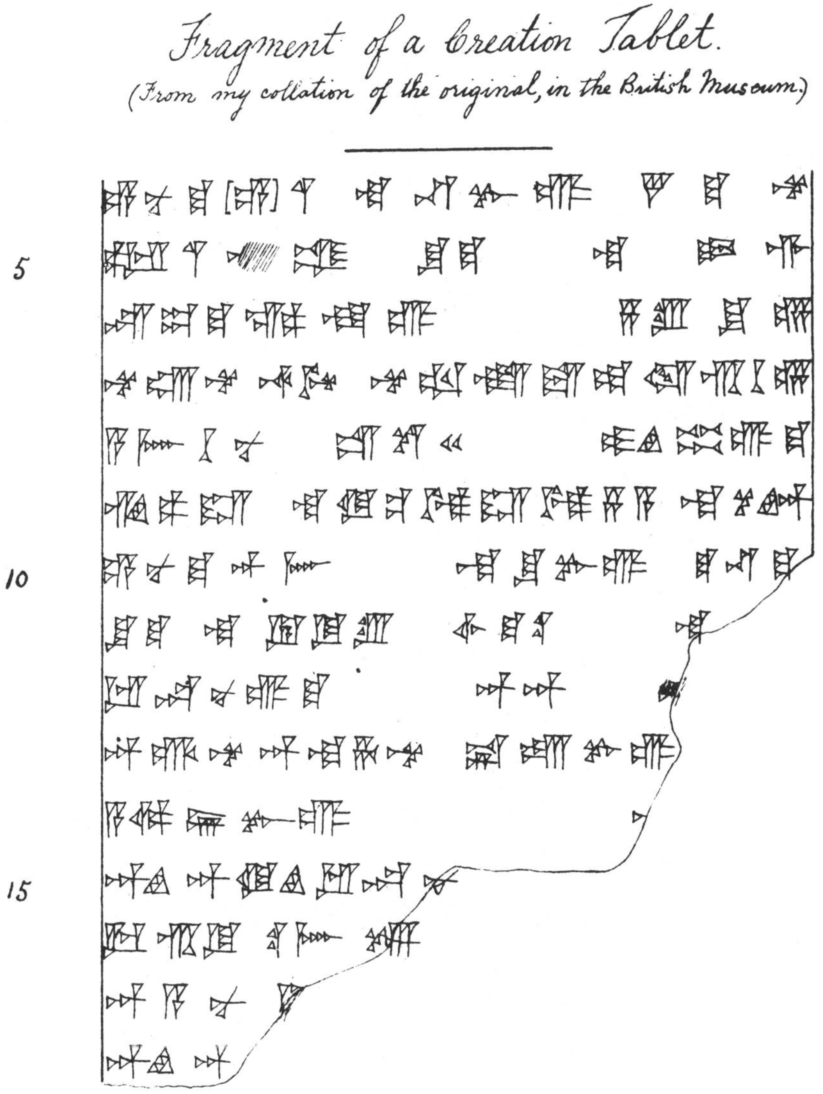

Fragment of a Creation Tablet.
(From my collation of the original, in the British Museum.)

Fig. 13 Styles of cuneiform transcription: Lyon.
This early simple style was designed for use by students.
The figures have been separated to make for easier reading.

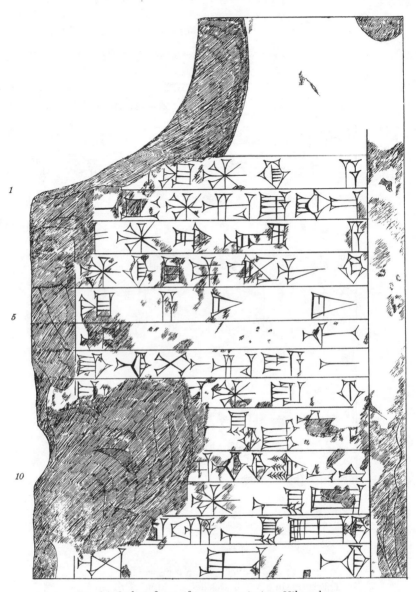

Fig. 14 Styles of cuneiform transcription: Hilprecht.
Hilprecht initiated an exact style that, although clear, reproduced the
distracting aspects of the tablet itself.

Reverse.

Col. IV. _Col. III._ _Col. II._ _Col. I._

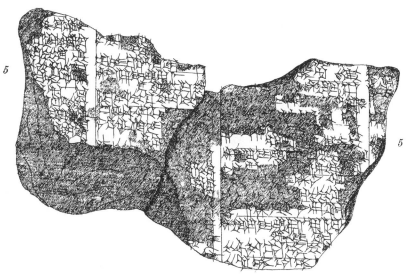

5

5

Obverse. _Reverse._

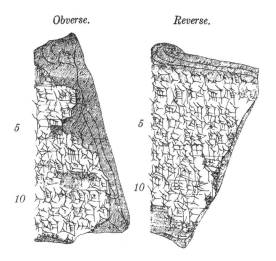

5 5

10 10

Fig. 15 Styles of cuneiform transcription: Radau.
Radau (and Arno Poebel) carried Hilprecht's techniques to an extreme.
The copy was beautiful but fussy.

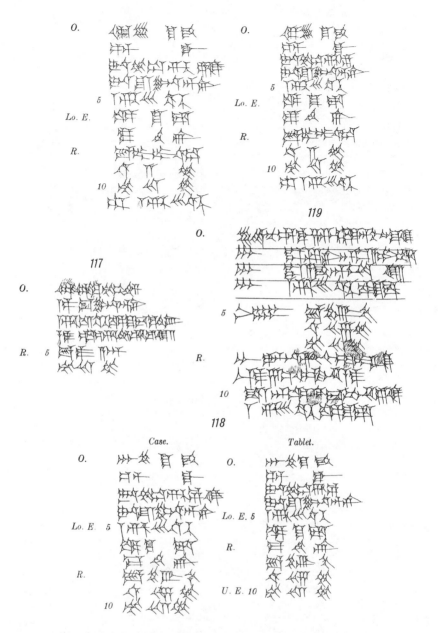

Fig. 16 Styles of cuneiform transcription: Clay.
In contrast to Hilprecht, Clay designed his transcriptions for easy readability.
Note that even lines indicating the edges of the tablets are missing.

Origin.[7] The Amorites possessed a Semitic culture that was common to both Mesopotamia and Israel. Hebrew-like religion and literature grew up there, separate from Babylonian influence. The Israelite tradition could not be derived from Mesopotamia.

Scholars tore into the "Amurru theory," especially because of Clay's religious partisanship. They treated his philological understanding derisively. Yet Clay spent the last fifteen years of his life, from 1910 to 1925, defending his ideas. His persistent, if unsuccessful, attempts to arrange an expedition focused on a search for the city of the Amorites. A sympathetic figure in his dispute with Hilprecht, Clay showed himself at Yale to be much like his mentor. His scholarly imbroglios became personal and nasty as Clay's peers rejected most of his assertions about the Amorites. At the same time Clay scored two triumphs. He presciently pointed to Syria as an area for exploration, where the French later excavated the Amorite city of Mari. Clay also destroyed the hold of pan-Babylonianism on American academics.[8] The interconnections of civilizations in the ancient East did not allow, his colleagues concurred, for the simple hegemony of the Babylonians.[9]

Slightly after Clay wrote, James Henry Breasted's *Ancient Times* carried forward the attack on pan-Babylonianism. But Breasted was a secular thinker, celebrated outside the academy. Early in the century Breasted made for himself an international reputation as an Egyptologist. Although he was renowned as an epigrapher, he appreciated archaeology and had, indeed, turned down an opportunity to collaborate with Sir Flinders Petrie.[10] Breasted sensed the complexities of the evidence and had a professional interest in moving the action away not just from the Babylonians but also from the Hebrews. He wanted, too, to take the story past the Israelites to the Greeks and Romans. In 1916 *Ancient Times* reached a far wider audience than had *Babel und Bibel* and *Amurru*, and it repudiated not only pan-Babylonianism but also a history centered on the Jews.[11]

Ancient Times introduced its readers most memorably to "the fertile crescent," the arc of culture that included Mesopotamia, Syria, and Palestine. Moreover, Breasted contended that civilization in the Near Orient had had a twin focus. Egypt and Mesopotamia passed on their heritage to the Greeks. Although they were superior, the Greeks did not begin ancient history but carried on a dual tradition from the East. From the Egypto-Babylonian culture, Breasted wrote, "we are able to push backward *up* the centuries and connect with the prehistoric stages which preceded civilization and developed into it." "[I]n the other direction we may follow *down* the centuries . . . to . . . Europe." This "vast cultural synthesis," said Breasted, embraced "the whole known career of man." The Near East of Egypt and Mesopotamia was "the keystone of the arch, with prehistoric man on one side and civilized Europe on the other."[12]

Breasted's achievement was to present this story of the youth of humanity in an accessible yet scientific style. He used the latest research and implied that expert wisdom supported him. *Ancient Times* examined cultures using standard categories of analysis and made comparative, systematic judgments. Breasted spoke about evidence and the way it warranted generalizations, satisfying readers that he was an impartial man of knowledge. Yet he showed that he knew what he was talking about without boring them or making the story incomprehensible. The narrative was sufficiently complicated to demonstrate the value of technical study in making advances over earlier, "unscientific" accounts. Yet Breasted wrote in a style that was popular, fluent, and intelligible enough to avoid the stigma that his work was useful only to "specialists and men of science."[13]

Later critics savaged Breasted because of the unilinear, evolutionary trajectory that led to a satisfaction with contemporary America as the bearer of the ideals of a smugly superior West. In addition to pervasively emphasizing men, he wrote that "the Great White Race was the fundamental carrier of civilization."[14] The book uncritically contemplated the positive nature of the victories of male human beings in western Europe but presumed that these victories were universal. Man "*has* raised himself by his own bootstraps," and the possibilities of "human advance" remained unlimited. Human betterment was cumulative. Technical aptitudes appeared: mathematical skills here, scientific attitude there. Social justice sprang up everywhere, and all flowed into a current that would become a flood. The line, in simplified form, went from Babylonia and Egypt to Greece and Rome to western Europe, and then the United States. "The rise of man," "the upward course of human civilization," and the "unconquerable buoyancy of the human soul" did not so much describe the process as drive it.[15] Later critics saw this vantage point as sexist, racist, and culturally imperialist.

One aspect of the critique of Breasted, however, received little attention. When his learned predecessors discovered the ancient Near East, they worried about the connection of the Near Orient to classical civilization and to Christianity. The pan-Babylonians, for example, puzzled about how to fit the Judeo-Christian world into a wider story that had its start in Mesopotamia, and Clay altered the story to put the Jews front and center again. For Breasted the Jews played a relatively minor role in the transitions that led to the modern world. A humane and flawless West replaced the idea of a Christian civilization as the end point of the civilizing process. Breasted had theological critics, too, who deplored the shift in twentieth-century thought about the deep past to "naturalistic" lines.[16] His elevation of the West must be seen in the context of a vision that dislodged Judeo-Christianity from a core role in the history of civilization.

Breasted's view became the conventional wisdom victorious in secondary schools and college classrooms. He deemphasized Western religion in a way different from that of pan-Babylonianism. His primary intellectual commitment was to Egypt, interest in which had always been secular, popular, and outside the collegiate setting. Appropriately enough, an Egyptologist with Breasted's ideas carried the day with educated Americans who were not necessarily scholars. Yet while Breasted was reworking later editions of *Ancient Times* at Chicago, a more academic and positive account of the role of Israel emerged. This account came from the pen of William Foxwell Albright, who became a hero to religiously inclined students.

Albright had an unusual career. Born to humble Protestant missionary parents in Chile at the end of the nineteenth century, Albright was handicapped by his extreme nearsightedness. His family returned to the United States in 1903, where his father ministered to one small Methodist church after another in the Midwest. There a farming accident maimed Albright's left hand, rendering it useless. In 1912 he was graduated from Upper Iowa University, and took a job as principal of a high school in the small German-speaking community of Menno, South Dakota. His physical limitations had led him to an occupation eminently suited to what such a Protestant family could expect of an intelligent and devoted son.

Then, however, Albright's life changed abruptly. He was not merely bookish and reclusive, but demonstrated great gifts, in particular a capacity for learning languages connected to his Bible upbringing. The *Orientalistische Literaturzeitung* accepted his essay on Akkadian while he was teaching in South Dakota. Albright had sent this essay to Paul Haupt and applied for admission to the Johns Hopkins program. On the strength of the article Haupt secured a University Fellowship in Semitics for Albright.[17]

Three years later Albright received his Ph.D. under Haupt and began an extraordinary life's work. His writing, like Haupt's, always displayed a sure sense of critical issues. His dissertation, "The Assyrian Deluge Epic," focused on that part of the Gilgamesh epic that dealt with Noah's Flood.[18]

Despite his seeming introversion, Albright had a sincerity and tact in dealing with others that early on made him a favorite among Orientalists. At the same time he was not afraid to state his own views forcefully. In his early and losing fight with Hilprecht to get Johns Hopkins into Near Eastern exploration, Haupt had shown an interest in excavation. Yet after his defeat, his work was in the higher critical, literary tradition. Albright was more of an archaeologist, and his reformed Christian affirmation deepened his differences with Haupt. Yet he treated Haupt with respect without being servile or hypocritical, and Haupt admired Albright's abilities without approving of his substantive outlook.[19]

Albright was employed as a research fellow after receiving his doctorate and then went to ASOR in Jerusalem in 1919, becoming acting director in

1920–21 and director the following year. In his first year in Palestine he mediated arguments between Albert Clay and John Peters.[20] His letter of introduction to Clarence Fisher came from Breasted himself.[21]

Albright studied Palestine's ancient history, archaeology, and topography. Fisher trained everyone in Palestine in the 1920s, and Albright learned digging techniques from him. Albright supplemented them by examination of pottery and soon helped Fisher with the ceramics. Although Albright did not circumvent Fisher's horizontal orientation, Albright's investigation of pottery forced him to look more at layers of debris.[22] Fisher and Albright founded Palestinian archaeology as a distinct field. Albright's excavations set the standard, and he was foremost among the field-workers in conceptualizing a universal system of dates. His research combined literary analysis with archaeological methods using Fisher-Reisner excavating and ceramic-dating methods. His *Archaeology of Palestine and the Bible* (1932) took its place next to Edward Robinson's *Biblical Researches*. Albright would eventually be looked on as the definer of the field of biblical archaeology. For a time, however, his work and his intelligence threatened to make the study of Egypt and Mesopotamia orbit around that of the Holy Land. In his influential view, Palestine was both geographically and intellectually central to the ancient Near East.[23]

In the middle of his excavating career in 1929, Albright accepted Haupt's chair at Johns Hopkins, which had been vacant in Baltimore since the latter's death in 1926. He held the position until he retired in 1958. The successive tenures of Haupt and Albright at Johns Hopkins from the 1880s to the 1950s made Baltimore a key institution in the field. Albright's relationship with ASOR also ensured Johns Hopkins a reputation in archaeology even though the school did not have that essential adjunct to fieldwork, a museum.

Albright was not shy about pressing his own ideas. When he accepted the Baltimore position, he told Johns Hopkins's president that he would reorganize the school's doctoral training. It would move away from philology "to literature, religion, civilization—in short to history and archaeology." The "Oriental Seminary" must not fail to "attach due importance to the study and teaching of the Bible."[24] In the seminary he had, during his tenure, seventy-five advanced students who worked closely with him over the years. Fifty-seven received their doctorates, twenty-three on the Bible. They were called "the Baltimore School." One admiring pupil from a divinity school put it well: Johns Hopkins "seemed like a continuation of what we had already experienced, namely a strong Christian cultural bias, and an essentially apologetic approach to the subject of religion, especially Biblical religion in (or against) its environment; nevertheless the basis and the method were different." Yet even these students complained that toward the end of his career Albright became theologically dogmatic. He developed an embattled sense of the place of the Christian scholar in American culture.[25]

The American academy became secularized in the twentieth century, but secularization had an idiosyncratic, stutter-step, and crypto-dialectical character. Generalizations about secularization must be complex, as the case of Johns Hopkins shows. Albright is the exception who proves—in the sense of *tests*—the rule.

Albright's sectarian beliefs had always made him suspicious of Wellhausen, and his interest in nonliterary data left him open to pan-Babylonianism during his student days. But he realized that a concern for all the evidence need not lead to pan-Babylonianism. Excavating convinced him that using all the facts available would tell a different story.[26] His results were most significantly reported in *From the Stone Age to Christianity: Monotheism and the Historical Process* (1940), and the more specific review of the archaeological material pertaining to the history of Israel's religion, *Archaeology and the Religion of Israel* (1942).[27]

Albright argued that the religious systems of the ancient East emphasized the continuity of deity, nature, and humankind, and the need for harmony among them. But, he said, Israel did not fit this paradigm. Its system was dissimilar and untouched by Babylonian preconceptions. Pan-Babylonianism could not be correct. From the start, the dominant tenet of Hebrew thought was the absolute transcendence of God. There were monotheistic tendencies at work all over the ancient world, but they were partial or ineffectual. Moses created a new, superior religion through a creative insight. He represented an "abrupt break" and an "evolutionary mutation."[28] Archaeological evidence proved that the Wellhausen narrative of gradual growth and decline was wrong. The sources showed the biblical narrative to be historically accurate. The development was complex, but monotheism was there from the start, and there had been no decay. Moreover, the comparative data pointed to the uniqueness of Judaism. It had a special character unequaled as a "phenomenon of historical order."[29]

One critic wrote that Albright's archaeological approach typified the cheerful faith of American academics in empiricism and statistics.[30] And it is true that Albright self-consciously described himself as "positivist" in his method and adopted the logical empiricist view of science prominent in the 1940s and 1950s.

According to this view, archaeological history should explain matters in the way that the natural sciences presumably did. The investigator devised "midlevel theories," hypotheses that had the character of laws—relating supposed cause to supposed effect. If an ancient culture developed in a particular way, strata would appear thus. The archaeologist drew inferences from these hypotheses and tested them with relevant new information. This information consisted of the network of spatiotemporal facts that the archaeologist unearthed. If strata were thus, then we would find certain material remains and not others. The archaeologist uncovered the facts that confirmed or disconfirmed a putative law. If the facts corroborated the inferences drawn from a hypothesis, it was verified and might eventually reach the status of a warranted generalization, or even a law. If the data did not bear out the hypothesis, researchers looked for novel causal links. Investigators had to conjure up other hypotheses to account for the facts and subject the new hypotheses to further empirical verification. Archaeologists played off previously known facts, carefully improvised theories, and newly discovered facts, to create a science of humankind and an objective, realistic account of the early history of humanity.

Archaeologists constructed a true story from their facts rather than a false one by establishing such warranted hypotheses. The true story was composed of them. Scientific scholars distinguished their stories from others by planning ways in which supposed laws could predict the existence of new facts. True stories did not merely account for the already discovered material but could also find a place for material that turned up later. Despite his religiosity, Albright anticipated the "new archeology" of the 1960s: under the influence of scientific anthropology, the "new archaeologists" were to push conservative peers away from their old-fashioned fact gathering and impressionistic storytelling. But Albright's rhetorical emphasis on positivist science had a twist: he was not interested in hard social science as an end in itself, but as a tool to go beyond the limits of normal empirical understanding.

For Albright, the positivistic method of ascertaining truth produced a complicated story. But scientific objectivity was compatible with narratives that embodied values, as the history of the Hebrew people illustrated. There was progress in Judaism and in civilization, but it never took place in a simple fashion. Advance occurred indirectly through crises, and even progressive cultures might fall into decline. Although Albright saw upward directionality, it always had a tragic and ambiguous aspect.[31]

Albright designed his remarks on these issues for popular audiences and was short on argument. As he grew older, even his academic performances neglected elaborate statements, and he expounded his position through a series of ex cathedra utterances.[32] One sympathetic student said that even *From the Stone Age to Christianity* was "almost entirely programmatic in character."[33]

Yet the heart of Albright's ruminations was clear. Secularists—Breasted was one of his favorite examples—were not simply wrong in their attitude to human life. There was, after all, much in Albright's position that would justify a benign account of the history of civilizations. Rather, Breasted and his ilk did not look soberly at the religious dimension of various social orders over the long term. For secularists religion was infantile, a product of the childhood of the race. Science would replace it as the species matured. Breasted and his disciples easily assumed that a new, rational core would supplant the sense of the divine. In Albright's opinion, this view was facile and shallow. History and archaeology showed religion to be vital to all cultures. No known past culture of any kind had existed without religion, and Albright said that no experienced archaeologist expected to find one. The notion that the religious nucleus would give way over time to a more enlightened scientific one simply ignored the facts: civilization after civilization was built on religion and toppled when the spiritual sense degenerated. The secularists did not investigate with any depth how belief in the holy worked in culture.

They also did not, as they claimed, exorcise the teleology they said religion illicitly imposed on nature. Although Breasted's vision represented a dramatic and hard-won conceptual shift, science functioned theologically for Breasted. And he endowed human culture, under science, with a progressive, purposeful ethos. If secularists took the enduring character of religion in history seriously, they might wonder why the holy was critical and impossible to replace. Perhaps, reflected Albright, they would then begin to see it as intrinsic to the unfolding of human life and try to figure out how it might be understood as true.[34] Albright believed that he was just as scientific as his opponents. Science, nonetheless, was only a tool for him. He reserved the sacred values for religion.

One need not defend the ideas of men like Breasted (and John Dewey) to see the weaknesses in Albright's own vision. Albright really presupposed the veracity of Scripture. He privileged a text that all of modern scholarship argued had to be treated as skeptically as any other document. The archaeological data actually served only to verify what Albright believed in the first place. For Albright, God's revelation to humans depended in part on historical truths found in the Bible. Archaeology had its place in enriching and sustaining the narrative of the book. Albright based his beliefs on Christianity and postulated that other religious impulses would lead to monotheism. He *had* to find in the evidence a way to discredit the religion of science and to preserve traditional faith.

Indicating the way scholarship served religion in Albright's worldview, however, does not prove him wrong. If Albright's ideas were correct, we could expect to demonstrate them in more or less the way he suggested. Yet even if one accepted the whole of Albright's program, the conceptual gap underscored by the higher criticism remained. The complete vindication of Old Testament history would not in itself tell us anything about the truth of Judaism, Christianity, or reformed Protestantism. It is easy to see what Albright was driving at in his argument, but also where the weak point was. Dismissing the secularist's version of the role of religion in history undermined an ultimate and exclusive reliance on science. Our best scientific efforts pointed to the Bible as a basically accurate history and to Israel as unusual in its milieu. Albright wanted his auditors to infer that the historical truth of the Bible made Judeo-Christianity more plausible. But history, said the higher criticism, revealed only human, natural truth. Nothing the Bible told us about the development of old-time beliefs could confirm their supernatural purport. Albright could not go from the human story to that of God. The use of archaeology in Bible studies may have undermined the substantive conclusions about ancient history that scholars like Wellhausen expounded. Yet the new reading of the Bible did nothing to compromise the higher criticism, which ruled out the supernatural in history.

At this stage in his argument Albright's organismic philosophy of history found its place. Again, on this issue, although Albright did not write systematically, he was perhaps the most thoughtful scholar in ancient Near Eastern studies. In many branches of the humanities, secular thought was the norm. It was de rigueur to assume that religion was not a variable in one's outlook. Breasted exuded a complacency about the modern world, and his followers did not examine the tension between the eternal and the practical. On the other side, Oriental studies provided a core area in the academy in which the religiously inclined could lodge undisturbed. Faithful scholars neither defended their faith nor attacked its enemies. Neither the secular nor the religious was much of an object of professional controversy, especially as the accumulation of facts became the most prominent goal of scholars. Albright was different. He boldly excoriated the premises of colleagues like Breasted and also proclaimed his own faith and sought to make it defensible.

In addition to recovering the ancient Near East, the late nineteenth century and the twentieth century had unearthed early civilizations in India, Asia, and Latin America. Some of this investigation yielded ammunition for the internecine disputes of Orientalists over which Near Eastern culture was most important. But these formulations were minor compared to the syntheses generated by scholars who wanted to write a world history that would encompass all peoples.[35] Writers such as Christopher Dawson in *Progress and Religion* (1929), Karl Jaspers in *The Origin and Goal of History* (1949), and Eric Voegelin in *Order and History* (1952–75) worked in a newly created genre of historical writing. With all cultures as its area of inquiry, this genre aimed to tell a universal story.[36] These scholars asked what made civilizations rise. Why were they distinctive? How were they connected? Need they all have collapsed?

Critics have attacked the authors of this genre for importing into their writings a progressivism usually associated with Judeo-Christianity. Breasted avoided a commitment to the supernatural but gave scientific humankind a sort of religious telos. This presumption also characterized the least expansive synthesizers, such as Breasted, H. G. Wells in *The Outline of History* (1920), and William Hardy McNeill in *The Rise of the West* (1959).[37]

But the most spectacular efforts, such as Oswald Spengler's *Decline of the West* (1918) and Arnold Toynbee's *Study of History* (1934–61),[38] had more-powerful premises. These authors found in a grand master narrative the supernatural quality that was not there when events were examined piecemeal. Rather than smuggling a divine element into the struggles of humanity, Spengler and Toynbee contended that these struggles led us to an understanding of the supernatural. Albright turned to Toynbee when he expatiated on his organismic philosophy of history.

Toynbee argued that in the course of recorded history twenty-one civilizations had risen and fallen or would fall, according to a logic akin to what brought about birth and death in nature. Civilizations grew and decayed in four stages; they took root, bloomed, withered, and died. For Toynbee, religion was at the crux of the careers of civilizations, and the death agonies of successive civilizations left humankind at a higher level of spiritual consciousness. New civilizations were formed on the basis of this novel consciousness. Cultures rose and fell in cycles—episodes in the march of religion. But each cataclysm resulted in the progress of the soul from animism to pagan humanism to monotheism. Toynbee used the analogy of a wheel, which went around and around in a circular motion yet propelled a cart forward.[39] When he came to the present, Toynbee merged the bleak with the optimistic. Christianity produced Western civilization for him, and as the former receded, the West must go irreversibly downhill. Yet a new culture would grow up on the death of the old, with a concomitant higher awareness of the life of the spirit.

Albright objected to the anti-Christian dimension of Toynbee's ideas. Toynbee seemed to say that Christianity too would be surpassed, that it was only a chapter in the realization of the most enlightened religious affirmation.[40] But Albright perhaps saw Toynbee as less of a Christian thinker than he was. While surely heterodox, Toynbee was not a secularist, and even those close to Albright found him inordinately conservative and defensive during the period he was criticizing Toynbee.

What Toynbee did propose was clear. Although his critics rightly accused him of many factual errors, he was determined to get his story right and mired himself in historical detail and facticity. From the density of the data, the meaning of history appeared—the progressive fruition of the divine in time. If we had *all* the facts, their meaning would arise in an undeniable way that we could not conceive of when we operated from a more limited, fact-deprived perspective. The quantity of factual material would change the quality of our insight into events.

Even if Toynbee's Christianity was just a phase of the progressive development of divine ideas, Albright identified with reasoning like that of Toynbee. The spine of history was a restless spirit. It displayed ambiguity, interminable and only partial victories against the forces of darkness, a suspicion of meliorism, and a combination of humility and assurance. Only synthetic, organismic historical work would depict this spirit.

Albright made this point at the end of *From the Stone Age to Christianity*. "We have endeavored," he said, "to make the facts speak for themselves," though it might be difficult for the reader to "follow the unfolding scale of history." His treatment had "a double strand":

> First, the ascending curve of human evolution, a curve which now rises, now falls, now moves in cycles, and now oscillates, but which has always *hitherto* recovered itself and continued to ascend; second, the development of individual historical patterns or configurations, each with its own organismic life, which rises, reaches a climax, and declines. The picture as a whole warrants the most sanguine faith in God and in his purpose for man. . . . Every human culture has risen and fallen in its turn; every human pattern has faded out after its brief season of success. It is only when the historian compares successive configurations of society that the fact of real progress makes itself apparent.[41]

Albright's critique of Toynbee had a real sticking point, however. Albright dismissed the purveyors of comparative religion, important in liberal American religious circles. Nor would he truck with the even more fashionable "cultural relativists," significant in wider American intellectual circles. For him as for Breasted, some cultures were better than others, and some religions more adequate in understanding the eternal. With Breasted he held that the Near East was the crucible of world civilization, and Christianity its religious precipitate. Christianity was thus not to be understood in terms of world religions; they had to be understood in terms of it.[42]

Toynbee held out the possibility that something might transcend Christianity, but Albright assumed that nothing could. The evolution of Western civilization from the time of Christ might in some ways evidence decline, but concluding that something better would replace the Judeo-Christian tradition was inappropriate. Progress and its opposite were each riven with ambiguity. Even if one believed with Toynbee that religious insight progressed, one did not have to believe that Christianity would be surpassed. If time was bounded, if it came to an end, some religious insight had to prevail.

Although Albright did not spend much time clarifying these matters for his audiences, he did praise Eric Voegelin's *Order and History* as an alternative to Toynbee. Voegelin disputed the cyclical theories of history that he presumed Toynbee illustrated and, indeed, traced them back to the pre-Christian worldviews of the ancient Near East. Coming out of the ancient East, Israel introduced a new idea into humankind's cogitations on time. For Voegelin, Judaism saw history as the progressive realization of a certain kind of spiritual ideal.[43] Rather than the more-or-less cyclical view associated with Toynbee, Albright articulated an idea of historical development more in line with traditional Christianity, more reflective, that is, of what he presumed to be the actuality of historical experience.

Albright believed that human beings had to think in historical terms and that their history was of the nature of stories, of narrative. Stories had a *point*, and no one could think that history did not have a point. If all intelligent life were destroyed today forever, if history were to end, its end would probably be conceived as the conclusion to a failed project, but its end could not *not* be conceived. Stories implied a storyteller who stood outside the story and for whom the story had some meaning or other. Historians were, of course, human storytellers, but even supposing the business of writing history to be over entailed that a consciousness grasped that it was over. For Albright historicity was not just a mandatory category of human understanding but also implied a greater than human consciousness. It was nonrational for the secularist to allow that we thought historically yet to urge that the religiosity entailed by such thinking was illusory. What we had instead was a puzzle or, better, a mystery of some large significance.

The human story had to have a directionality grasped by consciousness. But how this occurred was beyond our ability to comprehend. Our reasoning powers were not the shipwreck of understanding, but human brains simply got lost when they tried to press any farther. This incomprehensibility was the indecipherable will of God in history that Albright would ask us ultimately to take on faith. For the faithful, redemptive religion was the *how* of the way stories related to the end, the aim, or the finish of history.

Albright urged that an appropriate philosophy of history could bridge the logical gap central to the secularism of the higher criticism. He hoped to convince his audiences that the whole of history would convey the supernatural dimension of the human story in a way that it could not when historians built more limited narratives. The factual compactness and scientific generalizations for which archaeology strove would enable the learned to leap over the chasm that the higher criticism had created. The whole of human history was greater than the sum of its parts.

Toynbee had a brief moment as a hero to educated Americans, while Albright (and Voegelin) influenced a comparatively small group of serious and religiously minded people. Breasted made his impact on a more superficial and wider group, the authors of textbooks and their students. He wrote *Ancient Times* for secondary schools, but it became a model for books in an even more important market, the college text in the course in Western civilization.

The textbook on the rise of the West embodied what one historian called a "cultural-historical archaeology." It had blossomed with the combination of evidence from epigraphy and excavation typical of the work of Petrie, Breasted, and Albright.[44] One emphasis was on identifying strata by ceramic analysis. The separation of strata based on different pottery types indicated successive episodes of abrupt change. The literary material, left mainly by rulers about their victories, verified the archaeology. The history of the ancient world displayed a sequence of violent, historically recorded (or archaeologically inferred) racial or ethnic conquests. The evidence recorded the diffusion and triumphs of vigorous groups. Such a history cohered with the lived experiences of Europeans from 1815 to 1945 and the historical writing on the earlier rise of the European state system. Moreover, it made credible why the European and American explorers in the twentieth century should find themselves with so much power in the ruins of the Middle East.

The focus on the Bible had a final, reinforcing effect. Although other interests were represented, study of the Old Testament guided the choice of places to excavate in the Near East. In the Near East the tools of biblical and classical archaeology—stratigraphy and pottery analysis—were not seriously used on remains later than the end of the Crusades. The "Late Arab" or "Turkish" period remained unexplored. The impression of desolation or decline in this period was stressed, furthering the notion of the unmitigated "rise" of the West.[45]

In 1911, Petrie had written *The Revolutions of Civilization*, a short book on these topics, of which he was inordinately proud. For Petrie, civilization had begun appropriately enough in Egypt and marched to Crete, Greece and Rome, and medieval Europe. Regular thousand-year periods of growth, conquest, and decay recurred. Although Petrie was not a fatalist as were his more adventurous kin, Spengler and Toynbee, he did fear Anglo-Saxon decline in the present. To avoid it, he relied on his understanding of the engine of change: a racial struggle in which hardier, more intelligent groups won out. Petrie consequently wrote that eugenics, voluntary sterilization, limitation of birth, and the like should be practiced in order to maintain his (English) civilization at its peak.[46]

More important than Petrie's peculiar racism was the way his premises typified those of all writers trying to grasp in empirical terms the rise and fall of cultures. More recent scholars have noted that the concentration on "catastrophism" as the motivating force of change ruled out gradualist ideas such as continuity and adaptation.

Overall, the poverty of data and the historically located imagination of scholars produced narratives of civilization that commentators could easily criticize as one-sided or prejudiced. As the sensibilities of academics shifted, or as they thought anew at a later time on the evidence, the sweeping stories altered too. Later in the century, images of invading hordes, flashing swords, and burning cities gave way to descriptions of economic reorganization, ecological change, and social tension. Recent scholars rendered interpretations of the material that were more abstract but less easy to visualize.[47]

Influenced at the end of the twentieth century by feminism, historians saw the slow growth of settled agriculture—a precondition of civilization—as exemplifying the rule of men over women. Culture was hierarchical, and women *became* unequal, and more domesticated as they had more children.[48] In *Black Athena* Martin Bernal relocated the rise of the West away from a European-oriented Greece to a Greece dependent on an Egypt (and Phoenicia) connected to black Africa.[49]

Textbooks in the more conservative tradition of Breasted tried to keep up, but it was hard. In the twentieth century, the complexity of the politics of the Near East and competing academic factions involved in the selection of textbooks complicated matters. Added to the dilemmas of scholarly synthesizers were the greater complexity of the evidence and the loss of the exemplar that Breasted had provided. Faced with complications, authors responded with eclecticism. The ancient world now had *more* marauding civilizations, but politicocultural progress was less clear. Authors stressed the role of women and the lives of individual women, and political themes gave way to fuller sketches of ancient social orders, family life, and religious practices. At the same time, writers fudged the origin of theological truth, although the significant place given to the Israelite people hinted that they were, at least for some of us, still special.[50]

Albright's hope that the scientific use of more facts would enable the truth of Christianity to appear was not fulfilled. Much of the general nonspecialist work of the Orientalist could be subject to the criticism that it mirrored present cultural assumptions as much as the learned grasp of objective knowledge. Indeed, the discoveries of specialists over time confirmed this criticism. Every archaeological achievement briefly promised to transform our understanding, usually of the Bible. Woolley of Ur early exemplified this process with the claims that he made for the Flood and the city of Abraham.[51] Later explorers, for example those at Nuzi, Ugarit, Mari, Jericho, and Ebla, made similar claims. Yet after the first thrill of discovery passed, it was found that new assemblages of data ultimately produced not knowledge but ever-altering interpretive stances.[52]

In general, the historiography of the history of civilizations gave some ammunition to relativists. There were no true histories; there was rather a changing series of frameworks that enclosed a more or less arbitrary selection of the facts and that displayed the cultural outlook of contemporary authors. The histories were as much about the present as about the past.

CONCLUSION

T HIS HISTORY of ancient Near Eastern studies in the United States has focused on the early expeditions to Babylonia, the growth of the university system, and the secularization of knowledge. The history has covered what I would call the formative period, from the last decades of the nineteenth century through the first decades of the twentieth, although I have skirmished with certain topics that fall outside this time. In the formative period, universities built a variety of fields in which scholars would study the ancient Near East. The complex administrative units in which Near Orientalists worked came into being. They inhabited oddly structured departments, or had eccentric relations with less odd departments in the university, or had awkward connections with college-affiliated museums. Ancient Near Eastern scholars at museums with no university ties or at schools of divinity might orbit intellectually around the university.

The structural features that defined the learned life of Orientalists appeared. A handful of schools struggled for preferment. Scholars vied to establish the primacy of a specific geographic area within the ancient Near East. The tension between field archaeology and epigraphy continued. The bureaucratically better-organized discipline of anthropology persistently pushed to transform what was perceived as the retrograde discipline of archaeology.

The problems that shaped the American ancient Near East also came into clear light. One paradigm for work was the decipherment of the documents and the reconstruction of the cultures that produced them. This paradigm uneasily coexisted with the similar goals that field workers hoped to obtain. Following Assyriology and Egyptology (as the study of languages), archaeology developed into an arcane specialty. The Bible as a fulcrum of study and as a bearer of truth only slowly gave way to less religiously oriented modes of inquiry. Gifted synthesizers continuously tried to make sense of the whole of the known past.

The ancient Near East in the United States was also *American*. The Americans intially modeled themselves on the Germans, as their penchant for German scholars and scholars trained in Germany revealed. But the personalities of the Germans and international political hostility ensured that this modeling was incomplete. More significantly, the role of the state in German higher education was more important than it was in the United States, as was the German reverence for hierarchy. The competition among private institutions in the United States blunted any national arrangements between scholars and the government, as the failures of Paul Haupt's various schemes testified, and Americans never realized the high goal of contemptuous expertise that Hermann Hilprecht set for them.[1]

In consequence, the organization of the field fell between what existed i Great Britain, where a few institutions promoted what were regarded as brilliant amateurs, and the system that produced German *Doktors*. The structure of the American ancient Near East was more pluralistic than its German counterpart. The structure was also more democratic. Although no one would deny the arcane nature of the studies, archaeological museum culture reached out beyond the academy. In addition, Bible scholars and Egyptologists, each group with effectively antithetical agendas, sought wide audiences.

The flavor of the academic field was more conventionally religious than that of its German and English peers. This condition reflected the long Protestant tradition in American higher education. At the same time, the Egyptian component of the ancient Near East furthered a popular religious comparativism.

It is more difficult to ascertain the influence of national boundaries on the substance of scholarship. In archaeology the United States copied the digging techniques of both the English and the Germans. As a result, American methods were perhaps more eclectic than those of other Western countries. Different techniques preserved and uncovered different information. But it is not possible to conclude that styles of excavation mandated different construals of the evidence. On the other side, the unique possession of documents almost exclusively dictated epigraphical advances. This underscored the international character of knowledge. National rivalries over exploration made sense only because scholars recognized that any nation could contribute to learning once it had secured the appropriate material.

Two connected themes have organized my stories of the digs, the disciplines, and the evolution of intellectual principles. The first is the connection of the Judeo-Christian framework to the suppositions of reasoning that, for Americans, came to clear consciousness in the ancient Near Eastern field. The second is the moral and epistemological dimension of the substance and organization of the knowledge in the field.

At the end of the nineteenth century a revolution occurred in the way reflective Americans comprehended the world. Instead of being an assumption of knowledge, Protestant theism became subject to study and analysis. This revolution was widespread. Theology virtually vanished as a discipline, ultimately to be replaced by religious studies. Philosophy ceased to anchor religion, and eventually philosophical techniques undercut earlier creeds. Historians and social scientists distanced themselves from the supernatural and reduced the sacred to political, economic, or psychic variables.

This phenomenon was surely not confined to the United States. Although matters other than Protestant theism were often at issue, the impulses one sees, typically, in John Dewey can also be found in Sir James Frazer, Max Weber, Sigmund Freud, and Emile Durkheim. The transition was not easily made. Many ostensibly secular scholars imbued some dimension of their nonreligious beliefs with a holy quality. Some, for example, gave the humanities or the scientific method an eternal value that had previously been more openly attached to religion. Numerous intellectuals had a thin surrogate for dogma, an unimpressive moralism puffed up with a vague spirituality. This tepid faith, indeed, was related to the explicit theologies of many religious liberals who also found the confrontation with modernism uncomfortable.

This appraisal is unsympathetic. These people forsook deep and important beliefs. Psychologically, they could be expected to find some sort of substitute, to rest for a while at a halfway house. We should give them the benefit of the doubt and realize that calling *providence* by the name *progress* represented an enormous conceptual shift. Early secularizers forswore the faiths of their fathers not only because of fashion, thoughtlessness, or peer pressure, but also because they no longer found gospel tenets credible.

In uncovering ancient life, scholars of the Near East contributed to this altered vision of the world. Many of them exuded a sense of the cosmos that was uncongenial to religion. Central to archaeological reasoning was the determination of the relation of objects in space and time. These objects became the crucial reality. Even in Bible studies the principles of the higher criticism were unavoidable. Academics conceded that acceptable explanations of the past must conform to what would pass muster in the present, and so accentuated the concern for the spatiotemporal. The dominance of this kind of thinking among twentieth-century intellectuals is a criterion of secularization. Archaeological thinking concentrated on what happened in the physical world; the thinking was *worldly*.

Such a world may be compatible with Scripture. It may simply be that the particular religious beliefs that crumbled in the nineteenth and twentieth centuries as ancient Near Eastern studies developed were restricted or provincial. It is still true that many of the intellectuals who imbibed, adhered to, or advanced Orientalist ideas relinquished a robust, Protestant, Bible-oriented theism, or relegated it to a minor place in their lives. Over succeeding generations, intellectuals gave up the clerical profession for the academic one.

The principles of the higher criticism and of archaeological reasoning fit into a complicated reordering of the worldview of the twentieth-century thinker. Their independent significance is debatable, and so is the role of academic students of the ancient Near East. But, along with Darwin's theories, the principles were crucial in this great transformation. Primarily at stake in natural selection was a substantive view about the origins of life. The new principles of reasoning put the morality of believers on the line, in contrast to that of historians (or scholars). The duty of scholars was to establish the grounds of beliefs not on what was wished for or hoped for, not on what had been learned from various authorities, but on what could be determined as true. The will to truth became primary.[2]

The academics who studied the ancient Near East may have been idiosyncratic in that they harbored in their midst an abnormally large group of practitioners who in some manner or other maintained doctrinal orthodoxy. But the secular inroads that were made even in the study of the Holy Lands—the sancta sanctorum of American religions—evidenced the grievous wounds that religion had suffered as the university system was perfected.

Both religious and nonreligious scholars were ordinary in relegating their affirmation to their private lives. Like most other professors, their professional careers eschewed the divine. Their careers called attention to the general failure of scholars to integrate their professorial ideals with a wider grasp of their place in the world. The erudite ignored the problems of belief created by the triumph of critical principles of explanation.

William Foxwell Albright was one of many students of the ancient Near East who adhered to a traditional faith. He was, however, one of the few who proclaimed his assurance in the face of the secular implications that seemed unavoidable in scholarly study. Albright grappled with the problem of showing that a transcendent God could be found in human history. He believed, simultaneously, in the principles of higher criticism and in eschatology. But it was unclear how the natural could translate into the supernatural, how the human story could have a nonhuman significance.

It has been easy for students of the ancient Near East writing the story of their enterprise to be proud of their accomplishments.[3] For more than two thousand years, the old Orient had been largely erased from the collective memory of humanity. Over a period of some seventy-five years, scholars recovered it.

On the other hand, some recent and formidable detractors have noted the quasi-colonial ambitions of the Westerners involved in this work. The censurers have urged that Orientalism was an intellectual stage of a materialistic industrialism.[4] The premises of Orientalist scholarship are so deeply tarnished by the acquisitive mentality of the West as to be worthless. On this view, Orientalism (and much scholarship in the humanities) mirrors imperialistic capitalism and takes a view of its object that is essentially distorted.

Much indeed can be said against the ideals of the late-nineteenth-century students of the ancient Near East in America, a subgroup of Orientalists. They were certainly sexist, racist, and homophobic. Primarily arrogant, well-to-do Protestants, they had little sense that their collective endeavor might be different from the common good. The self-interest, not to say self-aggrandizement, of individuals was staggering. Some later scholars have suggested that the style of male aggressiveness in scholarship was the same sort of thing at work in World War I.[5] The fruition of academic ideals in the Near East was linked to some of the least-pleasant aspects of the economic system.

A lot can be said, too, against the institutional bearers of ancient Near Eastern studies, against the ethos of the Victorian university. Built from newly won wealth, American colleges at the end of the nineteenth century expressed the same vices as the social order around them. They relished power and were ardent for rank. Academic managers were often more interested in promoting and protecting their own culture than in understanding the culture of others.

Looking at the history of this field over a long period lends weight to the critique of Orientalism. The imaginative or interpretive dimension of scholarship meant that persistent statements of scientific rectitude could not be sustained. Their protestations to the contrary, academics did not realize their aim to escape prejudice. The learned seemed always to be implicated in their milieu, in the way detractors argued.

Yet the world of Orientalist scholarship has something to recommend it. The learning that did take place was not theoretical, and it came to the fore in an intellectual enterprise that cost some of its purveyors cherished religious ideas. Creating the discipline was not a tea party, as the American campaigns demonstrated. At Nippur, Joseph Meyer died a wretched death on behalf of knowledge. The Orientalists were not arms dealers, nor were they high officials in the foreign service; they had their own concerns that differentiated them from the latter groups. These concerns resulted in the body of information we have about the ancient Near East and the principles of reasoning that have secured this information.

Three considerations that emerge from this study must undermine the most serious and only crucial censures of Orientalism. Orientalism may be the best example of the West's ability to appropriate "the other" for its own purposes, but it is also an excellent example of the persuasive case that can be made for the advance of knowledge and a modest degree of fairness in scholarly pursuits.

First, decipherment—illustrated in this book by the recovery of Sumerian—indicates that prolonged endeavor can result in the progressive recovery of the intentions of past peoples. It seems to me possible but foolish to throw out the achievements of the translation projects. One could argue that decoding the languages of the Egyptians and the Mesopotamians was, for example, some bizarre sort of Western imperial construction. But this is a high price to pay. The alternative is to accept that ancient people expressed certain beliefs about the world and that we are able to recover them.

The second consideration concerns the reasoning implicit in the development of stratified digging. The reasoning emphasized in archaeology stresses the fundamental character of spatiotemporal facts. The censure of Orientalism rightly recognizes that substantive information in the field is embedded in contested interpretations, and the censurer can easily jettison many conclusions about the history of any civilization and their connection to the present. But the positive significance of the facticity in the field remains untouched in practice. For the censurers have immediately gone on to establish alternative factual bases that allow them inventively to write supposedly better history, to urge that Orientalist work is subjective. The efforts of anti-Orientalists presuppose an aspect of the enterprise they disparage. To put the point another way: the censure is based on its own premise that only *other* scholars are hopelessly entangled in political commitments that undermine nonpartisanship. But this premise depends on the ability of anti-Orientalists to attend to overlooked facts established by techniques in part generated by Orientalist scholarship.

The third consideration concerns the principles involved in the higher criticism of the Bible. It is a minor irony in the censure of Orientalists that many proponents of the censure regarded the assault on Judeo-Christian verities as liberating. Orientalism itself was part of that assault. Unless the censure of Orientalism includes an attack on the higher criticism, the censure must fall short: the censure itself hinges on modes of argumentation that scholars of the ancient Near East helped legitimate. Orientalists aided in developing standards of evidence and reliable grounds for assertion that their detractors use to urge that Orientalist reasoning is suspect. The anti-Orientalists can only avoid accepting the intellectual premises of Western modernism by opening themselves to reasoning that committed Christians and Jews privately adopt.[6]

This history has shown that many learned conclusions were not compelled by the evidence but instead were produced by the culturally grounded inventiveness of scholars. This finding must enormously complicate our view of what careful inquiry can obtain; the finding makes claims to objectivity cautious and partial. Yet this history of the ancient Near East in the United States also suggests that censurers of Orientalism may have chosen the wrong vehicle to make any strong case against a prudent empiricism. Rather than demonstrating the bankruptcy of Western attempts to understand the human world around it, Orientalism supplied, at the least, the tools even its harshest censurers need to argue against it.

My story of the American ancient Near East illustrates something of what G. W. F. Hegel called "the cunning of reason in history." The narrative is one of the passions and self-interests of individuals, flawed in various ways and limited by their culture. The American university had an ambiguous relation to the philanthropy of the rich and to the aspirations of the cultivated. A scientific ethic constantly confronted both private and institutional aggrandizement. Personal, racial, and national prejudices frequently marred the work of scholars, and communities of learning often harbored the stupid, the ignorant, and the dishonest. Yet the meaning of the story—in this case the growth of knowledge—somehow overstepped these limitations, just as it had to come through them.[7]

ABBREVIATIONS

AG   Archives General, University Archives, University of Pennsylvania
AJA   *American Journal of Archaeology*
APS   American Philosophical Society
BA   *Biblical Archaeologist*
BL   Reisner-Hearst Letters, Bancroft Library, University of California,
        Berkeley
BMFA   Boston Museum of Fine Arts
HS   Hilprecht Sammlung, Friedrich Schiller University, Jena
HUA   Harvard University Archives
HVH   H. V. Hilprecht, *The Excavations in Assyria and Babylonia*
        (Philadelphia, 1904)
JAOS   *Journal of the American Oriental Society*
JBL   *Journal of Biblical Literature*
JHU   Johns Hopkins University Archives
LL   Central Records, Low Library, Columbia University
MA   University Museum Archives, University of Pennsylvania
ML   Morgan Library, New York
N   John Punnett Peters, *Nippur; or, Explorations and Adventures on the
        Euphrates*, 2 vols. (New York, 1897)
NR   Nippur Records, Museum Archives, University of Pennsylvania
OI   Archives of the Oriental Institute, University of Chicago
PHC   Hermann Vollrat Hilprecht, ed., *The So-Called Peters-Hilprecht
        Controversy* (Philadelphia, 1908)
RA   Rockefeller Archives Center, Tarrytown, New York
RL   Regenstein Library, Special Collections, University of Chicago
SIA   Archives of the Smithsonian Institution, Washington, D.C.
SM   Museum Records, Semitic Museum, Harvard University
UA   University Archives, University of Pennsylvania
VPSC   Special Collections, Van Pelt Library, University of Pennsylvania
YBC   Yale Babylonian Collection, Sterling Library, Yale University
YUA   Yale University Archives

NOTES

INTRODUCTION

1. Frank Harper to [William] Rainey Harper, 15 March 1889, 51/5, Presidents' Papers, 1889–1925, RL.

2. See Raymond Schwab, *The Oriental Renaissance: Europe's Rediscovery of India and the East, 1680–1880*, trans. Gene Patterson-Black and Victor Reinking (New York, 1984).

3. For the term "Orient," see Bernard Lewis, "The Question of Orientalism," in Lewis, *Islam and the West* (New York, l993), 100–105.

4. S. G. F. Brandon, "The Myth and Ritual Position Critically Considered," in *Myth, Ritual, and Kingship: Essays in the Theory and Practice of Kingship in the Ancient Near East and in Israel*, ed. S. H. Hooke (Oxford, l958), 261–91, discusses the cultural unity of the ancient Near East, as does H. Frankfurt, "The Ancient Near East," in *Orientalism and History*, ed. D. Sinoor (Bloomington, Ind., 1970), 1–15. Wolfram von Soden, *The Ancient Orient: An Introduction to the Study of the Ancient Near East*, trans. Donald G. Schley (Grand Rapids, Mich., 1994), 1–6, also makes an attempt at a definition.

5. On biblical archaeology, see Roger Moorey, *A Century of Biblical Archaeology* (Cambridge, England, 1991). On the early history of Semitic studies, see "Proceedings of the Society, May, 1885," *JAOS* 13 (1889): cclxvi–cccvi, and Morris Jastrow, Jr., "Recent Movements in the Historical Study of Religion in America," *Biblical World*, n.s., 1 (1893): 24–32.

6. See Shuly Rubin Schwartz, *The Emergence of Jewish Scholarship in America: The Publication of the Jewish Encyclopedia* (Cincinnati, l991), 1–16.

7. Paul Ritterband and Harold S. Wechsler, *Jewish Learning in American Universities: The First Century* (Bloomington, Ind., 1994), 237 n. 5.

8. Brian M. Fagan, *The Rape of the Nile* (Boston, 1975), 23; see also Charles Breasted, *Pioneer to the Past: The Story of James Henry Breasted, Archaeologist* (Chicago, 1943), 159.

CHAPTER ONE

1. The summary that follows is based on my own *Churchmen and Philosophers: From Jonathan Edwards to John Dewey* (New Haven, 1985), although that book underestimates the persistence of Christian commitment among academics at the end of the century.

2. On the missionaries, see David H. Finnie, *Pioneers East: The Early American Experience in the Middle East* (Cambridge, Mass., 1967); the best source on the touring pilgrimages is Lester I. Vogel, *To See a Promised Land: Americans and the Holy Land in the Nineteenth Century* (University Park, Pa., 1993).

3. See John T. Irwin, *American Hieroglyphics: The Symbol of the Egyptian Hieroglyphics in the American Renaissance* (New Haven, 1980), and John A. Wilson, *Signs*

and Wonders upon Pharaoh: A History of American Egyptology (Chicago, 1964), 35–123.

4. Edward Robinson, *Biblical Researches in Palestine, Mount Sinai, and Arabia Petraea in 1838* (New York, 1841). A second important treatise followed and incorporated a later exploration: Robinson, *Biblical Researches in Palestine and the Adjacent Regions: A Journal of Travels in the Years 1838 and 1852*, 2d. ed. (London, 1856).

5. For Germany, see Carl Diehl, *Americans and German Scholarship, 1770–1870* (New Haven, 1978); for New Haven, see Louise Stevenson, *Scholarly Means to Evangelical Ends: The New Haven Scholars and the Transformation of Higher Learning in America, 1830–1890* (Baltimore, 1986).

6. On Whitney, see Michael Silverstein, ed., *Whitney on Language* (Cambridge, Mass., 1971), and Stephen Alter, "William Dwight Whitney and the Science of Language" (Ph.D. diss., History, University of Michigan, 1993). See also Julie Tetel Andersen, *Linguistics in America, 1769–1924: A Critical History* (London, 1990).

7. The critical literature about Harper is minimal. See the interpretation and bibliography in James P. Wind, *The Bible and the University: The Messianic Vision of William Rainey Harper* (Atlanta, 1987).

8. For the story of comparative philology, see Garland Cannon, *The Life and Mind of Oriental Jones: Sir William Jones, the Father of Modern Linguistics* (Cambridge, England, 1991), and Maurice Olender's illuminating *Languages of Paradise: Race, Religion, and Philology in the Nineteenth Century* (Cambridge, Mass., 1992).

9. See Nathaniel Schmidt, "Early Oriental Studies in Europe and the Work of the American Oriental Society, 1842–1922," *JAOS* 43 (1923): 1–14, and Rosane Rocher, "History of the AOS" (1971), typescript in Rocher's possession.

10. William Hayes Ward, "Address before the American Oriental Society in 1893," *JAOS* 16 (1896): lx.

11. For the work of the one most relevant to this study, see *Oriental Studies: A Selection of the Papers Read before the Oriental Club of Philadelphia, 1888–1894* (Boston, 1894), esp. 7–10.

12. Warren J. Moulton, "The American Palestine Exploration Society," *Annual of the American Schools of Oriental Research* 8 (1926–27): 55–78.

13. For a good early history, see Ward, "Address before the American Oriental Society," lix–lxiv.

14. On this issue, see D. G. Hart, "American Learning and the Problem of Religious Studies," in *The Secularization of the Academy*, ed. George M. Marsden and Bradley J. Longfield (New York, 1992), 195–233.

15. On Wellhausen, see the special issue of *Semeia* 25 (1982), "Julius Wellhausen and His *Prolegomena to the History of Israel.*"

16. R. E. Clements, *A Century of Old Testament Study*, 2d ed. rev. (London, 1983), has an excellent discussion of the debates over the higher criticism.

17. Bruce Metzger, David Goldstein, and John Ferguson, eds., *Great Events of Bible Times: New Perspectives on the People, Places, and History of the Biblical World* (New York, 1987), 8.

18. See Jerry Wayne Brown's meticulous *Rise of Biblical Criticism in America, 1800–1870* (Middletown, Conn., 1969).

19. On this issue, see William M. Calder III, ed., *The Cambridge Ritualists Reconsidered* (Atlanta, 1991).

20. The first edition of James Frazer's *Golden Bough: A Study in Comparative Religion* appeared in two volumes. On Frazer, see Robert Ackerman, *J. G. Frazer: His Life and Work* (Cambridge, England 1987).

21. On Smith and his context, see T. Beidelman, *W. Robertson Smith and the Sociological Study of Religion* (Chicago, 1974), and Calder, *Cambridge Ritualists Reconsidered.*

22. On comparative religion, see Jastrow, "Recent Movements," and Morris Jastrow, Jr., *The Study of Religion* (London, 1901), esp. vii–xi.

23. For a good example of this attitude—both at the end of the nineteenth century and more recently—in the related field of church history, see David W. Lotz, "Philip Schaff and the Idea of Church History," in *A Century of Church History: The Legacy of Philip Schaff*, ed. Henry W. Bowden (Carbondale, Ill., 1988), 1–35.

24. The story of Smith and Eliot is well told in Warner M. Bailey, "William Robertson Smith and American Bible Studies," *Journal of Presbyterian History* 51 (1973): 299–300. Toy's influence is suggested by Bailey's having gotten his first name wrong.

25. On the Wolfe Expedition and its background, see "Nippur's Little-Known Pioneers," exhibition copy, MA; Ritterband and Wechsler, *Jewish Learning in American Universities*, 29–30; and N, 1:1–3.

26. See Ward, "Report on the Wolfe Expedition," *New York Independent*, 20 May 1886, and N, 1:3–5.

27. The information on Peters is from the Yale Alumni Records, Yale University, New Haven; "Nippur's Little-Known Pioneers"; Peters, AG; and Joshua Lawrence Chamberlain, *Universities and Their Sons* (Boston, 1901), 6:399–400. Information on his appointment at Penn comes from the Penn *Catalogue*, 1886–1894, and Minutes of the Trustees, 1886, UA.

28. Peters's views are taken from his articles: John Punnett Peters, "Biblical Antiquities," *New York Evening Post, Supplement*, May and June 1884; "Babylon in New York," *New York Evening Post*, 27 February 1885; "Nineveh in Philadelphia," *Philadelphia Sunday School Times*, 30 May 1885; "The Times of Isaiah Now Recoverable," *Philadelphia Sunday School Times*, 21 November 1885; "Daniel and the Monuments," *Philadelphia Sunday School Times*, 23 January 1886; and "Babylonia and the Bible," *New York Standard of the Cross and the Church*, 31 March 1888.

29. For the story of Edward Clark and the university's involvement, see "Nippur's Little-Known Pioneers"; Percy C. Madeira, Jr., *Men in Search of Man: The First Seventy-five Years of the University Museum of the University of Pennsylvania* (Philadelphia, 1964), 15–17; and the surviving documents in 3/10, NR. The account Peters gives from memory is especially interesting. See John Punnett Peters, "Thirty Years' Progress in Semitics," in *Thirty Years of Oriental Studies: Papers Presented at the Anniversary of the Oriental Club of Philadelphia* (Philadelphia, 1918), 23–25.

30. On Pepper, see William Pepper II, AG; *The Monument to William Pepper, Provost of the University of Pennsylvania* (Philadelphia, 1900); and Stevenson to Bitter, 30 June 1897, Secretary-Letterbook 1, MA.

31. See William Pepper II, AG, and Pepper's speech to the board, December 1889, Pepper Papers, vol. 3, VPSC.

32. For a typical history of the sort of people who supported Penn, see David P. Contosta, *A Philadelphia Family: The Houstons and Woodwards of Chestnut Hill* (Philadelphia, 1988).

33. Haynes to Edward Clark, 8 December 1894, 8/3, NR.

34. Pepper/Stevenson, Directors Files, 3/1, MA.

35. For a more detailed account of the museum's founding, see Richard L. Zettler, "Excavations at Nippur, the University of Pennsylvania, and the University's Museum," in *Nippur at the Centennial: Papers Read at the 35e Rencontre Assyriologique Internationale, Philadelphia, 1988* (Philadelphia, 1992), 325–36.

36. Gordon to Harrison, 8 September 1913, UPT 50 H 319, 1913, Correspondence, UA.

37. These issues in museum culture are treated, for a more recent period, in Ivan Karp and Steven D. Lavine, eds., *Exhibiting Cultures: The Poetics and Politics of Museum Display* (Washington, D.C., 1991).

38. For the role of the nomad in the vision of the Near East, see John Tracy Luke, "Pastoralism and Politics in the Mari Period: A Re-examination of the Character and Political Significance of the Major West Semitic Tribal Groups on the Middle Euphrates, ca. 1828–1758 B.C." (Ph.D. diss., University of Michigan, 1965), esp. 1–2, 8–38, and the notes thereto. A good introduction to the role of the White City is Alan Trachtenberg, *The Incorporation of America: Culture and Society in the Gilded Age* (New York, 1982), esp. 211–14.

39. See Colin Renfrew, "The Great Tradition and the Great Divide: Archaeology as Anthropology?" *AJA* 84 (1980): 291.

40. On anthropology versus archaeology, see Curtis M. Hinsley, "From Shell-Heaps to Stelae: Early Anthropology at the Peabody Museum," 51–59; on museums and anthropology, see Ira Jacknis, "Franz Boas and Exhibits: On the Limitation of the Museum Method of Anthropology," 75–111, and George W. Stocking, Jr., "Philanthropoids and Vanishing Cultures: Rockefeller Funding and the End of the Museum Era in Anglo-American Anthropology," 112–45, all in *Objects and Others: Essays on Museums and Material Culture*, ed. George W. Stocking, Jr. (Madison, Wisc., 1985).

41. This discussion is indebted to Steven Conn's dissertation, "To Organize and Display: Museums and American Culture, 1876–1926" (Ph.D. diss., University of Pennsylvania, 1994), esp. 97–174. See also Regna Darnell, "The Emergence of Academic Anthropology at the University of Pennsylvania," *Journal of the History of the Behavioral Sciences* 6 (1970): 80–92.

42. See his testimony in *PHC*, 59.

43. Noorian letters, Nippur Letter Books, vol. 2, to Ward, 3 June 1889, NR.

44. Frank's letters to Rainey during the expedition reveal the former's character clearly. For his cigars, see the letter of 18 June 1888, and for the quote, 19 February 1889, in 51/5, Presidents' Papers, 1889–1925, RL.

45. For biographical details on Haynes, see Haynes, AG, and "Nippur's Little-Known Pioneers."

46. Noorian letters, Nippur Letter Books, vol. 2, 22 July 1889, Hilprecht to Pepper, 15 October 1888, Peters to Pepper, 11 December 1888, 3/14, NR.

47. For biographical details on Hilprecht, see Hilprecht, AG; for his appointments, see Minutes of the Trustees, 1886, UA.

48. N, 1:9.

49. Frank Harper, "Hilprecht-Peters Controversy by a Contemporary Third Party Who Was Present," file 2, Frank Harper Papers, OI; Frank Harper to Rainey Harper, 15 March 1889, 51/5, Presidents' Papers, 1889–1925, RL.

50. On Haupt, see Hugh Hawkins, *Pioneer: A History of the Johns Hopkins University, 1874–1889* (Ithaca, N.Y., 1960), 158–59. On Hilprecht and Haupt, see Haupt to Pepper, 29 April 1896, and Pepper to Haupt, 1 June 1896, Pepper Papers, vol. 7, VPSC.

51. Sayce to Haupt, 18 August 1883, Sayce-Haupt Correspondence, Near Eastern Studies Records, JHU.

52. For this story, see Jerrold S. Cooper, "From Mosul to Manila: Early Approaches to Funding Ancient Near Eastern Studies Research in the United States," *Culture and History* 11 (1992): 151–55. The best primary source on this dispute is the material collected in "Correspondence with Paul Haupt and Others," series 201, box 11, folder 8, SIA.

53. For this fight, see 3/14, NR; Langley to Mitchell, 23 February 1888, Curatorial 1, 1888–93, MA; Haupt Letters, 1888–92, Gilman Papers, and Gilman to Bayard, 15 February 1888, Haupt Papers, JHU; and "Memorandum concerning National Expedition," series 201, box 11, folder 8, SIA.

CHAPTER TWO

1. N, 1:120.

2. See Neil Asher Silberman, "Desolation and Restoration: The Impact of a Biblical Concept on Near Eastern Archaeology," *BA* 54 (1991): 76–77.

3. Traditional texts on Near Eastern politics and diplomacy give the best flavor of how educated Europeans viewed their role in the Turkish Empire and Mesopotamia: See Patrick Kincross, *Ottoman Centuries* (New York, 1977); Stephen Hensley Longrigg, *Iraq, 1900 to 1950: A Political, Social, and Economic History* (Oxford, 1953); William Miller, *The Ottoman Empire and Its Successors, 1801–1927 . . .*, rev. and enl. ed. (Cambridge, England, 1966); and Karl Wittek, *Rise of the Ottoman Empire* (London, 1938).

4. For these developments and the sources for the quotations in this paragraph, see the letters from Peters to Edward Clark in the summer and fall of 1888, 3/8, 3/14, NR. It is hard to know the extent to which the American view of the Ottomans was merely a cultural prejudice. For a treatment of the Turkish bureaucracy, see Carter Vaughn Findley, *Ottoman Civil Officialdom: A Social History* (Princeton, 1989).

5. Hilprecht to Pepper, 30 November 1888, 3/14, NR.

6. E.g., N, 1:194.

7. Pepper to Goode, 1 August 1888, 3/14, NR.

8. For a discussion of the problematic aspects of Schliemann's work as well as a (critical) introduction to the man, see David A. Traill, *Excavating Schliemann: Collected Papers on Schliemann* (Alpharetta, Ga., 1993).

9. I have used two standard secondary sources to summarize the story of the

decipherment of cuneiform and the reconstruction of Mesopotamian civilization in the nineteenth century: Seton Lloyd, *Foundations in the Dust: The Story of Mesopotamian Exploration*, rev. and enl. ed. (London, 1980), and Brian M. Fagan, *Return to Babylon* (Boston, 1979). Another charming account is C. J. Gadd, *The Stones of Assyria: The Surviving Remains of Assyrian Sculpture, Their Recovery, and Their Original Position* (London, 1936). Herman Hilprecht's narrative of nineteenth-century Mesopotamian exploration in *Explorations in Bible Lands* (Philadelphia, 1903) was, early on, recognized as outstanding. My own summary is meant not only to convey information but to indicate the historical conventions accepted by Assyriologists and their educated followers at the turn of the century.

10. An excellent and early narrative of decipherment is Holger Petersen, *The Discovery of Language: Linguistic Science in the Nineteenth Century*, trans. John Spargo (Bloomington, Ind., 1931).

11. Quoted in William H. Stiebing, Jr., *Uncovering the Past: A History of Archaeology* (Buffalo, N.Y., 1993), 94–95.

12. See Metzger, Goldstein, and Ferguson, *Great Events of Bible Times*, 8.

13. The flavor of Layard's story is conveyed in Arnold C. Brackman, *The Luck of Nineveh: Archaeology's Great Adventure* (New York, 1978), but see also Gordon Waterfield, *Layard of Nineveh* (London, 1963).

14. Quoted in H. W. F. Saggs, *Assyriology and the Study of the Old Testament* (Aberystwyth, Wales, 1969), 11.

15. Paul Ziff, in *Semantic Analysis* (Ithaca, N.Y., 1960), discusses the conceptual underpinnings of this method.

16. For one version of this process, see Wallace E. A. Budge, *The Rise and Progress of Assyriology* (London, 1925), 223–41 and 283–90, esp. 288–89.

17. Quoted in Fagan, *Return to Babylon*, 116.

18. Sources of information about the "duplicate" sculptures include: Cyrus Adler, "The Beginnings of Semitic Studies in America," in *Oriental Studies Dedicated to Paul Haupt*, ed. Cyrus Adler and Aaron Ember (Baltimore, 1926), 323; Gadd, *Stones of Assyria*, 86–87; William J. Hinke, "An Alabaster Slab of Ashur-nasir-pal," *Auburn Seminary Record* 8 (1912–13): 20–27; Morris Jastrow, Jr., "The Ashurnasir-pal Slabs Belonging to the New York Historical Society," *JAOS* 14 (1890): cxxxviii–ix; and S. Merrill, "Assyrian and Babylonian Monuments in America," *Bibliotheca Sacra* 32 (1875): 320–25.

19. Austen Henry Layard, *Discoveries among the Ruins of Nineveh and Babylon . . .* (London, 1853), 477.

20. The issue of the integrity of Mesopotamian civilization has been taken up by Norman Yoffee, "The Collapse of Ancient Mesopotamian States and Civilizations," in *The Collapse of Ancient States and Civilizations*, ed. Yoffee and George L. Cowgill (Tucson, Ariz., 1988), 44–68, and Yoffee, "Too Many Chiefs? (or, Safe Texts for the '90s)," in *Archaeological Theory: Who Sets the Agenda?* ed. Yoffee and Andrew Sherratt (Cambridge, England, 1993), 64–71. See also Joseph A. Tainter, *The Collapse of Complex Societies* (Cambridge, England, 1988).

21. Glyn Daniel and Colin Renfrew, *The Idea of Prehistory*, 2d ed. (Edinburgh, 1988), 62.

22. Peters's views are taken from the sources listed in chap. 1, n. 28.

23. N, 1:121, 161; Haynes manuscript, chaps. 1, 3, 17, 10/2, NR.

24. N, 1:86, 250, 267; Haynes manuscript, chaps. 2, 5, 10/2, NR.

25. N, 2:310–11, 345.

26. N, 1:196–97; 2:6, 45, 47, 61.

27. Hilprecht's view can be found in his letters to Pepper in the fall of 1888, 3/14, NR.

28. Hilprecht to Pepper, 14 January 1889, Peters to Edward Clark, 14 January 1889, 3/14, NR. For a later rendition of the story, see Biography Collection, William H. Witte interview, 26 July 1953, 4, MA.

29. Noorian letters, Nippur Letter Books, vol. 2, 18 August 1889, NR; N, 1:190.

30. Pepper to Peters, Pepper to Hilprecht, 18 December 1888, 4/1, Pepper to Hilprecht, 26 March 1889, 4/2, NR.

31. Haynes manuscript, chap. 5, 10/3, NR; HVH, 304, 355; N, 1:105, 222, 227, 280; 2:63, 73.

32. See the extracts from Peters's letters to Clark in early 1889, 3/8, and the letters themselves, 4/2, NR.

33. HVH, 323, 357; see also N, 1:231–34.

34. N, 1:27, 253; 2:267.

35. HVH, 304, 314–15.

36. Hilprecht to Pepper, 24 February 1889, 4/2, NR.

37. See "An Appeal . . . ," 10 March 1889, in 3/8, NR.

38. Harper and Hilprecht to Pepper, 1 April 1889, 4/2, NR.

39. Hilprecht to Pepper, 26 March, 1 April 1889, 4/2, NR.

40. Preliminary Report 3, 26 February 1889, 3/8, NR.

41. Hilprecht to Pepper, 10 February 1889, 4/2, NR.

42. Hilprecht to Pepper, 24 February 1889, 4/2, NR.

43. A. H. Sayce, *A Primer of Assyriology* (London, 1894), 22.

44. N, 2:109, 140.

45. See "The University Archaeological Association" (1890), Directors Files, 2/4, MA.

46. N, 1:279–93.

47. Haynes manuscript, chap. 8a, 10/3, NR.

48. Noorian letters, Nippur Letter Books, vol. 2, 14–24 April, NR.

49. N, 1:288.

50. Ibid.

51. Pepper to Harper, 20 June, 3 July 1889, 4/3, NR.

52. For example, see Haynes to Pepper, 29 June 1889, 3/6, NR.

53. Hilprecht to Pepper, 25 April 1889, 4/2, NR.

54. Hilprecht to Pepper, 12 December 1888, 3/14, NR.

55. Peters to Pepper, 11 December 1888, to Edward Clark, 23 December 1888, 4/1, to Edward Clark, 6 January 1889, 4/3, NR.

56. Noorian letters, Nippur Letter Books, vol. 2, 25 February 1890, NR.

57. Peters to Pepper, 16 May 1890, 4/4, NR.

58. Noorian letters, Nippur Letter Books, vol. 2, 27 April 1890, NR.

59. Pepper to Peters, 1 April 1890, Peters to Pepper, 16 June 1890, 4/4, NR.

60. Peters to Edward Clark, 28 October 1889, 4/2, Peters to Pepper, 23 August 1890, 3/14, NR.

61. Pepper to Peters, 7 June, 18 June 1890, 4/4, NR.

62. Peters to Pepper, 17 July 1890, 3/14, NR.

63. Pepper to Low, 25 April 1891, Low to Pepper, 4 May 1891, 4/6, NR.

64. Peters to Pepper, 20 June 1891, 3/14, NR; notes of "Special Meeting of the Babylonian Exploration Fund," Directors Files, 2/2, MA.

65. Peters to Pepper, 23 June 1891, 3/14, NR.

66. Peters to Clark, 10 August 1891, 4/7, NR.

67. Peters to Pepper, 17 July 1890, 3/14, NR.

CHAPTER THREE

1. For a discussion, see Carl T. Jackson, *The Oriental Religions and American Thought: Nineteenth-Century Explorations* (Westport, Conn., 1981), 179–86.

2. This fascinating story is told in Alter, "William Dwight Whitney," chap. 10, and Rocher, "History of the AOS," 45–51.

3. "Semitic Studies in America: Addresses at the Meeting of the American Oriental Society," *Hebraica* 5 (1888–89): 76–91.

4. For information on Harrison, see his biographical files in AG.

5. 23 April 1894, Pepper Papers, vol. 5, VPSC.

6. See Harrison, AG.

7. For information, see Stevenson's AG file, and Margaret S. Drower, "The Early Years," in *Excavating in Egypt: The Egypt Exploration Society, 1882–1982*, ed. T. G. H. James (Chicago, 1982), 9–36.

8. See her recollections in Curatorial 2/6, MA.

9. For the evidence, see Pepper/Stevenson, Directors Files, 3/1, 3/2, and 3/3, MA. On the general problem of clandestine Victorian relations, see Altina L. Walker, *Reverend Beecher and Mrs. Tilton: Sex and Class in Victorian America* (Amherst, Mass., 1982). I am indebted to Charles Rosenberg for insight on this topic.

10. Pepper/Stevenson, 157–58 (August 1894), Directors Files, 3/2, MA.

11. Harrison to Joseph Harris, 5 January 1895, UPB 65.1, box 3, Archaeology Correspondence, 1900–1903, UA; Harrison to Museum Board of Managers, 8 January 1895, Directors Files, 4/2, MA.

12. *Report of the Board of Managers . . . 1893* (Philadelphia, 1894), 4.

13. Harrison to the board, 8 January 1895, Directors Files, 4/2, MA.

14. Harrison to Pepper, 5 February 1895 (emphasis added), Harrison to Pepper, 1 January 1895, UPB 65.1, box 3, Archaeology Correspondence, 1894–99, UA.

15. Minutes of the Dr. Pepper Testimonial Committee, Building Committee, 1893 (inside back cover), MA.

16. Stevenson to Harrison, 15 February 1895, UPB 65.1, box 3, Archaeology Correspondence, 1894–99, UA.

17. Peters to Harrison, 11 March 1892, UPB 65.1, box 3, Archaeology Correspondence, 1900–1903, and Pepper to Hilprecht, 25 April 1892, AG Arch-Museum, 1892, 1, UA; Hilprecht to Stevenson, 28 March 1892, Curatorial 1, 1888–92, MA.

18. Hilprecht, "King List," n.d., UPB 65.1, box 3, Archaeology Correspondence, 1900–1903, UA.

19. Hilprecht to Harrison, 13 April 1900, UPB 65.1, box 3, Archaeology Correspondence, 1894–97, UA; Hilprecht to Pepper, n.d., 12/4, NR.

20. See Minutes of the Trustees, 1891–93, and Hilprecht to Pepper, 21 March 1893, AG, 1893, Archaeolgy, UA.

21. Burk to Harrison, 26 July 1892, UPB 65.1, box 3, Archaeology Correspondence, 1900–1903, Hilprecht to Pepper, n.d., AG, 1893, Archaeology, UA.

22. Haynes to Peters, 8 and 30 December 1893, 13/3, and 21 July 1894, 8/1, NR.

23. Edward Clark to Haynes, 6 June 1894, 11/4, NR.

24. See Dan Rottenberg, *Fight On Pennsylvania: A Century of Red and Blue Football* (Philadelphia, 1985), 12–13; Info Files, Athletics, Football, 1892–1973, UA; and "The Discovery of Professor Van Saabrandt," Curatorial 5, Hilprecht Controversy, uncatalogued, 2, MA.

25. Edward Clark to Peters, 7 August 1895, 12/1, NR.

26. Haynes to Peters, 17 March, 14 July 1894, 11/4, 21 July 1894, 8/1, NR.

27. Peters to Edward Clark, 18 and 8 June 1894, 11/4, NR.

28. Haynes manuscript, 2d typed version, chap. 12, 10/3, NR.

29. Haynes to Edward Clark, 10 May 1894, 8/1, NR.

30. For Meyer, see his AG file and "Nippur's Little-Known Pioneers."

31. All quotations from Meyer are taken from his journal, 7/5, NR. In a few cases I have silently made minor corrections.

32. Peters to Haynes, 1 September 1894, 11/4, and Peters to Edward Clark, 22 October 1894, 11/2, NR; Edward Clark to Haynes, 4 September 1894, UPB 65.1, box 3, Archaeology Correspondence, 1891–94, UA.

33. Meyer journal, 7/5, NR; Haynes to Peters, 25 August 1894, UPB 65.1, box 3, Archaeology Correspondence, 1891–94, UA.

34. Meyer journal, 9/5, Haynes to Peters, 27 October 1894, 8/3, NR.

35. Peters to Clark, 10 November 1894, 11/3, Peters to Haynes, 14 December 1894, 11/2, 25 January, 13 February, 5 January 1895, 11/7, NR.

36. Peters to Pepper, 27 March 1895, 11/1, and Peters to Clark, 5 January 1895, 11/7, NR.

37. Haynes to Peters, 1 December, 10 November 1894, 8/3, 5 January 1894, 10/5, and 2 February 1895, 10/4, NR.

38. Haynes to Peters, 1 and 15 December 1894, 8/3, and Sundberg to Pepper, 5 December 1894, 11/2, NR.

39. Pepper to Edward Clark, 16 January 1895, Edward Clark to Haynes, 21 February 1895, and Peters to Haynes, 22 January 1895, 11/7, NR.

40. Resume: Babylonian Committee, 10 December 1894; Edward Clark to Haynes, 18 December 1894; see also Hilprecht to Haynes, 11 December 1894, and Pepper to Edward Clark, 14 January 1895, 11/2, Haynes to Pepper, 13 and 29 April 1895, 10/4, Edward Clark to Haynes, 7 June 1895, and Pepper to Edward Clark, 23 June and 18 July 1895, 12/1, NR.

41. Haynes to Peters, 12 January 1895, 8/3, and Sundberg to Pepper, 27 February 1895, 11/7, NR.

42. Sundberg to Pepper, 27 February 1895, Pepper to Peters, 21 March 1895, Pepper to Edward Clark, 7 March 1895, 11/7, Edward Clark to Pepper, 25 April 1895, 11/1, Hilprecht to Edward Clark, 15 March 1895, 11/7, 22 and 30 April 1895, 11/1, and Peters to Pepper, 18 March 1895, 11/7, NR.

43. Hilprecht to Edward Clark, 21 May 1895, 11/1, 20 August 1895, 12/1,

1 September 1895, 7 February 1896, 11/7, Hilprecht to Pepper, 19 August 1895, 12/1, and Pepper to Edward Clark, 23 August 1895, 12/1, NR.

44. Blockley to Edward Clark, 23 May 1895, and Hilprecht to Pepper, 16 August 1895, 12/1, NR.

45. Lyon to Peters, 14 August 1895, Pepper Papers, vol. 6, VPSC; Hilprecht to Pepper, 20 August 1895, Petrie to Pepper, 18 August 1895, Pepper to Duncan, 7 September 1895, 12/1, and Duncan to Pepper, 4 November 1895, 12/2, NR.

46. Duncan to Pepper, 4 November 1895, 12/2, NR.

47. Haynes to Edward Clark, 1 June 1895, 12/1, and 28 September, 2 November 1895, 10/4, NR.

48. Haynes to Edward Clark, 7 and 21 December 1895, 10/4, NR.

49. Haynes to Edward Clark, 8, 15, and 29 February 1896, 12/3, NR.

50. Babylonian Committee Minutes, 17 February 1896, Directors Files, 4/2, MA; Duncan to Edward Clark, 3 February 1896; see also Haynes to Edward Clark, 12 March, Duncan to Clark, 15 March, and Duncan to Pepper, 11 May 1896, 12/3, NR.

51. Pepper to Petrie, 24 March 1896, Petrie to Pepper, 12 May 1896, and Pepper to Edward Clark, 1 June 1896, 12/3, NR.

52. Duncan to Edward Clark, 6 August 1896, 13/5, Duncan to Edward Clark, 12 October 1896, 13/9, and Duncan to Clarence Clark, 16 October 1896, 13/5, NR.

CHAPTER FOUR

1. Address by Daniel Baugh (1898), 29, MA.

2. Clarence Clark to Edward Clark, 1 and 8 August 1898, 17/6, NR; Building Committee Minutes, 1895–98, 12 August 1896, MA.

3. The best summary of his travels is in a memo, ca. May 1905, Hilprecht Papers, 1901, AG.

4. Hilprecht to Harrison, 20 July 1894, 24 April, 29 March, and 23 March 1897, UPB 65.1, box 3, Archaeology Correspondence, 1894–99, UA.

5. Hilprecht to Harrison, 23 March 1897, UPB 65.1, box 3, Archaeology Correspondence, 1894–99, UA; Hilprecht to Edward Clark, 28 May 1901, Hilprecht Papers, 1901, AG.

6. Hilprecht to Harrison, 20 July 1894, 18 December 1897, UPB 65.1, box 3, Archaeology Correspondence, 1894–99, UA.

7. Hilprecht to Harrison, 23 March, 18 December, 1897, UPB 65.1, box 3, Archaeology Correspondence, 1894–97, UA; memo, ca. May 1905, and Hilprecht to Edward Clark, 20 December 1901, Hilprecht Papers, 1901, AG; Hilprecht report, December 1898, Curatorial 1, Reports, MA.

8. Hilprecht to Harrison, 1 August 1898, UPB 65.1, box 3, Archaeology Correspondence, 1884–99, UA.

9. Hilprecht to Harrison, 21 January 1895, 23 March, 12 May, 19 October 1897, 8 November 1898, UPB 65.1, box 3, Archaeology Correspondence, 1894–99, UA.

10. Hilprecht to Harrison, 23 March 1897 and 3 April 1900, UPB 65.1, box 3, Archaeology Correspondence, 1894–99, UA.

11. Hilprecht to Edward Clark, 22 March 1900 and other dates, Curatorial 1, 1898–1900, Stevenson to Clark, 9 May 1900, Secretary-Letterbook 4, 21 November 1899 to 20 February 1901, MA.

12. On publications, see memos, 1896–99, Museum, 1892–1904, AG; Curatorial 4, Publications, 1896–1905, esp. Edward Clark to Pepper, 22 June 1896, MA.

13. Hilprecht to Harrison, 12 December 1896, UPB 65.1, box 3, Archaeology Correspondence, 1894–99, UA.

14. For a summary, see Peters to Edward Clark, 30 January 1897, 12/3, NR.

15. Hilprecht to Harrison, 12 and 18 December 1896, UPB 65.1, box 3, Archaeology Correspondence, 1894–99, UA.

16. See Haynes manuscript, all versions, 10/2, NR.

17. See the correspondence with Putnam's from Hilprecht and others, 12/4, esp. Hilprecht to Pepper, n.d. [1897], 12/1, NR.

18. Hilprecht to Edward Clark, 4 December 1898, 17/9, NR.

19. Haynes to Edward Clark, 27 June 1893, 17/6, NR.

20. See Fisher file, AG.

21. See Diane Taylor's account, "History in an Attic," MA, and, in the primary sources, especially Edward Clark to Harrison, 30 September 1898, UPB 65.1, box 3, Archaeology Correspondence, 1894–99, UA.

22. Hilprecht to Pepper, 27 July 1898, Peters to Edward Clark, 25 August 1898, 17/6, 8 September 1898, 17/9, NR.

23. Itinerary, 12/3, NR.

24. My account is based on the following: J. H. Haynes field notes, 14/6, Cassandria Haynes field notes, 15/1, Geere diary extracts, 16/2, J. H. Haynes diary, 16/3, NR, and Hilprecht Tagebuch, HS.

25. Geere's memoir, *By Nile and Euphrates: A Record of Discovery and Adventure* (Edinburgh, 1904), is a charming expression of the mind of the imperial traveler, but far less revealing than the diary.

26. Babylonian Committee Minutes, 31 May 1899, Directors Files, 2/2, MA; Hilprecht to Harrison, 11 June 1899, UPB 65.1, box 3, Archaeology Correspondence, 1891–93, UA.

27. Hilprecht to Harrison, 18 June 1899, Harrison Papers, UA.

28. The following account of Hilprecht's views is drawn from his weekly reports to Edward Clark, March to May 1900, 19/9, NR, and Reports from the Babylonian Expedition under Hilprecht, 1900, AG.

29. Geere diary, 16/2, NR.

30. Hilprecht Tagebuch, 25 March 1900, HS.

31. This comparison of Mrs. Haynes and Mrs. Hilprecht occurs later, in Hilprecht to Edward Clark, 7 July and 20 December 1901, Hilprecht Papers, 1901, AG.

32. Hilprecht Tagebuch, 10–14 March 1900, HS.

33. *PHC*, 96, 121–27.

34. Hilprecht Tagebuch, 12 March, 20 April 1900, HS.

35. Hilprecht Tagebuch, 21 April 1900, HS.

36. Hilprecht to Harrison, 3 April 1900, UPB 65.1, box 3, Archaeology Correspondence, 1900–1903, UA.

37. Corrected Hilprecht draft, 15 November 1901, Hilprecht Papers, 1901, AG.

38. Harrison to Hilprecht, 14 June 1901, Harrison Letterbook, UA. For the text of the agreement, see Directors Files, 15/9, MA.

39. Hilprecht to Newbold, 23 February 1901, UPB 65.1, box 3, Archaeology Correspondence, 1900–1903, UA.

40. Babylonian Committee Minutes, Fifth Babylonian Expedition, 18 May 1903, Directors Files, 2/13, MA.

CHAPTER FIVE

1. For descriptive surveys of the field, see Adler, "Beginnings of Semitic Studies in America," 317–28; William Rosenau, "Semitic Studies in American Colleges," in *Yearbook of the Central Conference of American Rabbis, 1896* (Cincinnati, 1897), 99–13; and C. Wade Meade, *Road to Babylon: The Development of U.S. Assyriology* (Leiden, 1974).

2. See Ernest W. Saunders, *Searching the Scriptures: A History of the Society of Biblical Literature, 1880–1980* (Chicago, 1982).

3. On the AIA, see Homer A. Thompson, "In Pursuit of the Past: The American Role, 1879–1979," *AJA* 84 (1980): 263–70.

4. On the schools, see Philip King, *American Archaeology in the Mideast* (Philadelphia, 1983).

5. I tell this story in *Churchmen and Philosophers*; the figures are from Thomas H. Olbricht, "Intellectual Ferment and Instruction in the Scriptures: The Bible in Higher Education," in *The Bible in American Education: From Source Book to Textbook*, ed. David Barr and Nicholas Piediscalzi (Philadelphia, 1982), 101–5.

6. Jerry Wayne Brown's work is critical here: see his *Rise of Biblical Criticism*.

7. On Norton, I am indebted to conversations with James Turner, who is working on a biography of Norton; see also Donald Preziosi's useful essay, "The Question of Art History," in *Questions of Evidence: Proof, Practice, and Persuasion across the Disciplines*, ed. James Chandler, Arnold T. Davidson, and Harry Harootunian (Chicago, 1994), 203–26.

8. For the troubles of the anthropologists, see Hinsley, "From Shell-Heaps to Stelae," 51–59.

9. Yellow sheet, n.d., General Correspondence, 1880s-1930s, SM.

10. On the museum, see *Addresses Delivered at the Formal Opening of the Semitic Museum of Harvard University . . .* (Cambridge, Mass., 1903); E. E. Braithwaite, "The Semitic Museum of Harvard University," *Records of the Past* 4 (1905): 243–51; and Jacob Schiff, "Report of the Committee on the Semitic Languages for the Years 1893–1905," SM. On Schiff, see Cyrus Adler, "Jacob Henry Schiff, A Biographical Sketch," *American Jewish Yearbook* 23 (1921–22): 21–64; Adler, *Jacob H. Schiff: His Life and Letters* (New York, 1928); and David Lyon, "Relations of Jacob Schiff to Harvard University," David Lyon Papers, HUA. On Hilprecht and Lyon, see Hilprecht to Harrison, 21 January 1895, and Putnam to Lyon, 18 January 1895, UPB 65.5, box 3, Archaeology Correspondence, 1894–99, UA.

11. This wonderful story is best told in David Lyon's narrative, "Relations of Jacob Schiff."

12. See Reisner, Biography, Archives, BMFA; Reisner to Hearst, 7 December 1899, BL; and Hearst to Culin, 24 July 1900, Hearst Correspondence, Directors Files 8, MA.

13. See George A. Reisner, *The Early Dynastic Cemeteries of Naga-Ed-Der*, University of California Publications in Egyptian Archaeology, vol. 2, part 1, Hearst Egyptian Expedition (Leipzig, 1908), v–viii. The California story is told well in

Timothy H. H. Thoresen, "Paying the Piper and Calling the Tune: The Beginnings of Academic Anthropology in California," *Journal of the History of the Behavioral Sciences* 11 (1975): 257–75.

14. Wilson, *Signs and Wonders upon Pharaoh*; 144–45.

15. See Ritterband and Wechsler, *Jewish Learning in American Universities*, 104.

16. Walter Muir Whitehill, *Museum of Fine Arts, Boston: A Centennial History* (Cambridge, Mass., 1970), 1:246–65.

17. David Lyon, "A Half Century of Assyriology," *Biblical World* 8 (1896): 134, 136.

18. Reisner to Hearst, 25 September, 9 November, and 7 December 1899, BL.

19. Reisner to Eliot, 19 October 1906, Eliot Papers, HUA.

20. Reisner to Hearst, 13 February, 30 April, and 15 May 1900, BL.

21. Whitehill, *Museum of Fine Arts, Boston*, 1:246–65; Reisner to Hearst, 16 March 1907, Old Hearst Papers, 1-A-7, Egyptology, BMFA.

22. See Lyon, "Relations of Jacob Schiff."

23. A good appraisal of Gilman is given in Darryl Hart, "Faith and Learning in the Age of the University: The Academic Ministry of Daniel Coit Gilman," in Marsden and Longfield, *Secularization of the Academy*, 107–45.

24. Adler announcement, Haupt Letters, 1886–87, Langley to Haupt, 15 February 1888, Haupt Letters, Gilman Papers, JHU.

25. Cyrus Adler's autobiography is *I Have Considered the Days* (Philadelphia, 1945).

26. On Goode, see Curtis M. Hinsley, Jr., *Savages and Scientists: The Smithsonian Institution and the Development of American Anthropology, 1846–1910* (Washington, D.C., 1981), 91–94, and Sally Gregory Kohlstedt, ed., *The Origins of Natural Science in America: The Essays of George Brown Goode* (Washington, D.C., 1991), esp. Kohlstedt's introduction, "George Brown Goode, 1851–1896," 1–21, and Goode's "Museums of the Future," 342–45.

27. Adler announcement, Haupt Letters, 1886–87, Gilman Papers, JHU.

28. For the AOS, see Rocher, "History of the AOS." For Haupt's imperialism, see Cooper, "From Mosul to Manila," 151–55, and Moshe Perlmann, "Paul Haupt and the Mesopotamian Projects," *Publications of the American Jewish Historical Society* 47 (1958): 154–75. Later, when the United States acquired the Philippines, Haupt urged the AOS to use this instance of American imperialism to have the government give financial support to American studies of Asian cultures (see Cooper, "From Mosul to Manila," 155–57).

29. Cyrus Adler, "Beginnings of Semitic Studies in America," 324–26; Langley to Haupt, 15 February 1888, Haupt Letters, Gilman Papers, JHU.

30. Paul Haupt, "Important Talk," 27 October 1884, Haupt Papers, Haupt to Gilman, 1 November 1884, Haupt to Gilman, rec'd 17 August 1885, Gilman draft reply, Memos, 1 December 1885 and 12 January 1886, Haupt Letters, Gilman Papers, JHU.

31. See, e.g., *JAOS* 14 (1890), 16 (1894), and 17 (1894).

32. Yellow sheet, n.d., General Correspondence, 1880s–1930s, SM.

33. Ward to Greene, 18 May 1910, and Ward to Morgan, 22 September 1911, Ward Letters, ML. On Ward and Morgan, I am indebted to conversations with the late Dr. Edith Porada.

34. Gottheil to Low, 25 May 1895, and Low to Gottheil, 18 June 1895, Gottheil Files, LL.

35. For Schiff's giving patterns, see Adler, "Jacob Henry Schiff," esp. 38–43, and Ritterband and Wechsler, *Jewish Learning in American Universities*, 281 n. 14 and 299 n. 96.

36. See Gottheil Letterbook, 1906–8, Rare Books and Archives, Butler Library, Columbia University, and Butler-Morgan Correspondence, Morgan Files, LL.

37. See esp. the C. H. Johns and I. Elias Gejou files, ML.

38. Adler, "Beginnings of Semitic Studies in America," 326–27; Lyon, "Half Century of Assyriology," 134; and *In August Company: The Collections of the Pierpont Morgan Library* (New York, 1993), 49.

39. My appraisal of Morgan is my own, but I am indebted to the work of Jean Strouse on the financier and to Neil Harris's "Collective Possession: J. Pierpont Morgan and the American Imagination," in his *Cultural Excursions: Marketing Appetites and Cultural Tastes in Modern America* (Chicago, 1990), 250–75.

40. See Albert Clay, ed., *Babylonian Records in the Library of J. Pierpont Morgan* (New Haven, 1912–22), and Clay, ed., *A Hebrew Deluge Story in Cuneiform and Other Epic Fragments in the Pierpont Morgan Library* (New Haven, 1922).

41. Morgan to Hadley, 3 January 1910, King to Hadley, 4 January 1910, Yale Corporation Records, Yale Corporation Minutes, 14 January and 21 February 1910, YUA.

42. See Clay Letters, 1909–10, ML.

43. Prince to Butler, 12 February 1913, Prince Files, LL.

44. See "James Buchanan Nies," exhibition copy, and Nies will, YBC.

45. Reisner, Biography, Archives, BMFA.

46. Olbricht, "Intellectual Ferment and Instruction," 110–13.

47. On Harper, see Robert W. French, "The Watershed of the American Biblical Tradition: The Chicago School, First Phase, 1892–1920," *JBL* 95 (1976): 8–11.

48. J. Dyneley Prince, "Robert Francis Harper, 1864–1914," *American Journal of Semitic Languages and Literature* 31 (1914–15): 91.

49. Adler to Langley, 27 October 1899, series 1, box 3, Langley-Adler Correspondence, SIA.

50. Bible Land Exploration, box 108, folder: Pledge, 3 July 1903, Rockefeller Family, 2-OMR, Educational Interests, RA.

51. Confidential Report no. 1, box 108, folder: Pledge, 3 July 1903, Rockefeller Family, 2-OMR, Educational Interests, RA.

52. See Hilprecht to Houston, 20 June 1905, Curatorial 5, HVH, uncatalogued 2, MA.

53. Edgar James Banks, *Bismya; or, The Lost City of Adab: A Story of Adventure . . .* (New York, 1912); *The Expedition of the Oriental Exploration Fund (Babylonian Section) of the University of Chicago* (Chicago, 1904).

54. Suzanne Marchand, *The Rise and Fall of German Philhellenism* (Princeton, forthcoming).

55. Laffan to Greene, 24 May 1909, Laffan Letters, ML; Banks to Clay, 22 May 1913, Banks, 1913–22, YBC; Harper-Breasted Correspondence, 5, U of C Semitic Languages, 1913, Breasted's Office Files, OI.

56. Lieshman to Banks, 15 May 1905, Banks to Judson, 25 April 1906, 9 October 1911, 51/7, Presidents' Papers, 1889–1925, RL.

57. Banks to Judson, 25 April 1906, 51/7, Presidents' Papers, 1889–1925, RL; Shelf List, Banks, Edgar, RA.

58. Lieshman to Banks, 15 May 1905, Frank Harper to Hilprecht, 25 March 1905, 51/7, Presidents' Papers, 1889–1925, RL.

59. Lieshman to Laffan, 10 March 1909, Laffan, YBC; Gates to Rockefeller, 5 November 1910, box 108, folder: Pledge, 3 July 1903, Rockefeller Family, 2-OMR, Educational Interests, RA.

60. Hilprecht to Houston, 20 June 1905, Curatorial 5, HVH, uncatalogued 2, MA.

61. Breasted to Frank Harper, 12 June 1907, U of C Semitic Languages, 1907, Breasted's Office Files, OI.

62. Reisner to Eliot, 2 August 1905, Eliot to Reisner, 25 August 1905, Eliot Papers, HUA.

63. On Breasted, see Breasted, *Pioneer to the Past*, and Wilson, *Signs and Wonders upon Pharaoh*, 130–43.

64. Frank Harper's impact on Breasted is cited again and again in Breasted, *Pioneer to the Past*, esp. 120–22, 131–33.

65. See the correspondence among the Rockefeller intermediary F. T. Gates, Harper, and Breasted in box 108, folder: Pledge, 3 July 1903, Rockefeller Family, 2-OMR, Educational Interests, RA.

66. Jeffrey Abt is at work on a biography of Breasted, and his astute approach is hinted at in "James H. Breasted and the Oriental Institute, 1894–1935," *Research Reports from the Rockefeller Archive Center* (spring 1993): 1–4.

67. James Henry Breasted, *The Oriental Institute of the University of Chicago: A Beginning and a Program* (Chicago, 1922), 1.

68. James Henry Breasted, "The Place of the Near Orient in the Career of Man and the Task of the American Orientalist," *JAOS* 39 (1919): 159–84; Breasted, *Oriental Institute*; Breasted, *The Oriental Institute of the University of Chicago* (Chicago, 1931); and Thorkild Jacobsen and John A. Wilson, "The Oriental Institute: Thirty Years and the Present," *Journal of Near Eastern Studies* 8 (1949): 236–47.

69. See Haupt to Gilman, March 1892, Haupt Letters, Gilman Papers, JHU, and Ryke Borger, "Altorientalische Lexikographie Geschichte und Probleme: Zur Vollendung von W. vonSoden, Akkadisches Handworterbuch," *Nachrichten der Akademie der Wissenchaften in Gottingen I. Philogogisch-Historische Klasse*, no. 2 (1984): 84–93.

70. Breasted, "Place of the Near Orient," 180.

71. Breasted, *Oriental Institute* (1931), 54.

72. "Future and Development of the Oriental Institute," n.d., box 112, folder: General Pledges, 29 December 1923 Pledge, Rockefeller Family, 2-OMR, Educational Interests, RA.

73. Breasted, "Place of the Near Orient," 180–81.

74. Breasted, *Pioneer to the Past*, 218.

75. For the striking case of Semitic languages, see Ritterband and Wechsler, *Jewish Learning in American Universities*, 39–44.

76. On Wilbour, see Wilson, *Signs and Wonders upon Pharaoh*, 99–109; on Davis, see John Romer, *Valley of the Kings* (London, 1981), 183–244.

77. For the Boston Museum, I am indebted on this point to an interview with Peter Manuelian, 2 August 1994.

78. Laffan to Clay, 11 June 1909, Clay to Laffan, 26 June 1909, Laffan Files, YBC.

79. Fisher file, 1918–29, Leonard Woolley file, 1926–27, YBC.

80. Expeditions file, 1899–1922, YBC.

81. Ferris J. Stephens, "History of the Babylonian Collection," *Yale University Library Gazette* 36 (1961–62): 132.

82. For a nice statement on the role of museums, see Lyon, "Half Century of Assyriology," 125.

83. The issue touched on in my story is broached more fully in Robert F. Arnove, ed., *Philanthropy and Cultural Imperialism: The Foundations at Home and Abroad* (Bloomington, Ind., 1980), especially the essay by Barbara Howe, "The Emergence of Scientific Philanthropy, 1900–1920: Origins, Issues, and Outcomes," 25–54.

84. For a stimulating account of this problem, see Baruch Halpern, *The First Historians: The Hebrew Bible and History* (San Francisco, 1988).

85. Barbara Zink MacHaffie, "Monument Facts and Higher Critical Fancies: Archaeology and the Popularization of Old Testament Criticism in Nineteenth-Century Britain," *Church History* 50 (1981): 327–28.

86. On biblical archaeology, see Moorey, *Century of Biblical Archaeology*, and Homer O. Thompson, *Biblical Archaeology* (New York, 1987).

87. Haynes manuscript, chap. 17, 10/2, NR.

88. James A. Montgomery, "Oriental Studies in the University," *General Magazine and Historical Chronicle* 36 (1933–34): 206.

89. See Mark Noll, *Between Faith and Criticism: Evangelicals, Scholarship, and the Bible in America*, 2d ed. (Grand Rapids, Mich., 1991), and Edgar Krentz, *The Historical-Critical Method* (Philadelphia, 1975).

90. David G. Hogarth, ed., *Authority and Archaeology: Sacred and Profane: Essays on the Relation of Monuments to Biblical and Classical Literature* (London, 1899), v–xiv. For a reprise of the same position, see Milar Burrows, *What Mean These Stones: The Significance of Archaeology for Biblical Studies* (New Haven, 1941).

91. This is the conclusion I draw from George A. Barton, "Higher Archaeology and the Verdict of Criticism," *JBL* 32 (1913): 260.

92. For comparative religion, see Eric J. Sharpe, *Comparative Religion: A History*, 2d ed. (LaSalle, Ill., 1986); Jastrow, "Recent Movements," and Samuel Noah Kramer, *In the World of Sumer: An Autobiography* (Detroit, 1986), 209–13. Robert S. Shepard, *God's People in the Ivory Tower: Religion in the Early American University* (Brooklyn, N.Y., 1991), is a monograph on the subject. For a survey of related developments, see Murray G. Murphey, "On the Scientific Study of Religion in the United States, 1870–1980," in *Religion and Twentieth-Century American Intellectual Life*, ed. Michael J. Lacey (New York, 1989), 136–71.

93. For a sense of Haupt's religiosity and of his self-importance, see his "Bible and Babel," *Johns Hopkins University Circulars* 22 (June 1903): 47–51.

94. For putting the problem this way, I am indebted to Van A. Harvey, *The Historian and the Believer* (New York, 1966).

95. I see this compromise as a descendant of that discussed by Robert N. Proctor, *Value-Free Science? Purity and Power in Modern Knowledge* (Cambridge, Mass., 1991), 33–38.

CHAPTER SIX

1. See the clipping file in Hilprecht, 952, AG.

2. Hilprecht to Edward Clark, 15 and 22 January 1903, Hilprecht Reports, Curatorial 1, MA.

3. Newspaper reports in Hilprecht, 952, AG. For other mentions of a new expedition, see Hilprecht to Harper, 11 December 1902, Curatorial 1, 1901–5, and Osborne to Hilprecht, 16 May 1903, Curatorial 1, 1906–10, MA.

4. Hilprecht to Charles W. Eliot, 11 December 1902, Eliot Papers, HUA.

5. Hilprecht, 952, AG.

6. Clay to Smith, 28 February 1904, UPB 65.1, box 3, Archaeology Correspondence, 1900–1903, UA.

7. Dodson memo, Hilprecht, 952, AG.

8. Hilprecht to Harrison, 30 November 1904, and memo, "Dr. Hilprecht," n.d., UPB 65.1, box 3, Hilprecht Papers and Data, 1905, UA.

9. See Hilprecht to Harrison, 6 April 1904, and Clay to Harrison, 7 April 1904, UPB 65.1, box 3, Archaeology Correspondence, 1900–1903, UA; see also Williams to Stevenson, 3 July 1904, Directors Files, 7/1, MA.

10. Stevenson to Harrison, 19 November 1904, UPB 65.1, box 3, Archaeology Correspondence, 1904–8, UA. The Myhrman case was a major one. See Directors Files, 15/9, MA.

11. Minutes of the Board of Managers, May 1904, and Fisher to Houston, 16 March 1905, Curatorial 5, Hilprecht Controversy, uncatalogued 2, MA.

12. Myhrman to Gordon, 28 July 1911, Directors Files, 15/9, MA.

13. See the correspondence from Hilprecht and Jastrow to Pepper in Archaeology, 1893, AG, and Hilprecht to Stevenson, 9 December 1902, Curatorial 4, Hilprecht Controversy, MA.

14. Paul Ritterband and Harold Wechsler, "A Message to Lushtamar: The Hilprecht Controversy and Semitic Scholarship in America," *History of Higher Education Annual* 1 (1981): 8–11 (and the material cited therein in UA); Wechsler, "Pulpit or Professoriate: The Case of Morris Jastrow," *American Jewish History* 74 (1985): 338–55.

15. See, among many other works, Jastrow, *Study of Religion*. For the quality of Jastrow's work, see the appraisal by William A. Clebsch, "Apples, Oranges, and Manna: Comparative Religion Revisited," *Journal of the American Academy of Religion* 49 (1981): 5, 9–10.

16. See the funeral service in *Sara Yorke Stevenson* (Philadelphia, 1902), 62.

17. For a discussion, see Jacob J. Finkelstein, "Bible and Babel," *Commentary* 26 (July–December 1958): 431–44.

18. Friedrich Delitzsch, *Babel and Bible* . . ., trans. and with an introduction by C. H. W. Johns (New York, 1903), 2–3.

19. Jews who were more conservative thought Delitzsch's lecture was anti-

Semitic. Jastrow was thus put in opposition to both confessional Protestants and Jews. See Schwartz, *Emergence of Jewish Scholarship*, 137.

20. *Philadelphia Sunday School Times*, 29 November 1902, in Curatorial 4, Hilprecht Publications (ser. 1), MA.

21. Stevenson to Harrison, 26 May 1904, UPB 65.1, box 3, Archaeology Correspondence, 1904–8, UA; Hilprecht to Clark, 22 January 1903, Curatorial 1, Hilprecht Reports, MA.

22. Gottheil to Hilprecht, 29 November 1907, Gottheil Letterbook, Archives, Rare Books and Archives, Butler Library, Columbia University.

23. Harper, "Hilprecht-Peters Controversy."

24. See "The American Oriental Society, April 22, 1903," *Nation*, 30 April 1903, 352.

25. *PHC*, 22, 32.

26. Bodine to Stevenson, 22 January 1905, and Stevenson to Baugh, 1 February 1905, Directors Files, 7/2, Stevenson to Baugh, 12 March 1905, Curatorial 5, Stevenson, 1902–6, Curatorial 4, Hilprecht Controversy, Barton to Stevenson, 23 February 1907, Curatorial 5, Hilprecht Controversy, MA; Ranke to Harrison, 22 June 1905, UPB 65.1, box 3, Hilprecht Papers, 1905, UA.

27. Ranke to Harrison, 7 April 1905, UPB 65.1, box 3, Hilprecht Papers, 1905, UA.

28. See the newspaper clippings in Curatorial 5, 672 and 673, MA.

29. I have cited this in the version used during the hearings: HVH, Hilprecht's reprint of his contribution to *Explorations in Bible Lands*, 526n.

30. See Stevenson's summary of events to Harris, 6 March 1905, Secretary Letterbook 7, MA.

31. For a lighthearted treatment of this issue, see John L. Hess, *The Grand Acquisitors* (Boston, 1974).

32. "Last Will and Testament of Herman Vollrath Hilprecht," Office of Register of Wills, City Hall, Philadelphia; Charlotte Brodkey Moore, "Description and Analysis of the Bronze and Lead Objects in the Herman V. Hilprecht Collection, the University Museum of Pennsylvania" (Ph.D. diss., University of Pennsylvania, 1969), xlvii–xlviii.

33. Stevenson to Harris, 1 April 1905, Curatorial 5, Stevenson, 1902–6, Stevenson to Bodine, May 1904, Directors Files, 7/2, MA; see also Stevenson chronology and notes, Curatorial 5, Hilprecht Controversy, uncatalogued 2, MA.

34. Fisher's most compelling statement on this and many other points is in a draft letter to a newspaper of 19 April 1908, Curatorial 5, uncatalogued 1, MA. The best enumeration of the collection, whose contents were subject to all these hazards, is given by Samuel Noah Kramer, "The Tablet Collection of the University Museum," *JAOS* 67 (1947): 321–22.

35. *PHC*, 60.

36. Clay to Harrison, 10 March 1903, UPB 65.1, box 3, Archaeology Correspondence, 1900–1903, UA; Ward to Fisher, 18 March 1906, 17/7, NR.

37. Stevenson chronology and notes, Curatorial 5, Hilprecht Controversy, uncatalogued 2, MA.

38. *PHC*, 66.

39. Stevenson to Baugh, 12 March 1905, Peters to Stevenson, 5 September 1905,

Curatorial 4, Hilprecht Controversy, MA; Clay to Langdon, 30 March 1918, Langdon, 1918–25, YBC.

40. Stevenson to Pepper, 23 March 1905, Curatorial 5, Stevenson, 1902–6, MA.

41. Hilprecht, 972, AG; *PHC*, 19; Furness memo, 1905, Directors Files, 7/4, MA.

42. Clay marginalia on his copy of *PHC*, 124, YBC.

43. Stevenson to Boyd, 1 April 1905, Stevenson to Baugh, spring 1905, Curatorial 5, Stevenson, 1902–6, MA.

44. *PHC*, 267–71.

45. See the Gottheil Letterbook for February and March 1907, Rare Books and Manuscripts, Butler Library, Columbia University.

46. *PHC*, 331.

47. Jastrow to Lyon, 19 March 1905, Letters, 1884–1913, Lyon Papers, HUA.

48. *PHC*, 329–32.

49. Edward Clark to Harrison, 25 March 1904, UPB 65.1, box 3, Archaeology Correspondence, 1900–1903, Houston to Hilprecht, 6 January 1908, 6 November 1907, Houston Letterbook, 21 February 1906–3 June 1908, Harrison to Hilprecht, 24 January 1908, UPB 65.1, box 3, Archaeology Correspondence, 1904–8, UA.

50. Clay to Harrison, 28 March 1904, UPB 65.1, box 3, Archaeology Correspondence, 1900–1903, UA.

51. See clipping in Curatorial 4, 1910, MA.

52. Hilprecht to Houston, 23 April 1908, Curatorial 1, 1906–10, MA.

53. Hermann V. Hilprecht, *The Earliest Version of the Babylonian Deluge Story and the Temple Library of Nippur* (Philadelphia, 1910).

54. See the analysis and citations in George A. Barton, "Hilprecht's Fragment . . . ," *JAOS* 31 (1911): 30.

55. See the Hilprecht-Robinette correspondence for April 1910, Hilprecht Papers, 1910, AG.

56. Ibid.; see also Barton, "Hilprecht's Fragment."

57. Clay to Greene, 29 March 1910, Johns file, ML.

58. See the clippings in Curatorial 5, 672 and 673, MA.

59. Hilprecht to Gordon, 24 January 1910, Curatorial 5, Hilprecht Controversy, uncatalogued 1, MA.

60. See the correspondence in Curatorial 2, Gordon-Clay, MA.

61. See the 1910 correspondence in Directors Files, 4/13, MA.

62. Hilprecht to Harrison, 4 March 1910, Curatorial 5, uncatalogued 1, MA.

63. Memo to Gordon and Hilprecht, 21 March 1910, Harrison Papers, Letter book, UA.

64. Gordon to Hilprecht, 23 April 1910, Curatorial 1, 1906–8, Hilprecht to Gordon, 25 April 1910, Curatorial 5, Gordon Case, MA.

65. Hilprecht Anniversary Volume (Leipzig, 1909).

66. Hilprecht to president and board of trustees, 29 April 1910, Curatorial 5, uncatalogued 1, MA.

67. Board of Managers Reports, 20 May, 17 June, and 21 October 1910, Directors Files 5, Reports to the Board, MA.

68. David Contosta, in *A Philadelphia Family*, 20, 40, suggests the pro-German orientation before World War I that went with being a Hilprecht supporter.

69. Houston to board of trustees, 14 November 1910, Harrison Letterbook, UA.

70. *Report in re Resignation of Dr. Herman V. Hilprecht* (Philadelphia, n.d. [ca. 1911]); *Copies of Letters* (Philadelphia, n.d. [ca. 1912]).

71. Radau to Sallie Crozer, 4 August 1911, Radau to Hilprecht, 31 July 1911, Curatorial 5, uncatalogued 1, MA.

CHAPTER SEVEN

1. For an introductory discussion, from which I have taken what follows, see W. F. Badé, *A Manual of Excavation in the Near East: Methods of Digging and Recording of the Tell en-Nasbeth Expedition in Palestine* (Berkeley and Los Angeles, 1934), 60–61.

2. The best example of this sort of archaeological book of advice is Flinders Petrie, *Methods and Aims in Archaeology* (London, 1904); see also Margaret Drower, *Flinders Petrie: A Life in Archaeology* (London, 1985), 277–79.

3. This assessment is William Foxwell Albright's in *History, Archaeology, and Christian Humanism* (New York, 1964), 114.

4. See Mark Bowden, *Pitt Rivers: The Life and Archaeological Work of Lieutenant General Augustus Henry Lane Fox Pitt Rivers, DCL, FRS, FSA* (Cambridge, England, 1991).

5. Drower, *Flinders Petrie*, 137; Bowden, *Pitt Rivers*, 92–93; Richard Burleigh and Juliet Clutton Brock, "Pitt Rivers and Petrie in Egypt," *Antiquity* 56 (1982): 208–9.

6. Peters to Edward Clark, 29 April, 13 June 1889, Hilprecht to Pepper, 24 February 1889, 4/2, NR.

7. Peters to Edward Clark, 18 October 1898, 17/9, NR.

8. Harper, "Hilprecht-Peters Controversy."

9. Haynes to Peters, 30 April 1894, Nippur Letter Books, vol. 3, Haynes Letters, Haynes to Edward Clark with Hilprecht marginalia, 3 August 1895, 10/6, NR; Haynes to Peters, 25 August 1894, UPB 65.1, box 3, Archaeology Correspondence, 1891–94, UA.

10. Hilprecht to Clark, 13 December 1894, 11/2, NR.

11. See Daniel and Renfrew, *Idea of Prehistory*, 110, and Fagan, *Return to Babylon*, 212–22.

12. Clarence Fisher, *Excavations at Nippur: The Topography and City Walls* (Lancaster, Pa., 1905).

13. Hilprecht Tagebuch, 20–24 March 1900, HS.

14. For Robert Koldewey see his *Die Tempel von Babylon und Bor* (Leipzig, 1911).

15. Drower, *Flinders Petrie*, 429–30. In addition to the specific works cited, the following discussion of Petrie, Reisner, and Fisher is indebted to the excellent dissertation by Thomas William Davis, "A History of Biblical Archaeology" (Ph.D. diss., University of Arizona, 1987), esp. 59–120.

16. Flinders Petrie, "Sequences in Prehistoric Remains," *Journal of the Royal Anthropological Institute of Great Britain and Ireland* 29 (1899): 295–301; see also Drower, *Flinders Petrie*, 160–63.

17. Seymour Gitin, "Stratigraphy and Its Application to Chronology and Terminology," in *Biblical Archaeology Today*, ed. Avraham Biran (Jerusalem, 1985), 100.

18. Drower, *Flinders Petrie*, 254.

19. See William Foxwell Albright, *From the Stone Age to Christianity: Monotheism and the Historical Process* (Baltimore, 1940), 23–25.

20. Drower, *Flinders Petrie*, 251–54.

21. The best source on Bliss is Jeffrey A. Blakely, "Frederick Jones Bliss: Father of Palestinian Archaeology," *Biblical Archaeology* 56 (1993): 110–15.

22. Drower, *Flinders Petrie*, 264; see the obituary of George Andrew Reisner by H. E. Winlock in *American Philosophical Society Yearbook, 1942* (Philadelphia, 1942), 370.

23. Peter Der Manuelian, ed., "George Andrew Reisner on Archaeological Photography," *Journal of the American Research Center in Egypt* 29 (1992): 1–34. Such professional techniques were becoming commonplace, in part because of Reisner's example. See Douglas R. Givens, *Alfred Vincent Kidder and the Development of Americanist Archaeology* (Albuquerque, N.M., 1992), 25, and Badé, *Manual of Excavation*, 13.

24. See Wilson, *Signs and Wonders upon Pharaoh*, 148–50, and Drower, *Flinders Petrie*, 430–31.

25. G. Andrew Reisner, "Egyptology, 1896–1928," in *The Development of Harvard University since the Inauguration of President Eliot, 1869–1929*, ed. Samuel Eliot Morison (Cambridge, Mass., 1930), 241–47; see also Reisner, "Principles, Methods, and General Results," in *Harvard Excavations at Samaria, 1908–1910*, by George Andrew Reisner, Clarence Stanley Fisher, and David Gordon Lyon (Cambridge, Mass., 1924), 1:31–90.

26. For an astute treatment of some of these themes, see Kenneth Hudson, *A Social History of Archaeology* (London, 1981).

27. For an account of the delays that kept the Americans in Egypt, see Neil Asher Silberman, *Digging for God and Country: Exploration, Archaeology, and the Secret Struggles for the Holy Land, 1799–1918* (New York, 1982), 171–76; on Jastrow and Lyon, see the 1906 letter from Jastrow to Lyon, Lyon Letters, 1884–1913, Lyon Papers, HUA.

28. Reisner to Gordon, 29 December 1910, 25 February 1911, Directors Files, 17/12, MA; Fisher to Clay, 19 September 1918, Fisher, 1918–29, YBC.

29. Harper to Hilprecht, 25 March 1905, 51/7, Presidents' Papers, 1889–1925, RL; see also the correspondence between Clay and Fisher, Fisher, 1918–29, YBC.

30. Clarence Fisher, *The Excavation of Armageddon* (Chicago, 1929); Badé, *Manual of Excavation*, 15–18; G. Ernest Wright, "The Phenomenon of American Archaeology in the Near East," in *Essays in Honor of Nelson Glueck: Near Eastern Archaeology in the Twentieth Century*, ed. James A. Sanders (New York, 1970), 14–16, and Philip J. King, "The Influence of G. Ernest Wright on the Archaeology of Palestine," in *Archaeology and Biblical Interpretation: Essays in Memory of D. Glenn Rose*, ed. Leo G. Perdue, Lawrence E. Toombs, and Gary Lance Johnson (Atlanta, 1987), 18–19.

31. See Gus W. Van Beek, "Albright's Contribution to Archaeology," in *The Scholarship of William Foxwell Albright*, ed. Gus W. Van Beek (Atlanta, 1989), 64–65.

32. John A. Wilson, "James Henry Breasted—The Idea of an Oriental Institute," in Sanders, *Essays in Honor of Nelson Glueck*, 50.

33. Drower, *Flinders Petrie*, 388–89.

34. Gitin, "Stratigraphy," 101–2.

35. R. E. M. Wheeler, *Archaeology from the Earth* (Oxford, 1954); Kathleen Kenyon, *Beginning in Archaeology* (New York, 1952); H. J. Franken and C. A. Franken-Battershill, *A Primer of Old Testament Archaeology* (Leiden, 1963); and Philip Barker, *Techniques of Archaeological Excavation*, 2d ed. rev. (New York, 1982).

36. Thompson, *Biblical Archaeology*, 124.

37. See M. J. Aitkin, *Science-Based Dating in Archaeology* (London, 1990), esp. 1–6.

38. Quentin Smith's *Language and Time* (New York, 1993) philosophically defends absolute time. For an example of the (nonphilosophical) social constructivists, see Johannes Fabian, *Time and the Other: How Anthropology Makes Its Object* (New York, 1983). A recent collection of essays suggesting the general orientation is John Bender and David E. Wellbery, eds., *Chronotypes: The Construction of Time* (Berkeley and Los Angeles, 1991). By extension, Timothy Mitchell's arguments in *Colonising Egypt* (Cambridge, England, 1988) could be applied to Petrie's work.

39. *PHC*, 179, 214.

40. Hilprecht to board of trustees, 12 November 1910, Directors Files, 15/9, MA.

41. Peters, "Thirty Years' Progress in Semitics," 33–34.

42. Silberman, *Digging for God and Country*, is an excellent study of this issue.

43. Glyn Daniel, *One Hundred Fifty Years of Archaeology*, 2d ed. (London, 1975), 311.

44. Seton Lloyd, *Twin Rivers*, 2d ed. (Oxford, 1947), 39.

45. Hudson, in *Social History of Archaeology*, quoting Colin Renfrew, 135–37.

46. Jane H. Kelley and Marsha P. Hanen, *Archaeology and the Methodology of Science* (Albuquerque, N.M., 1988), 360–61.

47. G. K. Chesterton, "The Honour of Israel Gow," in Chesterton, *The Father Brown Omnibus* (New York, 1935), 106–7.

CHAPTER EIGHT

1. Hilprecht to board, 16 December 1910, Curatorial 5, uncatalogued 1, MA (emphasis added).

2. Minutes of the board of managers, 20 January 1911, MA.

3. For a summary from Hilprecht's side, see Hilprecht to board, 21 June 1912, Hilprecht Controversy, 1912, AG.

4. Copies of clippings, August 1911, Curatorial 5, Hilprecht Controversy, uncatalogued 1, MA.

5. Clipping, 1 August 1911, Hilprecht, 952, AG.

6. Clay to Gordon, 18 June 1911, Curatorial 2, Clay, MA.

7. Hilprecht to trustees, 21 June 1912, Hilprecht Controversy, 1912, AG.

8. See the material in UPT 50 H 319, 1911, Correspondence, UA.

9. Minutes of the Trustees, 14 October 1912, UA.

10. See, e.g., clipping, 20 December 1913, Hilprecht, 1907, 954, AG.

11. For the quotation, see Hilprecht to Houston, 4 April 1912, 13.L., University Museum, Houston Papers, APS. This entire folder contains material on the reinstatement.

12. Sayce to Gordon, 18 November 1918, Directors Office, box 18, Gordon,

Budge to Gordon, 19 March 1915, Directors Office, box 18, Budge, Langdon to Rogers, 8 December 1915, Curatorial 5, Langdon, MA.

13. Langdon to Gordon, 15 June 1918, Curatorial 5, Langdon, MA. See C. J. Gadd, "Stephen Herbert Langdon, 1876–1937," *Proceedings of the British Academy* 23 (1937): 3–18.

14. On the genesis of *Murder in Mesopotamia*, see Agatha Christie, *An Autobiography* (New York, 1977), 469–518; Janet Morgan, *Agatha Christie: A Biography* (New York, 1985), 210–11; and Gillian Gill, *Agatha Christie: The Woman and Her Mysteries* (New York, 1990), 122–24.

15. Information on Hilprecht comes from an unpublished essay by Aage Westenholz, in Westenholz's possession.

16. Interview with Alessandro Pezzati, 27 December 1994.

17. Part of the story of the tablets can be pieced together by reading carefully Raphael Kutscher's circumspect work, *The Brockmon Tablets at the University of Haifa: Royal Inscriptions* (Haifa, 1989), 9, 49, 103. See also "Last Will and Testament of Herman Vollrath Hilprecht." The provenance of these tablets is an embarrassment to Assyriologists.

18. Jeffrey Tigay, *The Evolution of the Gilgamesh Epic* (Philadelphia, 1982), 138.

19. I have found the best analysis to be Thorkild Jacobsen, *The Treasures of Darkness: A History of Mesopotamian Religion* (New Haven, 1976), 209–18.

20. Tigay, *Evolution of the Gilgamesh Epic*, 373; Kramer, *In the World of Sumer*, 79.

21. The most critical example is Alexander Heidel's influential and much cited book, *The Gilgamesh Epic and Old Testament Parallels* (Chicago, 1946).

22. Morris Jastrow, Jr., *The Religion of Babylonia and Assyria* (Boston, 1898), 513–17.

23. Morris Jastrow, Jr., *The Civilization of Babylonia and Assyria* (Philadelphia, 1915), 444.

24. See Julian Morgenstern, "Morris Jastrow, Jr., as a Biblical Critic," *JAOS* 41 (1921): 324–26.

25. Morris Jastrow, Jr., "The Hebrew and Babylonian Accounts of Creation," *Jewish Quarterly Review* 13 (1901): 650–54.

26. Stephanie Dalley, trans., *Myths from Mesopotamia: Creation, the Flood, Gilgamesh, and Others* (New York, 1991), xvi, 40.

27. Tigay, *Evolution of the Gilgamesh Epic*, 131; Kramer, *In the World of Sumer*, 75.

28. Dalley, *Myths from Mesopotamia*, 45.

29. For an excellent account of this procedure, see John Gardner and John Maier, *Gilgamesh: Translated from the Sin-leqi-unninni Version* (New York, 1984), 280–90.

30. Paul Haupt, *Das Babylonische Nimrodepos* (Leipzig, 1891); R. Campbell Thompson, *The Epic of Gilgamesh: Text, Transliteration, and Notes* (Oxford, 1930), has an excellent summary of this philological study that collated, analyzed, and translated the essential tablets, 55–56.

31. See Jerrold S. Cooper, "Sumerian and Akkadian in Sumer and Akkad," *Orientalia* 43 (1973): 239–46.

32. Samuel Kramer, "Sumerian Literature: A General Survey," in *The Bible and the Ancient Near East: Essays in Honor of William Foxwell Albright*, ed. G. Ernest Wright

(New York, 1961), 258; "Sumerian Literature: A Preliminary Survey of the Oldest Literature in the World," *Proceedings of the American Philosophical Society* 85 (1942): 242.

33. Kramer, "Sumerian Literature: A General Survey," 253.

34. Budge, *Rise and Progress of Assyriology*, 109.

35. Kramer, *In the World of Sumer*, 44–45.

36. Samuel Noah Kramer, *From the Poetry of Sumer: Creation, Glorification, Adoration* (Berkeley and Los Angeles, 1979), 2–3.

37. Samuel Kramer, "Studies in Sumerian Phonetics," *Archiv Orientalni* 8 (1936): 21.

38. Kramer, *In the World of Sumer*, 129–30.

39. Thorkild Jacobsen, *The Harps that Once—Sumerian Poetry in Translation* (New Haven, 1987), xv.

40. Jean Bottero, *Mesopotamia: Writing, Reasoning, and the Gods*, trans. Zainabe Bahrani and Marc Van De Mierop (Chicago, 1992), 16, 20.

41. Ritterband and Wechsler, "Message to Lushtamar," 24.

42. Budge, *Rise and Progress of Assyriology*, 269–72, 284.

43. Morris Jastrow, Jr., and Albert T. Clay, *An Old Babylonian Version of the Gilgamesh Epic on the Basis of Recently Discovered Texts* (New Haven, 1920), 13–14.

44. Hugo Radau, "Miscellaneous Texts from the Temple Library of Nippur," in *Hilprecht Anniversary Volume*, 374–459; Radau, *Sumerian Hymns and Prayers* . . . (Philadelphia, 1911).

45. Kramer, *In the World of Sumer*, 46.

46. Ibid., 71–73; Kramer, "Langdon's *Historical and Religious Texts from the Temple Library of Nippur*—Additions and Corrections," *JAOS* 60 (1940): 234–57; and Kramer, "A Sumerian 'Paradise' Myth," *Crozer Quarterly* 22 (1945): 207–20. See also Budge, *Rise and Progress of Assyriology*, 193, and the candid obituary by Gadd, "Stephen Herbert Langdon."

47. Cyrus H. Gordon, *The Pennsylvania Tradition of Semitics* (Atlanta, 1986), 24.

48. Kramer, *In the World of Sumer*, 125–26, 38–39. On Chiera and Poebel, see Biography Files, AG.

49. See newspaper clippings for Jastrow, Alumni Records Files, UA, and Morris Jastrow, Jr., *The War and the Bagdad Railway: The Story of Asia Minor and Its Relation to the Present Conflict* (Philadelphia, 1918), esp. 1–16.

50. Langdon to Gordon and Langdon to Rogers, 8 December 1915, Curatorial 5, Langdon, MA; see also correspondence between Poebel and Gordon, 1913–20, Directors Files 17, Poebel, MA.

51. See Edward Chiera, *Sumerian Religous Texts* (Upland, Pa., 1924), 7, and Chiera, "Notes and Current Discussion," *Crozer Quarterly* 1 (1924): 93–94.

52. Poebel to Gordon, 12 September 1919, Directors Files 17, Poebel, MA; Sayce to Harrison, 26 November 1916, UPB 65.1, box 3, Archaeology Correspondence, 1904–8, UA. A good start on the Langdon-Jastrow fight, in which Jastrow tried to undermine Langdon's treatment of Chiera and Poebel, can be found in Morris Jastrow, Jr., "Sumerian Myths of Beginnings," *American Journal of Semitic Languages and Literatures* 33 (1917): 91–144, and the essays in *JAOS* 36 (1916). See also Peters's views as reported in the *New York Sun*, 31 February 1915. A bibliography of the material can be found in Ernst F. Weidner, *Die Assyriologie, 1914–1922* . . .

(Leipzig, 1923), 100–112. Albright later entered the fray with "Some Cruces in the Langdon Epic," *JAOS* 39 (1919): 65–90.

53. On Kramer's career, see Kramer, *In the World of Sumer*, 20–52, 142–67.

54. Ibid., 24.

55. Jastrow and Clay, *Old Babylonian Version*, 13–14; Thompson, *Epic of Gilgamesh*, 6; Stephen Langdon, "The Sumerian Epic of Gilgamesh," *Journal of the Royal Asiatic Society of Great Britain and Ireland* (1932): 911–47.

56. Kramer, *In the World of Sumer*, 78; Kramer, "The Epic of Gilgamesh and Its Sumerian Sources: A Study in Literary Evolution," *JAOS* 64 (1944): 7–23.

57. Jastrow and Clay, *Old Babylonian Version*. This publication, incidentally, was another attack by Jastrow on Langdon; see 13n and 15–16.

58. See Tigay, *Evolution of the Gilgamesh Epic*, esp. 39–54, 103, and, for various other views, 144.

59. In trying to grasp the difference between Akkadian and Sumerian, I have been helped by Edward Seidensticker, "On Trying to Translate Japanese," in *The Craft of Translation*, ed. John Biguenet and Rainer Schulte (Chicago, 1989), 142–53.

60. G. S. Kirk, *Myth: Its Meaning and Function in Ancient and Other Cultures* (Berkeley and Los Angeles, 1970), 119.

61. Tigay, *Evolution of the Gilgamesh Epic*, 51.

62. Dalley, *Myths from Mesopotamia*, xvii.

63. See Kramer's weak argument in *In the World of Sumer*, 82–84.

64. Barton, "Higher Archaeology," 260.

65. Tigay, *Evolution of the Gilgamesh Epic*, 22.

66. Kramer, *History Begins at Sumer*, 3d ed. (Philadelphia, 1981), 259.

67. Although decipherment differs from translation, some of the same problems occur in both areas. See Lawrence Venuti, *The Translator's Invisibility: A History of Translation* (London, 1995), and Edwin Gentzler, *Contemporary Translation Theories* (London, 1993). I am also indebted to Jenefer Coates for acquainting me with the work of the conference on Literary Translation in Higher Education, Warwick, England, December 1994.

CHAPTER NINE

1. Surveying this movement in America are Jurgen Herbst, *The German Historical School in American Scholarship* (Ithaca, N.Y., 1965), and Diehl, *Americans and German Scholarship*. Excellent on somewhat wider issues is Thomas R. Trautman, "The Revolution in Ethnological Time," *Man* 27 (1992): 379–97. Introductions to these questions in nineteenth-century intellectual history focus on England and Darwin, although the issues are broader. See John C. Greene, *The Death of Adam: Evolution and Its Impact on Western Thought* (New York, 1959).

2. For an excellent overview, see Herbert Hahn, *The Old Testament in Modern Research* (Philadelphia, 1954).

3. Robert William Rogers, in *A History of Babylonia and Assyria*, 6th ed. (New York, 1915), 1:249–73, gives a spirited contemporary account of the controversy. For a more recent perspective, Thomas B. Jones, ed., *The Sumerian Problem* (New York, 1969), is essential.

4. Herbert B. Huffmon, "*Babel und Bibel*: The Encounter between Babylon and the

Bible," *Michigan Quarterly Review* 22 (1983): 316–19; for a fuller treatment, see Reinhard G. Lehman, *Friedrich Delitzsch und der Babel-Bibel-Streit* (Freiburg, Germany, 1994).

5. Clay to Morgan, 6 April 1911, Clay file, ML.

6. Interviews with William Hallo and Benjamin Foster, 26 October 1993.

7. Albert Clay, *Amurru, the Home of the Northern Semites: A Study Showing that the Religion and Culture of Israel Were Not of Babylonian Origin* (Philadelphia, 1909).

8. Albrecht Goetze, "Professor Clay and the Amorite Problem," *Yale University Library Gazette* 36 (1961–62): 133–37.

9. William Foxwell Albright, "Professor Albert T. Clay—An Appreciation," *Journal of the Palestine Oriental Society* 6 (1926): 173–77.

10. Wilson, "James Henry Breasted," 43.

11. A predecessor to Breasted, less influential but equally interesting, is George Stephen Goodspeed, *A History of the Ancient World* (New York, 1904).

12. Breasted, "Place of the Near Orient," 168.

13. James Henry Breasted, *Ancient Times: A History of the Early World* (Boston, 1916). I have used the "library edition," which bore the title *The Conquest of Civilization* (New York, 1926). This volume has a foreword, v–xii, discussing issues of method. The quotation is from vii.

14. Breasted, *Conquest of Civilization*, 112. See also second edition of *Ancient Times* (Boston, 1935), 130–31.

15. See the comments in Wilson, "James Henry Breasted," 46–47, and Albright, *History, Archaeology, and Christian Humanism*, 226–27.

16. Wilson, "James Henry Breasted," 49.

17. Haupt to Albright, 27 May 1913, box 1, Albright Papers, APS.

18. See Haupt's report on the dissertation, 5 June 1916, box 1, Albright Papers, APS; see also Albright, "Some Cruces in the Langdon Epic."

19. Albright's own memories of this period were that he passed through a high-critical phase at Johns Hopkins and rejected secularism because of the archaeological evidence. On inspecting the evidence, I think this is dubious, as does Burke O. Long in his "Mythic Trope in the Autobiography of William Foxwell Albright," *BA* 56 (1993): 36–45. Long assembles the citations, but see also Albright to Haupt, 11 October 1922, box 3, Albright Papers, APS; Paul Haupt, "Recommendations for Appointments . . . ," 1917–18, Presidents' Papers, RG 2, series 1, 132–441, JHU; Leona Glidden Running and David Noel Freedman, *William Foxwell Albright: A Twentieth-Century Genius* (n.p., 1975), 47, 79; and William Foxwell Albright, "Professor Haupt as Scholar and Teacher," in Adler and Ember, *Oriental Studies Dedicated to Paul Haupt*, xxi–xxxii.

20. Running and Freedman, *William Foxwell Albright*, 69; Peters to Albright, 24 April 1921, box 2, Albright Papers, APS.

21. Running and Freedman, *William Foxwell Albright*, 65.

22. Davis, "History of Biblical Archaeology," 145–46.

23. Wright, "Phenomenon of American Archaeology," 22–30.

24. Albright to Ames, 13 June 1927, Albright to Goodnow, 26 January 1928, box 2, Albright Papers, APS.

25. David Noel Freedman, "W. F. Albright as an Historian," in Van Beek, *Scholar-*

ship of William Foxwell Albright, 35; Running and Freedman, *William Foxwell Albright*, 312–13; and Albright to family, 10 December 1969, Family Correspondence, Albright Papers, APS.

26. Albright, *History, Archaeology, and Christian Humanism*, 309. (The autobiographical sketch was written in 1948.)

27. Albright, *From the Stone Age to Christianity; Archaeology and the Religion of Israel*, 4th ed. (Baltimore, 1956). An earlier effort is equally interesting: Albright, *The Archaeology of Palestine and the Bible* (New York, 1932).

28. Albright, *From the Stone Age to Christianity*, 86. The same idea is at work in G. Ernest Wright, *The Old Testament against Its Environment* (Chicago, 1950).

29. Albright, *Archaeology and the Religion of Israel*, 176.

30. Hahn, *Old Testament in Modern Research*, 188.

31. Albright, *History, Archaeology, and Christian Humanism*, esp. 140.

32. See, for example, the Meisner Lectures at Cornell, 1951, box 18, Albright Papers, APS.

33. Running and Freedman, *William Foxwell Albright*, 397.

34. Albright, *History, Archaeology, and Christian Humanism*, 46–141.

35. For a survey of these historians, see Paul Costello, *World Historians and Their Goals: Twentieth-Century Answers to Modernism* (DeKalb, Ill., 1993).

36. Christopher Dawson, *Progress and Religion* (New York, 1929); Karl Jaspers, *The Origin and Goal of History* (New Haven, 1953); Eric Voegelin, *Order in History*, vol. 1, *Israel and Revelation*, (Baton Rouge, La., 1952), 34–162; see also Glenn Hughes, *Mystery and Myth in the Philosophy of Eric Voegelin* (Columbia, Mo., 1993), 70–88.

37. H. G. Wells, *The Outline of History: Being a Plain History of Life and Mankind* (New York, 1920); William Hardy McNeill, *The Rise of the West: A History of the Human Community* (Chicago, 1963).

38. Oswald Spengler, *The Decline of the West*, trans. Charles Francis Atkinson (New York, 1926–28); Arnold Toynbee, *A Study of History* (New York, 1934–61).

39. For my understanding of Toynbee I am indebted to Walter McDougall, "'Mais ce n'est pas L'Histoire': Some Thoughts on Toynbee, McNeill, and the Rest of Us," *Journal of Modern History* 58 (1986): 20–26.

40. Albright, *History, Archaeology, and Christian Humanism*, esp. 249, 253.

41. Albright, *From the Stone Age to Christianity*, 309–10.

42. My language, and the argument here about Albright, are indebted to the outstanding essay by John A. Miles, Jr., "Understanding Albright: A Revolutionary Étude," *Harvard Theological Review* 69 (1976): 151–75, esp. 161.

43. See Albright, *History, Archaeology, and Christian Humanism*, 261.

44. Bruce Trigger, *A History of Archaeological Thought* (Cambridge, England, 1989), 96–203, 250–54. This mode of explanation was, however, more than a fashion; for a more recent example of the style, see J. N. Postgate, "In Search of the First Empires," *Bulletin of the American Schools of Oriental Research* 293 (1994): 1–13.

45. This discussion is indebted to Silberman, "Desolation and Restoration," 76–87.

46. Flinders Petrie, *The Revolutions of Civilization* (London, 1911); see also Drower, *Flinders Petrie*, 302–4, 411, 428.

47. On this issue, see Silberman, "Desolation and Restoration."

48. For example, see Henry C. Boren, *The Ancient World: An Historical Perspective*, 2d ed. (Englewood Cliffs, N.J., 1986), 13–17, and D. Brendan Nagle, *The Ancient World: A Social and Cultural History*, 2d ed. (Englewood Cliffs, N.J., 1989), 4–6.

49. Martin Bernal, *Black Athena* (New Brunswick, N.J., 1987–91); see also the letter to the editor by William B. Branch, "History Didn't Begin in Mesopotamia," *New York Times*, 24 October 1990. For a fair-minded discussion, see the review articles in *American Historical Review* 97 (1992): 440–64; for more heat, see Paul O. Kristeller, "Comment on *Black Athena*," and the citation therein, *Journal of the History of Ideas* 56 (1995): 125–27.

50. For example, Nagle, *Ancient World*, 57–76.

51. The issue I am here taking up is examined from a somewhat different perspective by John Van Seters, *Abraham in History and Tradition* (New Haven, 1975).

52. For exemplary criticism of the use of Nuzi, see Barry L. Eichler, "Nuzi and the Bible: A Retrospective," in *Dumu-e2-dub-ba-a: Studies in Honor of Ake W. Sjoberg*, ed. H. Behrens, Darlene Loding, and Martha Roth (Philadelphia, 1989), 107–19.

CONCLUSION

1. The potency of the state is evidenced most dramatically in Suzanne Marchand's study of German classicists, *The Rise and Fall of German Philhellenism*.

2. This point is made most cogently by Van Harvey, *The Historian and the Believer* (New York, 1966). Francis Herbert Bradley's *The Presuppositions of Critical History* (Chicago, 1968) remains a crucial text.

3. See, for example, the works of Brian M. Fagan, in particular *Return to Babylon*; Glyn Daniel, *Man Discovers His Past* (London, 1966); and Lloyd, *Twin Rivers*.

4. Edward W. Said, *Orientalism* (New York, 1978), is the basic book here, but there are many recent texts making something of the same point: e.g., Fabian, *Time and the Other*; Billie Melman, *Women's Orient: English Women and the Middle East, 1718–1918* (London, 1992); Mitchell, *Colonising Egypt*; Mary Louise Pratt, *Imperial Eyes: Travel Writing and Transculturation* (London, 1992); and David Spurr, *The Rhetoric of Empire: Colonial Discourse in Journalism, Travel Writing, and Imperial Administration* (Durham, N.C., 1993). Said's later ruminations on his book are defanged: see Said, "Orientalism Revisited," *Times Literary Supplement*, 3 February 1995, 3–6. For a competent intellectual history of the background to Orientalism, see Albert Hourani, *Islam in European Thought* (Cambridge, England, 1991), 7–60. I have used "Orientalism" in a way that overlaps but is not congruent with Said's usage.

5. See the reasoning in such books as Michael C. C. Adams, *The Great Adventure: Male Desire and the Coming of World War I* (Bloomington, Ind., 1990); Gail Bederman, *Manliness and Civilization: A Cultural History of Gender and Race in the United States, 1880–1917* (Chicago, 1995); Mark Carnes, *Secret Ritual and Manhood in Victorian America* (New Haven, 1989); Mark C. Carnes and Clyde Griffen, eds., *Meanings for Manhood: Constructions of Masculinity in Victorian America* (Chicago, 1990); and David D. Gilmore, *Manhood in the Making: Cultural Concepts of Masculinity* (New Haven, 1990).

6. This issue appears sporadically in Chandler, Davidson, and Harootunian, *Questions of Evidence*, but see especially Barbara Herrnstein Smith's essay, "Belief and Resistance," and the response to it, 139–68. Fair-minded readers must judge for themselves the power of this argument.

7. In a somewhat different context, Robert N. Proctor takes up these issues in *Value-Free Science?* 262–71. It is worth stressing here that it is a cliché of scholarship that knowledge is embedded in culture; it seems to me now much more interesting to figure out how it manages, in some ways, to escape cultural constraints so that, for example, scholars can say truly that science is a social product.

ESSAY ON METHODS AND SOURCES

W RITING THE HISTORY of an academic field such as ancient Near Eastern studies requires a nuanced understanding of the institutional situation of the scholars, their cultural milieu, their personalities, and the structure of arguments in their disciplines and the changes in the arguments over time. The interpretative conclusions one reaches arise out of the density of the history. Although the nonideational aspects of the story are usually salient to the production of knowledge, I have never found it possible to reduce the knowledge to the nonideational. In the case of Near Eastern studies, there are also compelling grounds for saying that knowledge has progressed.

I have outlined in several places the presuppositions that govern the sort of intellectual history I have tried to write: *The Rise of American Philosophy: Cambridge, Massachusetts, 1860–1930* (New Haven, 1977), xvii–xix; *Churchmen and Philosophers: From Jonathan Edwards to John Dewey* (New Haven, 1985), 301–2; "Reply to Decker," *New Literary History* 23 (1992): pp. 307–10 (which lists other essays of mine); and "Confessions of an Intransigent Revisionist about Cultural Studies," *Diplomatic History* 18 (1993): 121–24. In general I believe that narrative has a crucial role in historical writing and that the theory implicit in it should be kept implicit in the presentation of research.

My strategy in writing this book was straightforward. Because of its importance and the accessibility and richness of its records, I used the Nippur Expedition as a case study to get at the complexities of institution building in ancient Near Eastern studies and at the adventure, dilemmas, and problematic quality of establishing field archaeology and decipherment as enterprises. The sources for studying this expedition are voluminous. They are certainly extraordinary in comparison with the other primary material available for examining the family of disciplines and institutions that this book investigates. Indeed, I have tried to guard against the problems created by the disproportions in the data that have happened to survive.

The Museum of the University of Pennsylvania houses the extensive records of the campaigns themselves and, in addition, curatorial and administrative records that touch on the expedition. William Pepper's papers are in the special collections of the Van Pelt Library at the university, and Charles Harrison's are in the University Archives. Substantial material from other participants is in the Museum Archives, but I was unable to locate the papers of John Peters or Morris Jastrow, Jr. Additional Hilprecht material is at the Hilprecht Sammlung in the Friedrich-Schiller University in Jena, and is described in Joachim Oelsner, "Der schriftliche Nachlass H. V. Hilprechts in der Hilprecht-Sammlung," in *Wissenschaftliche Beitrage der Friedrich-Schiller-Universität Jena 1980: Beitrage zur Ethnolinguistik. Gedenkschrift zum 100. Geburtstag von Ferdinand Hestermann* (Jena, 1980), 112–23, and Oelsner, "Zur Geschichte der 'Frau Professor Hilprecht-Sammlung Vorderasiatischer Altertumer in Eigentum der Friedrich-Schiller Universität Jena,'" in *Wissenschaftliche Beitrage der Friedrich-Schiller Universität Jena 1985: Zur Geschichte der klassischen Archaologies Jena-Krakow* (Jena, 1985) 46–53. I am indebted to Aage Westenholz of the Carsten Niebuhr Institute in Copenhagen for making a microfilm of this material available to me.

The wider organizational history depends on sources pertaining to many other institutions, although there are no records comparable in scope and depth to those about Nippur. The papers of the American Oriental Society are located in the society's headquarters in the Sterling Library at Yale University, where I was shrewdly assisted by Stanley Insler. The records of the American Schools of Oriental Research are in the Semitic Museum at Harvard University. Material pertinent to Jewish scholarship in Semitics at the end of the nineteenth century is housed in the Annenberg Research Institute in Philadelphia, in the papers of Cyrus Adler, Max Margolies, and Sabateo Morais.

There is a small collection of Paul Haupt papers at Johns Hopkins, and other useful material scattered in the records of its Oriental Seminar (variously designated) and the Gilman Papers, also at Johns Hopkins. The W. F. Albright Papers at the American Philosophical Society are extensive and useful; another trove of Albright material is in the files of the American Schools of Oriental Research at Harvard. The archives of the Smithsonian Institution have material pertinent to Johns Hopkins's role in Near Eastern studies in the period from 1880 to 1900. The papers of the Yale Babylonian Collection are located at Yale's Sterling Library; the Yale University Archives at the library contain other material in the papers of the presidents, of the Yale Corporation, of the treasurers, and of the librarians. Yale's story is connected to that of Columbia University and the Morgan Library. The Morgan Library's holdings in New York City are catalogued by the names of Morgan's correspondents. The Low Memorial Library at Columbia holds the central files of the administration; the Rare Books section in the Butler Library at Columbia has a letterbook of Richard Gottheil.

Harvard's role can be traced in the papers of presidents Eliot and Lowell at the Pusey Library and the records of the Semitic department at the Semitic Museum. In addition, at Pusey there is a small collection of G. Andrew Reisner papers, a large and only marginally useful collection of the Indologist Richard Lanman, and an exceptionally rich collection of David Lyon papers. The records of Reisner's early digs—second in completeness to the Nippur material—are at the Boston Museum of Fine Arts. Other correspondence relating to these digs is located in the Hearst Museum and Bancroft

Library at Berkeley; I am indebted to Henry May, David A. Hollinger, and Charles R. Katz for helping me locate and use this material.

At Chicago relevant primary sources are similarly divided. The presidents' papers—notably those of Rainey Harper—are located in the Regenstein Library and contain material on expeditions and funding. Those of the Oriental Institute, James Breasted, and Frank Harper are at the Oriental Institute. Chicago's long association with the Rockefeller interests can also be traced in appropriate material in the Rockefeller Foundation Archives in Tarrytown, New York.

Getting a handle on institutional history does not proceed separately from understanding the intellectual problems of ancient Near Eastern studies. For me this has proved inordinately difficult. I have brought to the task the skills of an intellectual historian and knowledge of the fin de siècle American university. In my previous studies of practices—philosophy, theology, and baseball—I had or was able to acquire what amounted to an insider's grasp of the craft. *Puritans in Babylon*, however, was written in ignorance of ancient epigraphy and without experience of archaeological fieldwork—the two fundamental kinds of expertise essential to ancient Near Eastern studies.

I have no knowledge of any Near Eastern languages, old or new, and this must remain a serious limitation, hardly mitigated by amateur attempts at studying Egyptian hieroglyphics or Akkadian (formerly Assyrian) grammar or by visiting tablet rooms. What I have done instead is to immerse myself in the periodical literature of the 1880–1930 period, and I believe I have an accurate sense of the debates. Although I have been incompetent independently to judge the quality of work in the field that depends on philological skills, I have been generously assisted by several experts who have treated me with exceptional courtesy: Aage Westenholz of the Carsten Niebuhr Institute; William Hallo and Benjamin Foster of Yale University; John Larson of the Oriental Institute; Peter Der Manuelian of the Boston Museum of Fine Arts; Jeffrey Tigay of the University of Pennsylvania; and Jerrold Cooper of Johns Hopkins. Finally, I have read with exceptional care the histories that scholars within the field have written and that I have cited. From the point of view of an intellectual historian, such histories have obvious and serious deficiencies. They also proceed with expert knowledge that I cannot hope to reproduce.

My problems as an archaeologist are equal to mine as an epigrapher; I have never been on a dig. To understand archaeological reasoning I have relied on a series of writings by the masters, among them Flinders Petrie, *Methods and Aims in Archaeology* (London, 1904); Clarence Fisher, *Excavations at Nippur: The Topography and City Walls* (Lancaster, Pa., 1905); G. Andrew Reisner, "Egyptology, 1896–1928," in *The Development of Harvard University since the Inauguration of President Eliot, 1869–1929*, ed.

Samuel Eliot Morison (Cambridge, Mass., 1930), 241–47, and "Principles, Methods, and General Results" in *Harvard Excavations at Samaria, 1908–1910,* by George Andrew Reisner, Clarence Stanley Fisher, and David Gordon Lyon (Cambridge, Mass., 1924), 1:31–90; Clarence Fisher, *The Excavation of Armageddon* (Chicago, 1929); William Foxwell Albright, *The Archaeology of Palestine and the Bible* (New York, 1932); R. E. M. Wheeler, *Archaeology from the Earth* (Oxford, 1954); and Kathleen Kenyon, *Beginning in Archaeology* (New York, 1952). Also to be consulted are W. F. Badé, *A Manual of Excavation in the Near East: Methods of Digging and Recording of the Tell en-Nasbeth Expedition in Palestine* (Berkeley and Los Angeles, 1934); H. J. Franken and C. A. Franken-Battershill, *A Primer of Old Testament Archaeology* (Leiden, 1963); Philip Barker, *Techniques of Archaeological Excavation,* 2d ed. rev. (New York, 1982); Thomas William Davis, "A History of Biblical Archaeology" (Ph.D. diss., University of Arizona, 1987); Joseph W. Michels, *Dating Methods in Archaeology* (New York, 1973); and M. J. Aitkin, *Science-Based Dating in Archaeology* (London, 1990).

I am also indebted to conversations with Murray Murphey of the University of Pennsylvania, James Sauer of Harvard, and Tjalling Waterbolk of the University of Groningen.

Readers who wish to see the sources on which my interpretation of this group of studies is based should track my notes, with the following proviso: although the sections on the Nippur dig itself are heavily documented by the primary sources, much of my feel for the story comes simply from reading, often many times, the various records of the expeditions. I have not been able to cite these completely, and there is no substitute for reading the extant evidence itself, especially if my account is unpersuasive.

The bibliographic references below do not reproduce, in another arrangement, the citations in the notes. Rather, I have tried to give the reader a sense of the major issues I take up in the book, and to point out material that shaped my thinking. I have ignored most works that appear in the notes and mentioned others that do not appear, and I have favored books with extensive bibliographies so that I need not summarize a listing that can be readily and more completely found elsewhere. Overall, I intend to introduce the interested reader to various works that have been important to the making of this volume.

History of Archaeology

Practitioners' history has severe limitations from my point of view. One is the isolation of "archaeology" as a separate endeavor before the turn of the twentieth century; another is the uncritical use of memoirs and narrative reports. But this sort of history also usually embodies a feel for excavation that is invaluable. An excellent overview is Bruce G. Trigger, "Writing the History of Archaeology: A Survey of Trends," in *Objects and Others: Essays on Museums and Material Culture*, ed. George W. Stocking, Jr. (Madison, Wisc., 1985), 218–35. Representative efforts include Glyn Daniel, *The Origins and Growth of Archaeology* (Baltimore, 1967); Daniel, *A Hundred and Fifty Years of Archaeology*, 2d ed. (London, 1975); Glyn Daniel and Colin Renfrew, *The Idea of Prehistory*, 2d ed. (Edinburgh, 1988); Kenneth Hudson, *A Social History of Archaeology* (London, 1981); and Neil Asher Silberman, *Digging for God and Country: Exploration, Archaeology, and the Secret Struggles for the Holy Land, 1799–1918* (New York, 1982)—an exception to the rule about practitioners' history.

There is much Marxist or quasi-Marxist writing in this field distinguished by its theoretical approach. Because it leaves out what its adherents would call much of the "superstructure," I find it lacking in nuance. Two examples are Thomas C. Patterson, "The Last Sixty Years: Toward a Social History of Americanist Archaeology in the United States," *American Anthropologist* 88 (1986): 7–26, and Bruce Trigger, *A History of Archaeological Thought* (Cambridge, England, 1989). Somewhat more complex is the collection of essays edited by Joan M. Gero, David M. Lacy, and Michael L. Blakey, *The Socio-Politics of Archaeology* (Amherst, Mass., 1983).

Much of the best work in this field focuses on archaeology in the New World, which has had a close connection with New World anthropology, or on English anthropology and the link in Britain between nineteenth-century archaeology and anthropology. These connections have suggested to many an overall relationship between archaeology and anthropology in which the former is subsumed by the latter. This assumption has been strengthened by the mature state of work in the history of anthropology, represented most significantly in the sustained writings of George W. Stocking, Jr. (see, e.g., his *Victorian Anthropology* [New York, 1987]). In ancient Near Eastern studies, however, the impact of anthropology and the connection between archaeology and anthropology were of less significance, except for the continuing attempts by anthropologists conceptually to reduce archaeology to anthropology.

History of Ancient Near Eastern Scholarship

Here we have more practitioners' history: Brian M. Fagan, *Return to Babylon* (Boston, 1979), and Fagan, *The Rape of the Nile* (Boston, 1975); the works of Seton Lloyd: *The Archaeology of Mesopotamia* (London, 1978), *Foundations in the Dust: The Story of Mesopotamian Exploration*, rev. and enl. ed. (London, 1980), and *Twin Rivers*, 2d ed. (Oxford, 1947); Philip King, *American Archaeology in the Mideast* (Philadelphia, 1983); C. Wade Meade, *Road* to Babylon: The Development of U.S. Assyriology (Leiden, 1974); and John A. Wilson, *Signs and Wonders upon Pharaoh: A History of American Egyptology* (Chicago, 1964). A different sort of study is Raymond Schwab, *The Oriental Renaissance: Europe's Rediscovery of India and the East, 1680–1880*, trans. Gene Patterson-Black and Victor Reinking (New York, 1984). Omar Carena, *History of the Near Eastern Historiography and Its Problems: 1852–1985*, part 1, 1852–1945 (Darmstadt, 1989), needs to be mentioned, as does William B. Dinsmoor, "Early American Studies of Mediterranean Archaeology," *Proceedings of the American Philosophical Society* 87 (1943): 70–104.

Celebratory histories of the Museum of the University of Pennsylvania include Percy C. Madeira, Jr., *Men in Search of Man: The First Seventy-five Years of the University Museum of the University of Pennsylvania* (Philadelphia, 1964), and Dilys Pegler Winegrad, *Through Time, across Continents: A Hundred Years of Archaeology and Anthropology at the University Museum* (Philadelphia, 1993). There is also Cyrus H. Gordon, *The Pennsylvania Tradition of Semitics* (Atlanta, 1986).

The United States and the Near East in the Nineteenth Century

Lester I. Vogel, *To See a Promised Land: Americans and the Holy Land in the Nineteenth Century* (University Park, Pa., 1993), is a comprehensive study of educated perception; the book has an enormous, learned bibliography. Less bibliographically comprehensive but more astute is Eduard van de Bilt, "'The Stern Fact, the Sad Self': American Travel Narratives about the Middle East, 1819–1918" (rev. Ph.D. diss., Cornell University, in the possession of the author at the University of Leiden). Other reliable monographs include R. L. Daniel, *American Philanthropy in the Near East, 1820–1960* (Athens, Ohio, 1970); John DeNovo, *American Interests and Policies in the Middle East, 1900–1939* (Minneapolis, 1963); David H. Finnie, *Pioneers East: The Early American Experience in the Middle East* (Cambridge, Mass., 1967); James Field, *America and the Mediterranean World, 1776–1882* (Princeton, 1969); Carl T. Jackson, *The Oriental Religions and American Thought: Nineteenth-Century Explorations* (Westport, Conn., 1981); and Robert Kaplan's tour to the present, *The Arabists: The Romance of an American Elite* (New York, 1993).

Textbooks

The evolution of genres of scholarship in a field is of some interest, especially in the field that produced the text in Western civilization. By the end of the nineteenth century American scholars were editing series of books that, although not designed expressly for students, did attempt syntheses of the scholarship pertaining to the ancient Near East and historical overviews in particular. For example, Charles Kent and Frank Sanders of Yale edited the Historical Series for Bible Students, for which George Stephen Goodspeed wrote *A History of the Babylonians and Assyrians* (New York, 1902). This book joined others, e.g., the important work by Robert William Rogers, *A History of Babylonia and Assyria*, 6th ed. (New York, 1915). Morris Jastrow, Jr., wrote a standard, *The Civilization of Babylonia and Assyria* (Philadelphia, 1915). Percy S. P. Handcock, *Mesopotamian Archaeology* (New York, 1912), is in the same vein and typifies attempts to be up to date with the latest United States developments. Jastrow himself edited a series of handbooks on the history of religion, and contributed *The Religion of Babylonia and Assyria* (Boston, 1898), one of many books whose orientation was that of comparative civilization. These volumes joined a venerable tradition of writing in Old Testament studies that now could be enriched by the new learning in archaeology and epigraphy. Two examples here are John Peters, *The Old Testament and the New Scholarship* (New York, 1902), and George A. Barton, *Archaeology and the Bible* (Philadelphia, 1916).

The true texts brought all these strands together, the most important being James Henry Breasted, *Ancient Times: A History of the Early World* (Boston, 1916), but a predecessor, George Stephen Goodspeed, *A History of the Ancient World* (New York, 1904), is outstanding. Goodspeed, who taught at Chicago with Breasted, antedated him in the conception of a "crescent" of civilization. An English publication, W. Cunningham, *An Essay on Western Civilization in Its Economic Aspects (Ancient Times)* (Cambridge, England, 1898), perhaps gave Breasted his title.

History of the Ancient Near East

From the tradition of books noted above come the volumes I relied on for my sense of ancient history: the relevant volumes of *The Cambridge Ancient History*, ed. I. E. S. Edwards et al., 3d ed. (Cambridge, England, 1975–); Hans J. Nissen, *The Early History of the Ancient Near East, 9000–2000 B.C.* (Chicago, 1988); and H. W. F. Saggs, *Civilization before Greece and Rome* (New Haven, 1989).

The Near East in the Nineteenth and Twentieth Centuries

Some orienting studies are W. S. Anderson, *The Eastern Question, 1774–1923: A Study in International Relations* (London, 1966); Paul Coles, *The Ottoman Impact on Europe* (New York, 1968); David Fromkin, *A Peace to*

End All Peace: The Fall of the Ottoman Empire and the Creation of the Modern Middle East (New York, 1989); Albert Hourani, *The Emergence of the Modern Middle East* (Berkeley and Los Angeles, 1981); Charles Issawi, *The Fertile Crescent, 1800–1914: A Documentary History* (New York, 1988); Bernard Lewis, *The Emergence of Modern Turkey* (New York, 1968); R. W. Seton-Watson, *Britain in Europe, 1789–1914* (Cambridge, England, 1938); and Stanford Shaw and Ezel Shaw, *History of the Ottoman Empire and Modern Turkey*, 2 vols. (Cambridge, England, 1977). A useful work on the cusp of ancient and modern life is Svend Aage Pallis, *The Antiquity of Iraq: A Handbook of Assyriology* (Copenhagen, 1956).

Sumer

On the recovery of Sumer I am indebted to many efforts that are scattered through the writing of Samuel Noah Kramer and that reflect on his craft: "Studies in Sumerian Phonetics," *Archiv Orientalni* 8 (1936): 18–33; "Langdon's *Historical and Religious Texts from the Temple Library of Nippur*—Additions and Corrections," *JAOS* 60 (1940): 234–57; "Sumerian Literature: A Preliminary Survey of the Oldest Literature in the World," *Proceedings of the American Philosophical Society* 85 (1942): 315–18; "The Epic of Gilgamesh and Its Sumerian Sources: A Study in Literary Evolution," *JAOS* 64 (1944): 7–23; "A 'Sumerian 'Paradise' Myth," *Crozer Quarterly* 22 (1945): 207–20; "Gilgamesh: Some New Sumerian Data," in *Gilgames et sa legende*, ed. Paul Garelli (Paris, 1960), 59–68; "Sumerian Literature: A General Survey," in *The Bible and the Ancient Near East: Essays in Honor of William Foxwell Albright*, ed. G. Ernest Wright (New York, 1961), 249–66; *From the Poetry of Sumer: Creation, Glorification, Adoration* (Berkeley and Los Angeles, 1979), 1–19; "Sumerian Literature and the British Museum: The Promise of the Future," *Proceedings of the American Philosophical Society* 124 (1980): 295.

Biographies

I have relied on biographies of many of my peripheral protagonists, but the genre does not attract interpretative skills. See Robert Ackerman, *J. G. Frazer: His Life and Work* (Cambridge, England, 1987); James P. Wind, *The Bible and the University: The Messianic Vision of William Rainey Harper* (Atlanta, 1987); Garland Cannon, *The Life and Mind of Oriental Jones: Sir William Jones, the Father of Modern Linguistics* (Cambridge, England, 1991); on Layard, see Arnold C. Brackman, *The Luck of Nineveh: Archaeology's Great Adventure* (New York, 1978), the charming *Man Who Found Nineveh* by

Robert Silverberg (New York, 1964), and Gordon Waterfield, *Layard of Nineveh* (London, 1963); Francis Newton Thorpe, *William Pepper, M.D., LL.D.* (Philadelphia, 1904); Margaret Drower, *Flinders Petrie: A Life in Archaeology* (London, 1985); Mark Bowden, *Pitt Rivers: The Life and Archaeological Work of Lieutenant General Augustus Henry Lane Fox Pitt Rivers, DCL, FRS, FSA* (Cambridge, England, 1991); William Chapman's outstanding essay "The Organizational Context in the History of Archaeology: Pitt Rivers and Other British Archaeologists in the 1860s," *Antiquities Journal* 69 (1989): 23–42; Cyrus Adler, *Jacob H. Schiff: His Life and Letters* (New York, 1928); T. Beidelman, *W. Robertson Smith and the Sociological Study of Religion* (Chicago, 1974); and Stephen Alter, "William Dwight Whitney and the Science of Language" (Ph.D. diss., University of Michigan, 1993).

Two men, James Henry Breasted and William Foxwell Albright, deserve further treatment. Information on the former can be found in Charles Breasted, *Pioneer to the Past: The Story of James Henry Breasted, Archaeologist* (Chicago, 1943). On Albright there is a growing literature; Leona Glidden Running and David Noel Freedman, *William Foxwell Albright: A Twentieth-Century Genius* (n.p., 1975), is an excellent guide to his papers. One might also consult David Noel Freedman, *The Published Works of William Foxwell Albright: A Comprehensive Bibliography* (Cambridge, Mass., 1975); Gus W. Van Beek, ed., *The Scholarship of William Foxwell Albright* (Atlanta, 1989); and the special issue of *BA*, "Celebrating and Examining W. F. Albright," *BA* 56 (1993). The most astute essay is John A. Miles, Jr., "Understanding Albright: A Revolutionary Étude," *Harvard Theological Review* 69 (1976): 151–75. Of Albright's own writings, the most revealing is *History, Archaeology, and Christian Humanism* (New York, 1964).

Jewish Scholarship

Distinctively Jewish scholarship in ancient Near Eastern studies has been at the border of my concerns, but my research has made me aware of its traditions. Harold Wechsler's work is the sine qua non here; see his "Pulpit or Professoriate: The Case of Morris Jastrow," *American Jewish History* 74 (1985): 338–55, and (with Paul Ritterband) "A Message to Lushtamar: The Hilprecht Controversy and Semitic Scholarship in America," *History of Higher Education Annual* 1 (1981): 1–17. Ritterband and Wechsler, *Jewish Learning in American Universities: The First Century* (Bloomington, Ind., 1994), has an especially rich collection of footnotes. See also "Semitic Studies in America: Addresses at the Meeting of the American Oriental Society," *Hebraica* 5 (1888–89): 76–91; Cyrus Adler, "The Beginnings of Semitic Studies in America," in *Oriental Studies Dedicated to Paul Haupt*, ed. Cyrus Adler and Aaron Ember (Baltimore, 1926), 317–28; Adler, *Jacob H. Schiff;*

Murray Friedman, ed., *When Philadelphia Was the Capital of Jewish America* (Cranberry, N.J., 1993); William Rosenau, "Semitic Studies in American Colleges," in *Yearbook of the Central Conference of American Rabbis, 1896* (Cincinnati, 1897), 99–113; and Shuly Rubin Schwartz, *The Emergence of Jewish Scholarship in America: The Publication of the Jewish Encyclopedia* (Cincinnati, 1991).

Bible Studies

A wide-ranging collection of secondary sources has been important in leading me to questions, beginning with the principal works of William Foxwell Albright: *The Archaeology of Palestine and the Bible; From the Stone Age to Christianity: Monotheism and the Historical Process* (Baltimore, 1940); *Archaeology and the Religion of Israel*, 4th ed. (Baltimore, 1956); and *History, Archaeology, and Christian Humanism.* See also R. E. Clements, *A Century of Old Testament Study*, 2d ed. rev. (London, 1983); Davis, "History of Biblical Archaeology"; Herbert Hahn, *The Old Testament in Modern Research* (Philadelphia, 1954); George M. Marsden and Bradley J. Longfield, eds., *The Secularization of the Academy* (New York, 1992); Roger Moorey, *A Century of Biblical Archaeology* (Cambridge, England, 1991); Ernest W. Saunders, *Searching the Scriptures: A History of the Society of Biblical Literature, 1880–1980* (Chicago, 1982); and Eric J. Sharpe, *Comparative Religion: A History*, 2d ed. (LaSalle, Ill., 1986). For the American context, see Jerry Wayne Brown, *The Rise of Biblical Criticism in America, 1800–1870* (Middletown, Conn., 1969), and John William Stewart, "The Tethered Theology: Biblical Criticism, Common Sense Philosophy, and the Princeton Theology, 1812–1860" (Ph.D. diss., University of Michigan, 1990).

Museums and Philanthropy

Sociologists have recently taken up systematically the relation of high culture, philanthropy, and capitalism. See, for example, the work of Paul DiMaggio, much of it cited in his article "Classification in Art," *American Sociological Review* 52 (1987): 440–55, but I have found this material too abstract. In the same genre are studies such as Frederick N. Bohrer, "The Times and Space of History: Representation, Assyria, and the British Museum," in *Museum Culture: Histories, Discourse, Spectacles*, ed. Daniel J. Sherman and Irit Rogoff (Minneapolis, 1994). More useful have been Robert F. Arnove, ed., *Philanthropy and Cultural Imperialism: The Foundations at Home and Abroad* (Bloomington, Ind., 1980); Daniel, *American Philanthropy in the Near East*; Daniel M. Fox, *Engines of Culture: Philanthropy and Art*

Museums (Madison, Wisc., 1963); Neil Harris, *Cultural Excursions: Marketing Appetites and Cultural Tastes in Modern America* (Chicago, 1990); John L. Hess, *The Grand Acquisitors* (Boston, 1974); Ivan Karp and Steven D. Lavine, eds., *Exhibiting Cultures: The Poetics and Politics of Museum Display* (Washington, D.C., 1991); Karp, Lavine, and Christine Mullen Kreamer, eds., *Museums and Communities: The Politics of Public Culture* (Washington, D.C., 1992); and Kathleen D. McCarthy, *Women's Culture: American Philanthropy and Art, 1830–1930* (Chicago, 1991). Most useful is the outstanding collection edited by George W. Stocking, *Objects and Others*. Steven Conn "To Organize and Display: Museums and American Culture, 1876–1926" (Ph.D. diss., History, University of Pennsylvania, 1994), has an excellent bibliography on museum culture.

Philosophical Assumptions

The presuppositions that Albright—and many anthropologists—thought were at the basis of scientific archaeology are elaborated in Carl Hempel, "The Function of General Laws in History," *Journal of Philosophy* 29 (1942): 35–48.

The project of examining the way in which archaeology reveals methodological commitment, the "philosophy of archaeology," has been the concern of Alison Wylie, many of whose essays are cited in Valerie Pinsky and Alison Wylie, eds., *Critical Traditions in Contemporary Archaeology: Essays in the Philosophy, History, and Socio-politics of Archaeology* (Cambridge, England, 1989), 152–53. See also Norman Yoffee and Andrew Sherratt, eds., *Archaeological Theory: Who Sets the Agenda?* (Cambridge, England, 1993). The best essay in this genre on archaeological reasoning is in Pinsky and Wylie's collection: Christopher Chippendale, "Philosophical Lessons from the History of Stonehenge," 68–79.

Reflections on the nature of time have often cropped up in this book. Two volumes by J. T. Fraser provide extensive bibliographical information about questions concerning temporality: *Time: The Familiar Stranger* (Amherst, Mass., 1987), and a work he edited, *The Voices of Time: A Cooperative Survey of Man's Views of Time as Expressed by the Sciences and the Humanities*, 2d ed. (Amherst, Mass., 1981). See, in addition, Charles M. Sherover, *The Human Experience of Time: The Development of Its Philosophic Meaning* (New York, 1975), and Jonathan Westphal and Carl Levenson, eds., *Time* (Indianapolis, Ind., 1993).

For surveys that are more historically oriented, see Jeremy Rifkin, *Time Wars: The Primary Conflict in Human History* (New York, 1987), and G. J. Whitrow, *Time in History: Views of Time from Prehistory to the Present Day* (Oxford, 1988). John Hedley Brooke, *Science and Religion: Some Historical*

Perspectives (Cambridge, England, 1991), 386–99, has a comprehensive bibliographical survey of questions connected to time in the nineteenth-century historical sciences.

A number of theorists have recently tried to argue for what has been called "the social construction of time"; see John Bender and David E. Wellbery, eds., *Chronotypes: The Construction of Time* (Berkeley and Los Angeles, 1991); Johannes Fabian, *Time and the Other: How Anthropology Makes Its Object* (New York, 1983); and Donald J. Wilcox, *The Measures of Times Past: Pre-Newtonian Chronologies and the Rhetoric of Relative Time* (Chicago, 1987). Deeper reflections that have shaped my thought include G. W. F. Hegel, *Reason in History*, trans. Robert S. Hartman (New York, 1953); Francis Herbert Bradley, *Appearance and Reality: A Metaphysical Essay* (London, 1916), and J. M. E. McTaggart's companion piece, "The Unreality of Time," *Mind* 17 (1908): 457–74; and George Henrik von Wright, "On the Logic and Epistemology of the Causal Relation" (1973), reprinted in *Causation*, ed. Ernest Sosa and Michael Tooley (New York, 1992), 105–24. Bradley's *Presuppositions of Critical History* (Chicago, 1968) examines these ideas in a more limited sphere, and needs to be supplemented by Van A. Harvey, *The Historian and the Believer* (New York, 1966).

At work in decipherment were certain notions about the determinability of translation that run against one main philosophical current. On this issue the reader should begin with Willard Quine's *Word and Object* (New York, 1960), and the opposed view of Noam Chomsky in *Reflections on Language* (New York, 1975). See also John R. Searle's ideas in *The Rediscovery of the Mind* (Cambridge, Mass., 1992).

I have not discussed the assumptions involved in making the physical world the bearer of intentionality, premises pertinent to deciphering the cuneiform and hieroglyphic writing. One can best get at these presuppositions philosophically by examining the work of Wilfrid Sellars, especially "Philosophy and the Scientific Image of Man," in his *Science, Perception, and Reality* (New York, 1963), 1–40. Also of interest is Avrum Stroll, *Surfaces* (Minneapolis, 1988).

During the period in which the field of ancient Near Eastern studies established itself, philosophers in the United States were proposing epistemological theories that in some ways mimicked the presumptions that I have found in the practice of these areas of inquiry. I have summarized the relevant work of the early Charles Peirce in *The Rise of American Philosophy*, 104–23. Also crucial is C. I. Lewis, *Mind and the Word-Order: Outline of a Theory of Knowledge* (New York, 1929).

INDEX

Abraham, 41–42, 48

Adler, Cyrus, 58, 105

Afej, 51–52

Agamemnon, 38

Akkadian, 5, 161; decipherment of, 39–41, 44; dictionary of, 112–13, 170–71; relation to Sumerian, 162–69

Albright, William Foxwell, 8, 18, 243; career and ideas of, 185–93, 199, 230n. 19

American Exploration Society, 62, 101–2

American Journal of Semitic Languages and Literatures, 99, 133

American Oriental Society (AOS), 21, 58–59, 99, 104, 113, 136

American Palestine Exploration Societies, 21

American Philological Association, 21

American School of Classical Study, 99

American School of Oriental Research (ASOR), 99, 118, 185–86

Amorites, 178, 183

Amurru . . . (1910), 178, 183

ancient Near East: as American, 196–97; at California, 102; at Chicago, 108–15; constructed, 4–7, 58–59, 99–100, 155–56, 205n. 4, 210nn. 9 and 20; and divinity schools, 119–20; at Harvard, 23–24, 100–104; at Hopkins, 24, 34–35, 104–7, 117–18; and museums, 114–19; at Penn, 28–29, 55–57, 59–60, 64–65, 78–81, 90–91, 102, 114, 131–33, 138–40; at Yale and Columbia, 107–8, 118–19, 178

Ancient Records of Egypt (1906–07), 111

Ancient Times (1916), 111–12, 114, 241; discussed, 183–85

Andover Theological Seminary, 100, 119

anthropology: compared with archaeology, 29–31, 105, 117, 156–57, 187–88, 196, 239; in museums, 30–31, 102–3, 105

anti-Semitism, 58–59, 101–4, 178

antiquities: and Arabs, 35–37, 46–47, 129; division of, 56–57; and Europeans, 37–41, 42–46; library of, 44, 52, 87–88, 90–91, 110, 127–31, 136–39; stolen, 49, 110–12, 154–55, 158–62, 227n. 17; types of, 64

Archaeological Institute of America, 25–26, 32, 99

archaeology, 65, 74–75, 186; and anthropology, 5, 29–31, 105, 156–57, 187–88, 196, 239; and architecture, 141–46, 146–49; emergence from adventuring, 30–31, 32–33, 141–46; ideas of, 52, 64, 142–52, 198–99; and Old Testament, 41, 42–45, 120–21; and philology, 45, 59, 118–19; and time, 152–57

Archaeology and the Religion of Israel (1942), 187

Archaeology of Palestine and the Bible (1932), 186

architecture: and archaeology, 141–46; at Nippur, 32–33, 52, 65, 70, 87–90, 143–45; Petrie on, 146–49; Reisner on, 149–52

Assurbanipal, 42, 46

Assyria, 42–46

Assyrian. *See* Akkadian

"Assyrian Deluge Epic, The," 185

Assyrian dictionary, 112–13, 170–71

Assyrian Manual (1886), 100

Assyriology: at Chicago, 109–12, 113; defined, 5, 58–59, 113; at Harvard, 104; at Hopkins, 106, 186–87; at Penn, 58–59, 131–32, 161; at Yale, 107–8, 116–17, 178

Authority and Archaeology (1899), 121

"Babel and Bible," 125–26, 135, 177–78

Babylon, 20, 41, 144–45

Babylonia, 5, 42, 46–47

Babylonian Exploration Fund, 3–4; expeditions of, 50–51, 54–57, 59, 63–67, 70, 73, 75, 77, 83–91, 124, 128–31, 144–46, 162; founded, 27–29, 31–34, 82–83

Baghdad, 4, 50, 67–68

Banks, Edgar James, 109–11, 129, 146

Barton, George, 136

Behistun, 39–40, 45, 165

Belzoni, Giovanni, 37

Bernal, Martin, 195

Bible: Albright on, 186–87; criticism of, 22–24, 120–21, 164–65; stories of, 22, 41–42, 135–36, 155–56, 169, 189; studies of in ancient Near East, 20–21, 58–59, 177–78

"Bible" (1875), 25

biblical archaeology, 5, 121–22, 185–87, 196

Biblical Researches (1841), 20, 186
Bismya, 109–11, 146
Black Athena (1987–1991), 195
Bliss, Frederick Jones, 149
Boston Museum of Fine Arts, 31, 102–4, 116
Botta, Paul Emile, 42–43
Bottero, Jean, 168
Breasted, James Henry, 8, 18, 122; career of, 111–14, 119, 170; ideas of, 183–85, 189, 193, 195, 241
British Museum, 37, 44–45
Brooklyn Museum of Fine Art, 115, 116
Brown, Francis, 119
Bruce, Thomas, 38
Budge, Wallace, 168
Business Documents of . . . Nippur (1898), 124
Butler, Nicholas Murray, 18, 107

Cairo Museum, 103
Calah, 43
Carter, Howard, 116
Chaldees, 41, 162
Chesterton, G. K., 157
Chiera, Edward, 169–71
Christie, Agatha, 161
civilizations, 8–9, 24, 126, 176–78, 183–95
Clark, Clarence, 18, 26, 78, 83–84
Clark, Edward White, 18, 26–27, 36, 50, 55–57, 63–67, 71, 73–77, 78, 83–84, 134
Clark Research Professorship, 90–91, 171
Clay, Albert, 17, 91, 110, 123, 139, 151, 171–72; career of, 107–8, 118; conflict with Hilprecht, 124, 126, 130, 135, 159; ideas of, 178, 182, 183
Columbia University, 31, 107–8
Commission of Arts and Sciences, 37
comparative civilization, 122
comparative religion, 121–22, 126, 190–95
Constantinople, 3, 35–36, 56–57, 63–64, 79, 138, 171
copying, techniques of, 178–82
cross-section, 147–48
Crozer, Samuel, 123
Crozer Theological Seminary, 123, 169, 170
cuneiform, 3; copying of, 178–82; decipherment of languages written in, 39–41, 43–46, 161–75
Cuneiform Inscriptions of Western Asia, 44
cunning of reason, 201–2

Darwin, Charles, 21, 23, 198
Darwinism. *See* evolution
Davis, Theodore, 116
Dawson, Christopher, 190
"Death of Gilgamesh," 171, 172
decipherment: of Akkadian, 39–41; of hiero-glyphic writing system, 37–38; presupposi-tions of, 173–75, 200, 246; of Sumerian, 167–73; techniques of, 44, 165–67
Decline of the West (1926, 1928), 191
Delitzsch, Friedrich, 7, 18, 140; controversy over, 125–26, 177–78, 221n. 19
Dewey, John, 8, 113, 189, 197
Discoveries among the Ruins of Nineveh and Babylon (1853), 43
divinity schools, 19, 100, 140; and ancient Near East, 119–20
divisions, of Nippur tablets, 56–57, 63, 79
Diwaniyeh, 51
Dörpfeld, Wilhelm, 142, 144
Duncan, John, 75–77, 84
Durkheim, Emile, 197

Earliest Version of the Babylonian Deluge Story (1910), 135
Early Babylonian Personal Names (1905), 124
Ebla, 195
Eden, 20–21, 22, 41
Edison, Thomas, 36
Egypt: as part of ancient Near East, 19, 37–38, 102–4, 111–12, 142, 144, 149–50, 185; Breasted in, 8, 111–12, 114; Napo-leon in, 37; Petrie in, 61, 146–49; Reisner in, 103–4, 149–50, 152
Egyptology: defined, 5; place in ancient Near East, 19, 103–4, 111–14, 115–17, 120, 122, 185, 197
Elamite, 40
Elgin, earl of, 38
Eliot, Charles William, 18, 25, 27, 100–101, 103–4, 111
Encyclopaedia Britannica, 25
England, and ancient Near East, 23–24, 39–41, 43–46, 139, 152, 160–61, 166–67, 197
epigraphy. *See* philology
Episcopal Divinity School, 26
Erech, 45, 163
ethnology, 29–30, 105–6
Euphrates, 51
evolution, 21, 23, 29–30, 105–6, 198, 208n. 38

Excavations at Nippur (1905), 146

expeditions, 195; at Bismya, 109–12; at the Gizeh Pyramids, 102–4; at Nippur, 46–54, 55–57, 59, 64–77, 83–90, 91, 123, 133, 143–44; in Palestine, 150–52; at Samaria, 102, 104, 150–51; at Tell el Hesy, 147–49; at Ur, 161, 195

explanations, 156–57, 235–36; Albright on, 187–93, 245

Explorations in Bible Lands (1903), 127–28, 131

Father Brown, 157

fertile crescent, 183

Field, Hasting Perez, 32, 55, 56

firman: for Bismya, 109–11; in Egypt, 103; at Nippur, 35–36, 56, 64, 129; in Samaria, 103, 104, 111

Fisher, Clarence, 17, 118, 124, 138, 145, 161, 162, 186; at Nippur, 83–90; in Palestine, 149, 151–52

Fisher-Reisner technique, 151–52, 186

Flood, the, 44, 135–36, 162–63

football, 66, 67

France, and ancient Near East, 37–38, 42–43, 166–67, 168

Franklin, Benjamin, 27

Franklin Sugar Refining Company, 59

Frau Hilprecht Sammlung, 160, 171, 235–36

Frazer, Sir James, 23, 45, 197

Freud, Sigmund, 197

From the Stone Age to Christianity (1940), 187, 188

G. P. Putnam's Sons, 82–83

Geere, Valentine, 75–77, 83–90, 145

Genesis, 41, 44

Germany: and ancient Near Eastern scholarship in the United States, 196–97; scholarship of, 6–7, 22–23, 44, 52, 87–88, 90, 125–26, 143–45, 160, 173–74, 176–78

Gilgamesh, 106: epic discussed, 162–69; Sumerian antecedents of, 171–73

Gilman, Daniel Coit, 18, 24, 104–7

Gizeh Pyramids, 102–4

Golden Bough (1890), 23–24

Goode, George Brown, 105–6

Gordon, George, 117, 136–38

Gottheil, Richard, 58, 107

Greece, 38

Grundzuge der sumerischen Grammatik (1923), 169

Hadley, Arthur Twining, 18, 108

Harper, Robert Francis, 17, 47; career of, 31–32; at Chicago, 109–12, 127, 131; at Nippur, 55, 56

Harper, William Rainey, 17, 31, 55, 99; career of, 20, 22, 26, 108–9, 112

Harrison, Benjamin, 105

Harrison, Charles Custis, 18; and Museum of the University of Pennsylvania, 136–39; as provost, 59–60, 62–63, 78–80, 132–33

Hartford Theological Seminary, 63, 119

Harvard University, 22; ancient Near Eastern studies at, 25, 58–59, 100–104, 117; and divinity, 120

Haskell, Caroline, 109

Haskell Museum, 109, 111–12

Haupt, Paul, 17, 24, 112, 117, 122, 166, 185, 196, 217n. 28; career of, 104–7; fight with Penn, 34, 49, 79, 131

Haynes, Cassandria Artella, 17, 131; at Nippur, 84–89

Haynes, John Henry, 17, 48, 121; and archaeology, 143–46; career of, 32; on fourth campaign, 83–91; and library, 87, 90, 127–28, 162–63; proposed book of, 82–83; on second campaign, 55–57; on third campaign, 59, 64, 65–77, 127–28, 131, 134

Hearst, Phoebe Apperson, 18, 101–2

Hearst Lecturers, 102

Hebraica, 99

Hebrew, as basis for the study of Akkadian, 5, 20, 40, 44

Hegel, G.W.F., 201–2

hieroglyphic writing system, 5, 37–38, 111–12

higher criticism, 22–24, 121–22, 176–78, 193, 197–99, 201; and Gilgamesh, 164–65; and religious belief, 8–9, 64–65, 155–56

Higher Learning in America, The (1918), 60

Hillah, 51, 68

Hilprecht Anniversary Volume (1910), 138, 139, 169

Hilprecht, Herman V., 7, 17, 36, 110–11, 122, 151, 178, 196, 227n. 17; and archaeology, 143–46; career of, 6–7, 33–34; in early twentieth century, 123–25; on expeditions, 46–54, 55–56, 63–66, 73, 83–91; in later 1890s, 78–83; leaving Penn, 158–62; on proposed fifth expedition, 91, 123;

Hilprecht, Herman V. (*cont.*)
  and Sumerian, 169–71. *See also* Peters-
  Hilprecht controversy
Hissarlik, 38
history: and explanation, 156–57; and
  higher criticism, 233nn. 6 and 7; organismic philosophy of, 183–95; and time,
  149, 152–57, 176–78, 226n. 38, 245–46
homosexuality, 89, 199
"Honour of Israel Gow, The," 157
Hot Springs, Arkansas, 67
Houston, Samuel, 133, 134, 138
Hymns and Prayers to Babylonian Gods
  (1911), 124

Iliad, 38
imperialism, 7–8, 199–200
Independent, 25
India, defined as scholarly area, 58–59, 113
Inscriptions de Sumer et Akkad (1905), 167
intellectual property, 158

Jacobsen, Thorkild, 168
Jaspers, Karl, 190
Jastrow, Morris, Jr., 18, 58, 170, 171–72,
  178; career of, 125–26; fights with Hil-
  precht, 128, 133, 151; ideas of, 164–66,
  168–69, 221n. 19
Jericho, 195
Jerusalem, archaeology of, 155–56
Jewish scholarship, 6, 122, 125–26, 173–74
jezireh, 51
Johns Hopkins University, 22; role in an-
  cient Near East, 24, 58, 104–7, 117–18,
  185–87; struggles with Penn, 34, 49, 79
Jones, Levering, 132
Journal of Biblical Literature and Exegesis, 99
Journal of Near Eastern Studies, 99
Journal of the American Oriental Society
  (JAOS), 21, 58, 99
Journal of the Royal Asiatic Society, 40
Judaism, 6, 24, 58–59, 101, 102, 125–26,
  164–65, 170, 173, 187, 188–190, 195
Judeo-Christianity, values of, 6, 58–59, 197–
  98

Kenyon, Kathleen, 152
Kermanshah, 39
Koldewey, Robert, 144–45
Kramer, Samuel Noah, 170–73
Kulturgeschichte, 29
Kuyunjik, 42

Laffan, William, 107–8
Laffan Professorship, 108
Lagash, 167
Lane, Gardiner Martin, 18, 103
Langdon, Stephen, 161, 169, 170, 174
Langley, George, 106
Lanman, Richard, 133–34
Larsa, 109
Layard, Henry, 43–46, 54, 65, 75, 127, 130,
  142, 146
Leben Jesu (1835–36), 23
Lee, Higginson, and Company, 103
Lloyd, Seton, 156
Louvre, 43
Low, Seth, 18, 107
Lowell, A. Lawrence, 18, 104
Lyon, David G., 75, 100–101, 103–4, 109,
  151
Lythgoe, Albert M., 104

Mallowan, Max, 161
Mari, 183, 195
*Mathematical, Metrological, and Chronologi-
  cal Texts . . .* (1906), 135
McNeill, William Hardy, 190
Mesopotamia, 41–42, 46–47; archaeology
  of, 141–46; European exploration in, 38–
  40, 45–46; as part of ancient Near East,
  4–6, 58–59, 103, 113, 116–17, 178,
  184–85
Metropolitan Museum of Fine Art, 25, 31,
  104, 107–8, 116
Meyer, Joseph, 67–75, 83, 89, 143, 200
Moore, George Foote, 100, 127
Morgan, J. P., 18, 25, 107–8, 116, 159, 178
Morgan Library, 107–8, 116–17
Moses, 22, 177
Mosul, 42–44
Murder in Mesopotamia (1936), 161
Murray, Thomas Chalmers, 24, 25
museums, 29–31, 114–19, 196; at Califor-
  nia, 102–3; at Chicago, 113–14; at
  Hopkins, 105, 117–18; at Penn, 27, 28–
  29, 60, 62–63, 80–82, 114, 136–40; at
  Yale, 118–19, 155. *See also* University of
  Pennsylvania Museum
Mycenae, 38
myth, 45, 135–36

Napoleon, 37
Naucratis, 147
Neo-Babylonian, 42

New Archaeology, 156–57, 187–88

New Testament, 23, 41

New York City, interest in Orient, 25–26, 107–8

New York Sun, 107

Nies, James Buchanan, 108

Niffer. *See* Nippur

Nimrud, 43

Nineveh, 42–44, 54

Nineveh and Its Remains . . . (1849), 43

Nippur, . . . (1897), 82–83, 146

Nippur, 37; planning for, 3–4; first campaign at, 46–54, 143; second, 55–57; third, 59, 64, 65–77, 143–44; fourth, 89–90; fifth, 91, 123, 133

Noah, 41, 44, 135–36

Norton, Charles Eliot, 99, 101

Nuzi, 195

Odyssey, 38

Old Persian, 39–40

Old Testament: and higher criticism, 20–25, 120–21, 155–56, 164–65, 177; stories of, 41–42, 135–36, 189

Oppert, Jules, 167

Order and History (1952–75), 190, 192

Orient, defined, 4–5, 205n. 3

Oriental Exploration Fund, 112

Oriental Institute (Chicago), 112–14, 119

Orientalism, analyzed, 4–5, 199–202, 232n. 4

Orientalistische Literaturezeitung, 185

Oriental Seminary, 105, 186

Origin and Goal of History (1949), 190

Ottoman Empire, 35–37, 51–52, 56–57, 118, 146, 209nn. 3 and 4

Outline of History, The (1920), 190

"Ozymandias," 8

Palestine, as part of ancient Near East, 19, 113, 147–51, 155–56

Pan-Babylonianism, 125–26, 177–78, 183, 187

Pennsylvania State University, 62

Pentateuch, 22, 26–27, 41, 164

Pepper, William, 18, 31, 33, 34, 114, 119; affair with Stevenson, 60–63, 74, 101–2, 212n. 9; career of, 27–28, 59–60; and first expedition, 47–54; and second, 55–57; and third, 63–64, 65, 73–74, 76, 77; and fourth, 78–79

Persepolis, 39–40

Persia, 38–40

Peters, John Punnett, 17, 101, 122; advises Penn, 83, 84, 85; archaeological ideas of, 52, 54, 142–43, 145, 146; career of, 26–27, 164; conflict with Hilprecht, 128–29, 131–33; and Hopkins, 34; and Nippur, 46–54, 55–57, 59, 63–67, 70–74; and Yale, 154–55. *See also* Peters-Hilprecht controversy

Peters-Hilprecht controversy, 79–83, 90–91, 127–40

Petrie, Flinders, 17, 61, 75, 77; ideas of, 142, 144, 146–49, 152–53, 194

Philadelphia, 3, 26–28, 58–59, 135

philanthropy, 120; and Harvard, 101–2; and Hearst, 101–2, 103, 120; and Morgan, 107–8, 178; and museums, 115–16; and Penn, 25–27, 50, 57, 90, 91; and Rockefeller, 111–12

philology, 20–21, 40–41, 44, 164–70; principles of, 173–75

photography: and Haynes, 32, 66, 70, 71; and Petrie and Reisner, 150

Pitt-Rivers, Julian, 142, 144

Poebel, Arno, 169–71

polychrome Bible, 106

pottery, and archaeology, 141, 147–49, 152–53, 193–94

Prince, John, 31, 36, 50, 107, 131

Proceedings of the Society for Biblical Literature, 99

professionalism, analyzed, 5–7, 19–24, 58–59, 97–98, 114–20, 155–56, 196–97

progress, 152–57, 173–75, 195, 199–202, 233n. 7; Albright on, 187–93; Breasted on, 183–85, 189

Progress and Religion (1929), 190

Prolegomena to the History of Israel (1878), 22

Protestantism, cultural ethos of, 19, 56–59, 198–99

provenance, 127–30, 136, 153–54

publishing, 81–83

racism, 184, 199

Radau, Hugo, 139–40, 169, 170

Ranke, Herman, 124

Ranke, Leopold von, 176

Rawlinson, Henry Creswicke, 39–40, 42, 44, 165, 166

Reisner, George Andrew, 18, 103–4, 149–52

. . . *Religion of the Semites* (1889), 24
Revolutions of Civilization, The (1911), 194
Rise of the West, The (1959), 190
Robert College, 32
Robinson, Edward, 20, 22, 155, 186
Robinson, James Harvey, 113
Robinson, Sallie Crozer, 123
Rockefeller, John D., 18, 22, 109, 110–11
Rockefeller, John D., Jr., 18, 111–12, 118
Rockefeller, Mrs. John D., 112
Roosevelt, Theodore, 111
Rosetta Stone, 37
Royal Asiatic Society, 40

Sacred Books of the Old Testament, The, 106
St. Michael's Church, 26, 64
Salisbury, Edward E., 20, 22
Samaria, 104, 150–51
Sankera, 109
Sarzec, Ernest de, 167
Schiff, Jacob, 18, 101–4, 150
Schliemann, Heinrich, 38, 142, 144
scribal quarter. *See* temple library
secularization, 3, 7–9, 22–24, 58–59, 121–
    22, 126, 155–57, 178, 183–93, 197–
    99
Semitic Museum (Harvard), 101–4, 109,
    117
Semitic studies, 5–6, 28, 125–26
sequence dating, 149, 153
seriation, 149
sexism, 184, 199
Shelley, Percy, 8
Smith, Edgar Fahs, 159
Smith, George, 44–45, 135, 162
Smith, Robertson, 24–25, 45, 100–101
Smithsonian Institution, 34, 104–7, 117–
    18
So-Called Peters-Hilprecht Controversy, The
    (1908), 133, 135. *See also* Peters-
    Hilprecht controversy
Society of Biblical Archaeology, 99
Society of Biblical Literature, 99
Spengler, Oswald, 191
Stevenson, Cornelius, 61
Stevenson, Sara Yorke, 17; affair with Pep-
    per, 60–63, 74, 101–2, 212n. 9; and Harri-
    son, 78, 80; and Hilprecht, 128, 129–30,
    131–32, 137, 139
Stillman, William James, 32
stratified digging, 141–46, 200–201
stratigraphy, 141–42, 147–49

Strauss, David, 23
Stuart, Moses, 20, 23
Study of History, A (1934–61), 191
Sumer, 3, 46, 166, 178, 242
Sumerian, 46, 161; and Akkadian, 162–69;
    decipherment of, 169–73; and Kramer,
    177–78
Sumerian Epic of . . . the Fall (1915), 169,
    170, 174
Sumerian Hymns and Prayers (1911), 169
Sumerian Religious Texts (1924), 170
Sunday School Times, 33, 63, 83
Sundberg, John, 72–73

tablets. *See* antiquities
Tell el Hesy, 147–49
Telloh, 167
tells, 37, 42, 147–49
temple library, 52, 127–30, 159, 162–63
textbooks, 111–12, 183–85, 194–95, 240–
    41
Thayer, Joseph Henry, 100
theft. *See* antiquities
theological schools. *See* divinity schools
Theory of the Leisure Class (1899), 60
Thureau-Dangin, François, 167
time. *See* history
Toy, Crawford, 25, 100, 207n. 24
Toynbee, Arnold, 8, 191–92
Trollope, Anthony, 9
Troy, 38
typology, 147–48

Ugarit, 195
Union Theological Seminary, 20, 119
University of California (Berkeley), 101–4,
    113, 120
University of Chicago, 22, 108–14, 119,
    120, 151, 170–71
University of Pennsylvania: and Harrison,
    59–60; and Hilprecht, 78–79, 132–33,
    139, 158–59; and Pepper, 27–29; and role
    in ancient Near East, 49–50, 50–51
University of Pennsylvania Museum: and an-
    thropology, 117; founding, 29; and Hil-
    precht, 79–83, 136–39, 161; and provosts,
    60–63, 114, 119
university system: as American, 196–97; ana-
    lyzed, 19–22, 27, 99–100, 132, 139–40,
    155–57, 158–62, 201–2; and museums,
    114–19
Ur, 41–42, 48, 109, 161, 195

Ur Committee, 109
Uruk, 45, 163

Valley of the Kings, 116
Veblen, Thorstein, 60, 190, 192
Voegelin, Eric, 190, 192

Ward, William Hayes, 17, 99, 107, 131;
    and Wolfe Expedition, 25–26, 58
Warka, 45
Weber, Max, 197
Wellhausen, Julius, 22–24, 42, 45, 165,
    177
Wells, H. G., 190
West, 4, 24, 28, 184, 199–202
Wheeler, Mortimer, 152
Wheeler-Kenyon method, 152

White City, 30, 208n. 38
Whitney, William Dwight, 17, 20, 22, 26,
    58, 104, 133
Wilbour, Charles, 115
Winlock, Herbert, 116
Wolfe, Catherine Lorillard, 18, 25
Wolfe Expedition, 25–26, 99, 107
Woolley, Leonard, 161, 195
World's Columbian Exposition, 30
World War One, 18, 159
Wright, G. Ernest, 231n. 28

Yale Babylonian Collection, 108
Yale University, 49, 107–8, 120, 154–55

zapiteh, 51
ziggurat, 52, 65, 144

Bruce Kuklick is Killebrew Professor of History at the University of Pennsylvania. Among his books are *To Every Thing a Season: Shibe Park and Urban Philadelphia, 1909–1976* (Princeton); *Churchmen and Philosophers: Jonathan Edwards to John Dewey*; and *The Rise of American Philosophy: Cambridge, Massachusetts, 1860–1930*.